more

more

more recipes with more veg
for more joy

MATT PRESTON

plum.   Pan Macmillan Australia

CONTENTS

INTRODUCTION

This book is about joy. The pure unadulterated pleasure that food can give you. These are recipes written for people who love to eat, who understand the glories of the table and that eating together is more than just about nutrition – carbs and protein – on a plate. Sharing a meal is one of the key things that makes us human. We should revel in that.

Sure, nutrition is important, and sure, it is great if recipes use fresh and easily accessed ingredients as these do, but these should be givens. At its simplest, the act of cooking is an act of love; an act of indulging those you love with something delicious.

This is a book about happiness. This is not the place for meanness and accusations; nor guilt and sacrifice – this is a place for simple recipes that will give you plate-licking pleasure and a certain abandonment that comes from the decadence of good food and an unfettered indulgence if you want it.

This is a book about vegetables and how to get more plant-based or plant-centric recipes into your repertoire. There are loads of vegetables, nuts and grains featured here because I love them and, I suppose in a way, this book is also a catalogue of my last few years of adventures and exploration with food, trying to redraw what is delicious and capture the happiness that good food can bring. Gone are the 'grey meat and potatoes' menus of the past. This is a book full of recipes that are so alive they pop with as much vibrant colour as they do vibrant flavours.

This is also a place of flexibility and we're not here to wag a finger. The recipes that follow are either vegetarian or vegan, but please feel free to use your favourite dairy, whether that's vegan, vegetarian or not, and if you do decide you'd like to add a little bacon or a slab of fish then we're not going to judge you. No one should – every little step each of us takes to ensuring our footprint on this planet is a little smaller should be applauded not questioned.

If this book had a motto it would be 'NO SACRIFICE'.

This whole book is a celebration of no sacrifice cookery. There is nothing missing in the recipes that follow – we've designed them to be packed with brilliant flavour and loads of contrasting textures.

They've been developed as an antidote to the dreaded, damp-cardboard vego meals of yesteryear. Those exercises in monastic monosyllabic blandness that are still peddled by some wellness bloggers and 'worthy' cookbooks; cookbooks too often written by people who don't love to eat; people who often fear rather than love food.

Food is not the enemy. It's a friend, but a friend that, like all friends, you need to respect and not abuse. It needs to be loved but not obsessed over – in any form; either through over-adoration or abrogation. Here we love food as much for the joy it brings as for the health it delivers.

So, maybe you want to eat more vegetables, or less meat, or try cooking some tasty vegan meals to broaden your repertoire and still put a broad smile on the faces of those you are feeding.

Maybe you want to save money by eating more plant-based meals, meals where nothing is missing, or maybe you just want to keep the vegan or vego in the family happy at dinnertime without having to cook two meals.

Maybe you are a long-term committed vegetarian or vegan just looking for some more tasty 'no sacrifice' recipes. Maybe you want to revel in what you've known for a long-time – that meat-free meals are so much more than three veg without a side of protein; they are meals that are harmonious, (ful)filling and never compromise on flavour. Or maybe, just maybe, you want to enjoy a meat-free Monday every so often and don't want to see this act as a sacrifice either.

Whatever your 'maybe' is, this book will help you get MORE!

Love and joy,

Matt

A note for vegans: Some wine and mustards, such as Dijon and grain which are made using verjuice or wine vinegar, may not be produced to the most stringent vegan standards. If this matters to you, take action accordingly and check that what you're using is fully vegan.

MY VEGETARIAN PANTRY

I felt it might be useful to list here what I'd like to find in my dream vegetarian pantry; if only to get you focused on the flavour bombs you can bring to bear on your cooking or elements you can add to bulk it up. Enjoy!

GRAINS & PULSES

In most instances, you can swap the grains and legumes in a recipe for what you have in your pantry. Just follow the instructions on the packet for how to cook them and then proceed with the recipe as instructed.

- Brown lentils
- Bulgur
- Couscous
- Farro
- Freekeh
- Pearl barley
- Puy lentils
- Quinoa
- Red lentils
- Rice, brown and white

CANNED GOODS

Always good to have on hand for a quick meal, there is nothing wrong with canned vegetables and legumes. They are cheap, convenient and last a long time loitering at the back of the pantry waiting to be turned into something delicious.

- Black beans
- Borlotti beans
- Cannellini beans
- Chickpeas
- Fava beans
- Kidney beans
- Lentils
- Sweet corn
- Tomatoes

(Don't forget to load your freezer with a few chillies, curry leaves, kaffir lime leaves, frozen corn, frozen peas, edamame, various suitable pastry, breadcrumbs, parsley, frozen cubes of stock and leftover lemon juice.)

DRIED HERBS & SPICES

Slowly build up your collection of dried herbs and spices and you'll always have flavour bombs on hand to create combinations that can spice up any dish.

- Allspice
- Bay leaves
- Cardamom pods
- Cayenne pepper
- Chilli powder/flakes/whole dried
- Cinnamon sticks
- Coriander seeds
- Cumin seeds
- Curry powder
- Dried oregano
- Dried thyme
- Dukkah
- Fennel seeds
- Fenugreek leaves
- Ground turmeric
- Mustard seeds
- Nigella seeds
- Nutmeg
- Paprika, smoked (especially), hot and sweet
- Sichuan peppercorns
- White pepper
- Za'atar

SAUCES & CONDIMENTS

Add immediate flavour to dishes or combine to make unique sauces and condiments to pimp up any dinner.

- Chipotles in adobo
- Coconut aminos (which is like a sweeter soy sauce)
- Curry paste
- Hoisin sauce
- Honey
- Kecap manis
- Ketchups
- Maple syrup
- Mirin
- Miso
- Nutritional yeast (to sprinkle on everything!)
- Peanut butter
- Shaoxing rice wine
- Soy sauce or tamari (gluten free)
- Sriracha chilli sauce
- Tabasco
- Tamarind puree
- Vegemite
- Vegetarian XO sauce

OILS & VINEGARS

Yes, oil for cooking, but build a small collection of different vinegars and you can create endless dressings to go with any number of dishes. Ditch the bought stuff and get creative!

- Apple cider vinegar
- Balsamic vinegar
- Black vinegar
- Coconut oil
- Extra virgin olive oil, for cooking and dressings
- Olive oil, for cooking
- Peanut oil, for high-heat cooking (think stir-fries)
- Rice wine vinegar
- Sesame oil
- Sherry vinegar
- Vegetable oil, for deep-frying
- Wine vinegar, red and white

NUTS & SEEDS

To add immediate texture and crunch to dishes, nuts and seeds are great to have on hand to add an extra dimension.

- Almonds, whole, blanched, flaked, slivered
- Hazelnuts
- Linseeds
- Peanuts (in all their forms)
- Pecans
- Pumpkin seeds
- Macadamias
- Sesame seeds, white and black
- Sunflower seeds
- Walnuts

PASTA & NOODLES

Stalwarts in every pantry, buy a few varieties and traverse European and Asian cuisines with ease. Here are some of the basics.

- 2-minute noodles (Don't sneer ... perfect for that pimped up bogan vego life saver late at night)
- Fettuccine
- Lasagne
- Macaroni
- Orecchiette
- Penne
- Ramen noodles
- Rice noodles, vermicelli, flat, thin
- Rice paper sheets
- Soba noodles
- Spaghetti
- Udon noodles

If you're here because you just want to get more veg into your diet and you are feeling less stringent, I'll leave it up to you whether you want to have the flexibility to include and use non-vego ingredients, such as Worcestershire sauce, fish sauce and oyster sauce.

D. F. V

For this book I felt it fitting to create a new acronym – D.F.V – which stands for Dirty, Filthy, Vegetarian. I have applied this catchy term to dishes within these pages that are decadent, naughty and overall just so damned good you'll wonder why you didn't get on the vegetarian bandwagon years ago. To celebrate their rightful elevation to D.F.V, I have given them their very own page, a la below.

Salads

These salads are the main event; not the sad bowl on the side that everyone ignores. They are all about texture, colour and flavour, whether it's an elegant plate of marinated silken tofu with a side of crisp wombok, sesame seeds and brown rice, a loaded quinoa san choi bao or my favourite, raw nachos. You'll also find loads of ideas for healthy plant-based lunchboxes for kids of all ages.

Avocado & friends

SERVES: 4 **PREP:** 20 mins **COOKING:** 40 mins

Our avocados are magnificent – no wonder they are so popular. But would they be so loved if they were called by their other old names of 'alligator pears' or, even worse, 'testicles'?

That last one is what the Aztecs called them when the conquistadors asked, 'What are those green fruit dangling in pairs from that tree over there?' when they arrived in what is now Mexico. Well, they would actually have called them 'āhuacatl', as that's the Nahuatl word for avocado.

Here we partner the avocado with other ingredients popular in Mesoamerican culture in the years before European incursion. They've hung together for so long it's no wonder they're such close mates.

250 g (1 cup) spelt (or you could use cooked brown rice to speed things up)
1 bunch coriander, leaves and stalks finely chopped
1 red onion, finely chopped
juice of 1 lime
60 ml (¼ cup) olive oil
sea salt and freshly ground black pepper
2 avocados, halved and sliced crossways
400 g mixed cherry tomatoes, halved
sliced pickled chillies, to serve
80 g Greek feta, crumbled (optional)

CHILLI BUTTER ROAST CORN
50 g butter, at room temperature
2 teaspoons chipotle sauce
finely grated zest of 1 lime
2 corn cobs, husks and silks removed

Preheat the oven to 200°C/180°C fan-forced.

To make the chilli butter roast corn, combine the butter, chipotle sauce and lime zest in a bowl. Place each corn cob on a piece of foil that is large enough to wrap it in. Dot the butter mixture evenly over the corn, then wrap up to enclose and place on a baking tray. Roast, turning halfway through, for 40 minutes or until tender.

Meanwhile, pour 500 ml (2 cups) of water into a large saucepan and bring to the boil over medium–high heat. Add the spelt, then reduce the heat to very low and cook, covered, for 25 minutes or until tender. Drain and set aside to cool.

Combine the spelt, coriander, red onion, lime juice and 2 tablespoons of the olive oil in a large bowl and toss until well combined. Season well and spoon onto a large serving platter. Top with the avocado slices.

Combine the tomatoes and remaining oil in a bowl. Season well, then arrange over the salad.

Open the foil parcels and spread any remaining chilli butter over the corn. Cut the corn off the cob, trying your best to keep the kernels together so you have little tiles of corn. Place on top of the salad with the pickled chillies and sprinkle with the feta (if using).

MEATY ADDITION: Slice 4 Barbecued or chargrilled chicken thigh fillets (see page 261) and place on top of the spelt base mixture with the avocado.

Barbecued potato salad with tamarind caramel, mint & yoghurt

SERVES: 6 PREP: 15 mins COOKING: 20 mins

Tamarind might well be my current favourite ingredient. Its heady dark sourness lurks in so many of my favourite recipes in this book and here it is, wonderful and corrupting the snowy tartness of yoghurt and fresh breath of mint like a hot motorbike-riding bad boy with malintent and a flagon of Fat Lamb. Oh, the stories!

1 kg kipfler potatoes, scrubbed and cut lengthways into 1 cm thick slices

2 tablespoons olive oil

sea salt and freshly ground black pepper

90 g (¼ cup) tamarind paste or puree

70 g (⅓ cup) brown sugar

125 g (½ cup) thick natural yoghurt

juice of ½ lemon

2 celery stalks, trimmed and finely chopped

2 spring onions, white and green parts thinly sliced

30 g (¼ cup) slivered almonds, toasted

¼ cup shredded mint, plus extra leaves to serve

Preheat a barbecue grill on high. Place the potato in a large bowl and drizzle with the olive oil. Toss until well coated, then season well and toss again. Grill the potato for 10 minutes on each side or until charred and tender.

Meanwhile, get your caramel ready. Combine the tamarind, sugar and 60 ml (¼ cup) of water in a small saucepan and stir over very low heat until the sugar has dissolved. Increase the heat slightly and bring to a gentle simmer (be careful as it can spit as it starts to bubble). Simmer for 5–7 minutes or until the syrup is nice and thick.

Combine the yoghurt and lemon juice in a jug and season well.

Place the celery, spring onion, almonds and shredded mint in a bowl and toss to combine.

Arrange half the potato slices on a serving platter. Dot half the yoghurt mixture and half the tamarind caramel on top, then sprinkle with half the celery mixture. Repeat the layers, then scatter with the extra mint leaves, a sprinkling of salt and serve.

 TIP: Change the mint to coriander, swap the almonds for toasted pumpkin seeds, whisk 3 tablespoons of cream cheese into the yoghurt and add a chopped tinned chipotle chilli in adobo sauce to the caramel to give this potato salad a Mexican twist.

MEATY ADDITION: Add 6 chopped rashers Crispy bacon (see page 268) to the celery mixture, or serve with Barbecued or chargrilled chicken thigh fillets (see page 261).

San choi bao for Buddha

SERVES: 4 as a starter **PREP:** 15 mins **COOKING:** 10 mins

Is san choi bāo the new pizza? Once a simple recipe for a lettuce cup filled with quail, chicken or minced pork and canned water chestnuts, it has become the template for a hundred Australian 'gourmet' variations, including snow peas or carrot, Mongolian lamb, tofu, duck or even a Thai or Laotian larb.

That's no small feat for a dish that has the scantest published history. Maybe it came here from southern China via Hong Kong? Maybe it comes from the Mandarin words for 'lettuce' (shēng cài) and 'bun' (bāo), or more accurately 'package'? Maybe it was part of the yuppification of Cantonese food in the 80s when prawn toast, XO sauce, crispy seaweed and a chilled glass of gewurz' or sweet riesling became popular in 'cool' Chinese places with square black plates.

Of course it might also have something to do with the Vietnamese translation of sân chơi ba ('three playgrounds'). Perhaps Buddha knows …

2 tablespoons peanut oil
150 g green beans, trimmed and sliced into coins
100 g snow peas, trimmed, strings removed and thinly sliced crossways
10 (about 150 g) lychees, peeled, halved and stones removed
1 bunch coriander, leaves picked, stalks and roots cleaned and finely chopped
3 cm knob of ginger, peeled and finely grated
2 long red chillies, deseeded and finely chopped
1 teaspoon Chinese five spice
140 g (¾ cup) cooked red quinoa
115 g canned water chestnuts, drained and cut into matchsticks
2 spring onions, white and green parts thinly sliced
1 tablespoon kecap manis
1 tablespoon Shaoxing rice wine
1 teaspoon sea salt
8 iceberg lettuce leaves
60 g (⅓ cup) roasted macadamias, roughly smashed

Heat half the peanut oil in a wok or large frying pan over high heat until smoking. Stir-fry the green beans and snow peas for 2–3 minutes or until starting to turn bright green, then transfer to a bowl.

Add the remaining oil to the wok or pan and stir-fry the lychee, coriander stalk and root, ginger and chilli for 2 minutes or until aromatic. Add the five spice and toss until well combined. Return the beans and snow peas to the wok or pan and add the quinoa, water chestnut and spring onion. Toss until heated through, then add the kecap manis, Shaoxing rice wine and salt, and toss for 2 minutes or until well combined.

Place all the lettuce leaves on a large serving platter. Spoon in the filling and top with the macadamias and coriander leaves.

MEATY ADDITION: Add a generous handful of Fried lap cheong (see page 268) with the green beans and snow peas.

Ancient grain salad version 22.0

SERVES: 4 **PREP:** 20 mins **COOKING:** 40 mins

Parsnips, swedes and turnips are like the forgotten members of the roast veg boy band that have been left behind by the solo success of pumpkins and sweet potatoes. No wonder those turnips are bitter.

However, the parsnip has more reason to be aggrieved. Is it because it doesn't have quite the same orange fake tan as the pumpkin or the sweet potato? Is it because, rather than possessing the smooth skin and elegant rounded shape of its rivals, the parsnip looks more like the long prosthetic nose of the witch in a Disney on Ice production of Snow White? Is it because sometimes it has a wooden heart?

These are all just excuses, so let's swing the spotlight onto the parsnip and watch it shine as a solo act!

4 parsnips, peeled and quartered
   lengthways
olive oil spray
sea salt and freshly ground
   black pepper
250 g (1 cup) whole freekeh
200 g Medjool dates, pitted and cut
   into thin strips
2 spring onions, white and green
   parts thinly sliced
45 g (½ cup) flaked almonds, toasted
⅓ cup coarsely chopped flat-leaf
   parsley, plus extra leaves to serve
⅓ cup coarsely chopped mint, plus
   extra leaves to serve
finely grated zest of 1 orange
75 g punnet pomegranate arils (that's
   the ruby-like seeds to you and me)
   or seeds of ½ pomegranate

POMEGRANATE & ORANGE DRESSING
2 tablespoons pomegranate molasses
2 tablespoons orange juice
2 tablespoons extra-virgin olive oil
sea salt and freshly ground
   black pepper

Preheat the oven to 200°C/180°C fan-forced. Line a baking tray with baking paper.

Place the parsnip in a single layer on the prepared tray, spray with olive oil and season well. Roast, turning halfway through, for 40 minutes or until tender and golden.

Meanwhile, place the freekeh and 750 ml (3 cups) of water in a saucepan over medium–high heat. Bring to the boil, then reduce the heat to low and simmer, covered, for 40 minutes or until tender. Drain.

To make the dressing, whisk together the pomegranate molasses, orange juice and olive oil in a jug. Season with salt and pepper.

Combine the freekeh, date, spring onion, almonds, chopped parsley and mint and half the orange zest in a bowl. Season well.

Transfer the freekeh mixture to a serving plate, then top with the roasted parsnip and drizzle with the dressing. Sprinkle with the pomegranate arils, parsley and mint leaves and remaining orange zest.

MEATY ADDITION: Serve with Barbecued or chargrilled lamb cutlets (see page 265) or Roast pork belly (see page 273) with some Labne (see page 52) on the side.

The golfer's salad

SERVES: 4 **PREP:** 15 mins (plus 1 hour marinating) **COOKING:** 5 mins

The golfer in question was Lucas Parsons and this recipe is inspired by a dish of tofu and oyster mushrooms he made in the first-ever season of **MasterChef.** *After tasting over 4000 dishes that is no small thing to remember, but it is a special idea that we've based this recipe on.*

60 ml (¼ cup) Shaoxing rice wine

60 ml (¼ cup) light soy sauce

1¼ tablespoons caster sugar

3 cm knob of ginger, peeled and finely grated

2 small red chillies, thinly sliced diagonally

300 g packet silken tofu, cut crossways into 8 slices

2 tablespoons orange juice

1 tablespoon rice wine vinegar

1 teaspoon sesame oil, plus extra for drizzling

½ wombok, finely shredded

300 g (2 cups) cooked brown rice

4 spring onions, white and green parts thinly sliced diagonally

40 g (¼ cup) sesame seeds, toasted

2 tablespoons peanut oil

200 g oyster mushrooms

Whisk together the Shaoxing rice wine, soy sauce and 1 tablespoon of the sugar in a bowl until the sugar has dissolved. Stir in the ginger and chilli.

Place the tofu in a shallow serving bowl and pour over the soy sauce mixture. Cover and place in the fridge, spooning over the marinade occasionally to make sure all sides of the tofu get a good coating. Leave to marinate for 1 hour.

Shortly before you are ready to serve, whisk together the orange juice, rice wine vinegar, sesame oil and remaining sugar in a jug.

Place the wombok, rice, spring onion and orange juice dressing in a bowl and toss to combine. Sprinkle with the sesame seeds.

Heat half the peanut oil in a large non-stick frying pan or wok over high heat. Add half the mushrooms and cook for 1–2 minutes on each side or until golden and tender. Place on top of the tofu. Repeat with the remaining peanut oil and mushrooms.

Drizzle the mushrooms and tofu with extra sesame oil and serve with the rice salad.

MEATY ADDITION: Shred 2 Poached chicken breast fillets (see page 261) and add to the rice salad.

Grilled plums with milky haloumi & rocket

SERVES: 4–6 **PREP:** 15 mins **COOKING:** 10 mins

Note to hardworking Michelle who tested and developed this recipe: I think this should be a 'salade tiède'. These were warm salads back in the days when rocket and raspberry vinegar were popular, so let's plate the plums straight from the grill. They need to be a little burnt in places.

Also, most people seem to want to tan up the haloumi so it gets squeaky but these days I almost love it more just warmed on one side only on a sheet of baking paper, either on a tray in the oven or on the barbecue flat plate. This way the cheese goes all mellow and soft, and cries little milky tears. This works particularly well with that pale, good-quality haloumi which is becoming increasingly common in supermarkets. The baking paper moderates the heat and makes the very tender haloumi far easier to plate warm onto the hot plums.

Note from Michelle to Matt (who is sounding more and more like some out-of-touch dilettante): Whatevs.

6 plums, halved and stones removed
olive oil spray
2 tablespoons pomegranate molasses
2 tablespoons olive oil
sea salt and freshly ground
    black pepper
2 radishes, cut into matchsticks
handful of baby rocket leaves
400 g haloumi, cut into 1 cm thick
    slices
35 g (¼ cup) hazelnuts, roasted and
    coarsely chopped

Preheat a barbecue grill on medium–high and a barbecue flat plate or frying pan over medium heat.

Spray the plums with a little olive oil, then cook on the grill for 2–3 minutes each side so they get a good charring and soften slightly but still hold their shape. Remove and keep warm.

While the plums are grilling, whisk together the pomegranate molasses and olive oil in a jug. Season well.

Toss the radish and rocket together in a bowl.

Carefully place a sheet of baking paper on the hot flat plate or frying pan, add the haloumi and cook on one side only for 1 minute or until soft and milky.

Transfer the plums to a serving plate. Place the slices of haloumi partly on the plums like a doona that's almost slipped off on a hot night.

Drizzle over the pomegranate dressing, then scatter over the rocket mixture and hazelnuts.

MEATY ADDITION: Serve with Barbecued or chargrilled pork cutlets (see page 271) as part of a shared meal.

Green goddess salad

SERVES: 6 PREP: 10 mins COOKING: 15 mins

George Arliss had two claims to fame. He was the first British actor to win an Academy Award — that was back in the early days of silent movies — and he also was the first movie star to have a salad dressing named for him. Paul Newman's claim was staked over 60 years later.

In an act of the sort of celebrity sycophancy popular among the great hotels of the late Victorian and Edwardian era (think Peach Melba, Pears Belle Helene and Pavlova), the Palace Hotel in San Francisco named the Green Goddess dressing in his honour after a smash-hit play he was touring with during 1923.

It seems to have been based on a green sauce for eel from the glory years of Versailles, but who really needs a sauce for eel these days?

1 kg baby coliban (chat) potatoes
200 g baby green beans, trimmed
2 baby cos lettuces, leaves separated
1 baby fennel bulb, thinly shaved
  (toss the shaved fennel in lemon
  juice to stop it turning brown)

CREAMY GREEN GODDESS DRESSING
1 large ripe avocado, roughly chopped
½ cup coarsely chopped flat-leaf
  parsley
2 tablespoons snipped chives
1 tablespoon coarsely chopped
  tarragon
2 tablespoons thick natural yoghurt
2 tablespoons freshly squeezed
  lemon juice
1 tablespoon olive oil
sea salt and freshly ground
  black pepper

Place the potatoes in a large saucepan and cover with cold water. Bring to the boil, then reduce the heat to medium and simmer for 10 minutes, adding the beans for the last 3 minutes. The potatoes should be just tender when pierced with a skewer and the beans bright green and tender crisp. Drain. Place the beans in a bowl of iced water to stop them cooking, then drain. Set the potatoes aside to cool.

While your potatoes cool, make the dressing. Place all the ingredients in a food processor and blitz until smooth.

Halve the potatoes and place in a bowl with the beans. Add half the dressing and toss until well combined.

Place the lettuce leaves in a shallow serving bowl or platter and spoon over the remaining dressing. Top with the potato salad and shaved fennel.

MEATY ADDITION: Sprinkle 200 g chopped Crispy bacon (see page 268) or Crispy prosciutto shards (see page 269) over the salad before serving. You could also mash 2 good anchovies into the dressing, which would be nice for pescatarians, especially if you serve this salad with some Pan-fried prawns (see page 275), too.

Raw nachos #14

SERVES: 6 **PREP:** 20 mins (plus overnight soaking) **COOKING:** 15 mins

19 July 2018 marked the end of my year celebrating the 75th anniversary of bartender Ignacio Anaya's single contribution to the world of gastronomy. For it was during World War II in 1943 that 'Nacho' knocked up the first 'nachos' for a group of air-force wives who had jumped the border into Mexico for a few lunchtime libations.

The year began with a doorstop feature of nine recipes for nachos in Taste magazine, written with food guru Michelle Southan. Then there were three recipes I demo'd at the Noosa Food and Wine Festival for delicious. magazine, which I developed with the lovely Warren Mendes, including the world's first breakfast nachos loaded with fried eggs and smashed avocado. I put nachos in my book that year, too, and, while all these recipes were seen by quite a few people, it was nothing like the millions around the world who saw me demo my black bean and corn nachos in a MasterChef MasterClass. (FYI, all these recipes are available online.)

While I think my efforts made a fitting celebration of Iggy's creation I felt slightly uncomfortable leaving it at 13 recipes. So here is just one more to take us past the unlucky number. Luckily, it's all vegan too.

175 g mini sweet capsicums,
   quartered
olive oil spray
400 g can black beans, rinsed
   and drained
1 tablespoon olive oil
3 limes
½ bunch coriander, leaves picked,
   stalks and roots cleaned and
   finely chopped
sea salt and freshly ground
   black pepper
150 g (1 cup) frozen corn kernels,
   just thawed
3 large avocados, roughly chopped
300 g mixed corn chips (blue and
   regular corn)
¼ iceberg lettuce, finely shredded
3 jalapeno chillies, thinly sliced
   (optional)

VEGAN SOUR CREAM
145 g (1 cup) raw cashews
boiling water
100 ml almond milk
1 tablespoon freshly squeezed
   lemon juice
1 teaspoon apple cider vinegar
1 teaspoon sea salt
freshly ground black pepper

Start the vegan sour cream a day ahead (don't worry, it will keep for up to 3 days in the fridge). Place the cashews in a heatproof bowl and cover with plenty of boiling water, then leave to soak for 24 hours. Drain the cashews and place in a high-powered blender. Add the almond milk, lemon juice, vinegar and salt and blend until smooth and creamy. Season to taste with pepper, then place in the fridge for 2 hours to chill and thicken.

Preheat a barbecue grill on medium–high or a large chargrill pan over medium–high heat. Spray the capsicum with olive oil and cook for 3–4 minutes on each side or until tender and charred. Transfer to a bowl and add the black beans, olive oil and juice of ½ lime. Finely chop half the coriander leaves and add to the bowl. Season well and toss to combine.

Add the corn to the grill or chargrill pan and cook, tossing, for 3–4 minutes or until slightly charred. Add to the bean mixture.

Place the avocado in a separate bowl. Add the coriander root and stalk and juice of 1 lime and mix until just combined – you want it to be chunky.

Arrange the corn chips and lettuce on a large serving platter. Top with the smashed avocado, bean mixture and jalapeno (if using). Roughly chop the remaining coriander leaves and scatter over the top.

Serve with the nutty sour cream and the remaining limes cut into wedges.

Devilled egg salad

SERVES: 4 **PREP:** 15 mins **COOKING:** 10 mins

'Don't you know there ain't no devil, it's just God when he's drunk,' growled the gravel-voiced, bar-room balladeer Tom Waits. And these eggs, first created in the 18th century, are certainly perfect drinking food. Perhaps that's why they are central to the Kentucky Derby and mint juleps, and known in Hungary as 'casino eggs'. Well then, as William Shakespeare wrote in **The Tempest,** *'Hell is empty and all the devils are here'.*

6 eggs
2 bunches asparagus, trimmed
85 g (⅓ cup) your favourite
   good-quality mayonnaise
3 teaspoons sriracha chilli sauce
smoked paprika, for sprinkling
½ bunch watercress, leaves picked
2 celery stalks, thinly sliced
1 Lebanese cucumber, thinly sliced

DILL MUSTARD VINAIGRETTE
60 ml (¼ cup) extra-virgin olive oil
juice of 1 lemon
2 teaspoons Dijon mustard
1 teaspoon raw sugar
1 tablespoon finely chopped dill
sea salt and freshly ground
   black pepper

Place the eggs in a saucepan filled with cold water and bring to the boil over high heat. Reduce the heat to medium and simmer for 6 minutes. Drain and refresh in iced water, then peel and halve the eggs lengthways.

While the eggs cook, make your dressing. Whisk together the olive oil, lemon juice, mustard, sugar and dill in a jug. Season well with salt and pepper.

Bring a frying pan of water to the boil, add the asparagus and cook for 2–3 minutes or until tender crisp. Drain and plunge the asparagus into a bowl of iced water to stop it overcooking. Drain. Cut the asparagus diagonally into 5 cm lengths.

Use a teaspoon to scoop out the egg yolks and place them in a bowl. Add the mayonnaise and sriracha, then mash with a fork until smooth. Place the egg white halves on a plate.

Spoon the egg yolk mixture into a piping bag fitted with a 1 cm fluted nozzle, then pipe it into the cavity of each egg white. (You could also just spoon it in or use a zip-lock bag with the corner cut off.) Sprinkle with paprika.

Combine the watercress, asparagus, celery and cucumber in a bowl. Transfer to a serving platter and place the devilled eggs on top. Drizzle with the vinaigrette and serve.

MEATY ADDITION: Serve with Barbecued or chargrilled chicken breast fillets (see page 260) or Barbecued white fish fillets (see page 275) as part of a shared meal.

TASTY ZEN: 9 VEGETARIAN LUNCHBOXES

for kids of all ages

I wrote a long article for my *delicious. on Sunday* column in your favourite Sunday newspaper about what makes a perfect lunchbox and how we've all got way too judgy about what we put in them. It would make the perfect introduction to this little section, but it's waaaay too long. So instead, read it online at delicious.com.au and see what follows as awesome ideas for the best plant-based lunchboxes.

LUNCHBOX 1

Place some leftover green fritters (see page 212) with some wedges of baby qukes, sliced hard-boiled egg, a handful of mixed herbs (mint, flat-leaf parsley, basil or whatever you have on hand) and a small pot of thick natural yoghurt swirled with mango chutney.

LUNCHBOX 2

Combine chopped and deseeded tomato, sliced cucumber, finely chopped red onion, green chilli and coriander leaves, and drizzle with lime juice. Serve with warmed leftover Dal makhani (see page 242), a handful of bhuja or chopped roasted peanuts, roti or Indian flatbreads and some thick natural yoghurt.

LUNCHBOX 3

Spread a thick slice of nice crusty
bread or a wrap of your choice
with mashed avocado and top with
a good slice of leftover meatloaf
(see page 170), thinly sliced brie
and some baby rocket. Finish with a
few good dollops of beetroot relish
and another slice of bread, or wrap
up and eat.

LUNCHBOX 4

Serve leftover Avocado and friends salad
(see page 12) with rinsed and drained
canned black beans or kidney beans,
baby cos lettuce leaves and corn chips
(optional). Have lime wedges on hand
for a last-minute squeeze.

LUNCHBOX 5

Place Beetroot and hazelnut falafels
(see page 222) on baby spinach and
zoodles, and serve with a little pot of
whipped feta, some fresh celery batons,
a handful of nuts and a fresh fig.

LUNCHBOX 6

Serve a portion of Zucchini slice 5.0 (see
page 149) with a good quarter of avocado
rubbed with lemon juice and a side salad of
rinsed and drained canned lentils, chopped
cherry tomatoes and very thin wedges of red
onion sprinkled with pomegranate arils and
mint leaves. Enjoy with flatbread and
a lemon wedge to squeeze over.

LUNCHBOX 7

Spread a long baguette with Green hummus (see page 58) or Pea and pumpkin seed pesto (see page 198). Sprinkle grated vegan cheese or cheese of your choice over leftover meatballs in tomato sauce (see page 118) and warm in the microwave until the cheese has melted. Scoop into the baguette and eat with gusto.

LUNCHBOX 8

Green lasagne (see page 99) with a side salad of shredded radicchio, flat-leaf parsley leaves and thinly sliced pear, sprinkled with chopped toasted hazelnuts. Drizzle with Instant blue cheese dressing (see page 43) and serve with quality sea salt grissini sticks.

Sifnos summer salad revisited

SERVES: 4 PREP: 15 mins COOKING: 20 mins

On a recent trip to Greece for a wedding I became obsessed with creating the perfect Greek salad, and experimented with changing the cheese and even adding fruit, such as peaches or watermelon, to support or replace the tomatoes or cucumbers. The most unusual and successful variation I tried was the addition of barley rusks in the manner they employ in Crete for their Dakos salad. This does a delightful job of soaking up the dressing, and adds some biscuity toastiness. These rusks are hard to find here so rather than use digestive biscuits (which taste oddly similar to me), we've employed toasted bread, which is sometimes used instead of rusks in Crete, too.

300 g sourdough bread, crusts
   removed and torn into large chunks
olive oil spray
6 ripe tomatoes, cut into large chunks
1 long cucumber, cut into large
   chunks
1 red onion, cut into thin wedges
120 g pitted Kalamata olives
2 teaspoons Greek dried oregano
   (or fresh oregano if it's growing in
   your garden)
juice of 1 lemon
2 tablespoons extra-virgin olive oil
sea salt and freshly ground
   black pepper
200 g cottage cheese
100 g Greek feta, crumbled
2 tablespoons finely chopped flat-leaf
   parsley (optional)

Preheat the oven to 180°C/160°C fan-forced.

Spread out the bread on a baking tray and spray with olive oil. Bake, turning once, for 20 minutes or until golden and crisp.

Combine the tomato, cucumber, onion, olives and oregano in a shallow bowl. Drizzle with the lemon juice and olive oil, then season and toss together.

Just before serving, add the bread and toss to combine.

Dollop teaspoons of the cottage cheese over the salad and scatter over the feta and parsley (if using).

 TIP: Use marinated macadamia feta (I like the one by Botanical Cuisine) for a vegan version of this salad, and dump the cottage cheese.

MEATY ADDITION: Serve with Barbecued or chargrilled lamb cutlets (see page 265).

The twofer salad

SERVES: 6 **PREP:** 20 mins (plus 30 mins pickling) **COOKING:** 10 mins

I can't remember why this is called the twofer salad. I suspect because it contains two of the most vaunted superfoods – one very 2017 (kale) and one very 1930s (grapefruit – star of the fad low-cal Hollywood Diet). Or it could be because it's named after a bloke called Christwofer who did me a favour once regarding an issue I had with a summons.

2 red or pink grapefruits
2 teaspoons maple syrup
1 teaspoon Dijon mustard (see note on page 129)
60 ml (¼ cup) olive oil
sea salt and freshly ground black pepper
1 small red onion, sliced as thinly as possible (use a mandoline if you have one)
2 teaspoons caster sugar
1 teaspoon sea salt
3 leeks, trimmed and cut into 1 cm thick coins
100 g chopped kale leaves, massaged with a little olive oil to soften slightly
1 baby fennel bulb, very thinly shaved (also with a mandoline if possible)

Peel the grapefruits. Holding the grapefruit over a bowl to catch the juice, use a sharp knife to cut away the white pith and remove the grapefruit segments, cutting close to both sides of the white membrane. Once you have removed the segments, give the remaining pith a squeeze to extract as much juice as possible. Repeat with the remaining grapefruit. Discard the pith and set the grapefruit segments aside.

Place 2 tablespoons of the grapefruit juice in a jug, along with the maple syrup, mustard and 2 tablespoons of the olive oil. Season with salt and pepper and whisk together.

Place the onion, sugar and salt in a bowl and add the remaining grapefruit juice (you should have at least 2½ tablespoons). Mix until well combined, then set aside for 30 minutes to pickle, turning occasionally.

Heat the remaining oil in a frying pan over medium–high heat. Add the leek and cook for 4–5 minutes each side or until tender, well charred and slightly burnt around the edges.

Combine the kale and fennel in a serving bowl or on a plate. Drain the onion and add to the salad, then top with the grapefruit segments and charred leek. Drizzle with the grapefruit dressing and serve.

 TIP: If you want to add some grains to this salad, combine 220 g (1 cup) of pearl barley or spelt and 750 ml (3 cups) of red wine in a large saucepan and bring to the boil. Reduce the heat to medium–low and simmer for 35 minutes or until the wine has been absorbed and the barley is tender but still a little bitey. Add 30 g of butter, then cover and allow to steam for 5 minutes. Use a fork to fluff up the grains, then set aside to cool. Toss through the kale mixture.

MEATY ADDITION: Serve with Barbecued or chargrilled chicken thigh fillets (see page 261) or Crispy-skinned salmon fillets (see page 275).

The impossible vegan caesar salad

SERVES: 4 **PREP:** 15 mins **COOKING:** 5 mins

Anyone on TV is a diva in some form or another – just ask their entourage. My diva antics are well reported. I like a car to drive me from the hotel all the way to the stage for my live shows and insist they drive three times around the town on the way back to ensure I'm not followed by ~~rabbit~~ … no no … rabid fans or the paparazzi. Or maybe that was someone else I once shared the bill with at a festival …

I only want the pineapple-filled squares from the block of 'Snack' in my rider.

Plus it's important that the minion carrying the mirror in front of me everywhere I walk never retreats too fast, or tries to look behind them.

In fact, the true measure of a diva is the ridiculous requests they make of those around them. And so it is with this recipe. I liked the title, so I demanded food guru Michelle create it for me. Now!

So make it and see how she went. She's praying for a few positive comments!!! You see, she knows what happened to the promoter who left the orange cream Snack squares in.

1 baguette, thinly sliced diagonally
olive oil spray
2 garlic cloves, peeled
4 baby cos lettuces, leaves separated
1 x quantity Carrot bacon (see
   page 133)
4 Brazil nuts

VEGAN CAESAR DRESSING
300 g silken tofu
2 small garlic cloves, crushed
2 tablespoons nutritional yeast
1 tablespoon capers, rinsed
   and drained
1 teaspoon mustard powder
2 tablespoons freshly squeezed
   lemon juice
sea salt and freshly ground
   black pepper

To make the dressing, place all the ingredients in the small bowl of a food processor and process until smooth and well combined. Transfer to a bowl.

Preheat a barbecue grill on high. Spray both sides of the baguette slices with olive oil. Cook in two batches for 2 minutes each side or until the bread is golden and charred. Rub one of the cut sides with the garlic cloves. Set aside.

Arrange the lettuce leaves, baguette croutons and carrot bacon on serving plates. Dollop with the dressing and finely grate the Brazil nuts over the top.

MEATY ADDITION: Replace the carrot bacon with 6 chopped rashers Crispy bacon (see page 268) or Crispy prosciutto shards (see page 269).

#Blessed bowls

If bowls are dead then see this as their swan song, a final death-bed aria to a life well lived. Maybe we can enact a resurrection. #blessed #foodasmedicine #bowledover.

You'll also find a dedicated hummus section here full of delicious dips that are perfect grazing food, or even as a dressing for meat and seafood if you wish.

#1 The #blessed Brazil rice bowl

SERVES: 4 **PREP:** 20 mins (plus 1 hour pickling) **COOKING:** 1 hour

I have a sneaking suspicion that the whole bowl thing might be over, but I feel that might break the heart of my publisher who still loves them and really wanted this section in the book. I have demurred because I think that doesn't make them any less delicious or superbly suited for the Australian climate, and not because she's the one signing the cheques … honestly.

1 celery stalk, thinly sliced, leaves reserved

2 tablespoons apple cider vinegar

2 teaspoons caster sugar

sea salt and freshly ground black pepper

4 baby fennel bulbs, tops trimmed and each bulb cut into 3 steaks, keeping the base intact, fronds reserved

2 tablespoons olive oil

400 g seedless red grapes, picked from the stems

3 × 250 g packets microwave black rice, heated following the packet instructions and cooled (you can also use red or brown rice, freekeh or barley)

180 g (¾ cup) Brazil nuts, coarsely chopped into a rubble, plus extra to serve

1 orange

1 head radicchio, leaves separated

INSTANT BLUE CHEESE DRESSING

150 g mild creamy blue cheese

200 g creme fraiche

1 tablespoon apple cider vinegar, plus extra if needed

pinch of sea salt

1 teaspoon caster sugar

Combine the celery, vinegar, sugar and 1 teaspoon of salt in a bowl. Set aside to pickle, tossing occasionally, for 1 hour, or longer if you have time. Drain.

Meanwhile, preheat the oven to 200°C/180°C fan-forced. Line a baking tray with baking paper.

Spread out the fennel on the prepared tray, drizzle with the olive oil and season with salt and pepper. Roast for 40 minutes. Turn the fennel over and add 300 g of the grapes, then roast for a further 15 minutes or until the fennel is golden and the grapes are all wrinkly.

While the fennel is cooking, make your dressing. Mash the blue cheese, creme fraiche and vinegar in a bowl. Season with the salt, sugar and more vinegar if needed. You want a good hum of vinegar to help pull the richness and salty pungency of the blue cheese back into line.

Combine the black rice and Brazil nuts in a bowl and set aside.

Cut the remaining grapes in half and toss with the pickled celery.

Peel the orange. Holding the orange over a bowl to catch the juice, use a sharp knife to cut away the white pith and remove the segments, cutting close to both sides of the white membrane. Once you have removed the segments, give the remaining pith a squeeze to extract as much juice as possible. Discard the pith and add the segments to the juice. Once the cooked grapes are ready, add them to the bowl and very gently toss.

Lay three radicchio leaves in the top left quadrant of each bowl. Pile in the Brazil rice, covering the base of the bowls. Place the fennel proudly in the bottom left quadrant, leaving some rice showing in between the fennel. Top with the orange and grape mixture, then the celery and grape mixture. Add a few dollops of the dressing and scatter with the reserved celery leaves, fennel fronds and extra chopped Brazil nuts.

MEATY ADDITION: Add 1 x quantity sliced Roast pork fillet (see page 272) to the bowls.

#2 The handmaid's tale undressed (& unrolled)

SERVES: 4 PREP: 20 mins (plus 2 hours standing) COOKING: 25 mins

It's a time-consuming pain to make rice paper rolls; some of us lack the dexterity to do it without the filling falling out or the rice paper tearing or drying out during our fumbles. Far better to find an easier Gilead way and just put all the makings in a bowl rather than a roll. Not handmade but still as tasty. Praise be!

2 large carrots, shredded with a
    julienne peeler or cut into long
    matchsticks
200 g rice vermicelli noodles
boiling water
3 long red chillies, deseeded and
    finely chopped
1½ teaspoons brown sugar
juice of 1 lime
75 g (1 cup) finely shredded
    iceberg lettuce
2 Lebanese cucumbers, thinly sliced
150 g shredded red cabbage
100 g bean sprouts, trimmed
400 g mixed cherry tomatoes, halved
1 bunch Thai basil, leaves picked
1 bunch mint, leaves picked
½ bunch coriander, leaves picked
110 g (⅔ cup) unsalted roasted
    peanuts, coarsely chopped
lime wedges, to serve

VEGAN 'FISH' SAUCE
80 ml (⅓ cup) soy sauce or tamari
8 dried shiitake mushrooms
3 nori sheets, torn into large pieces
1 teaspoon black peppercorns
1 teaspoon white miso paste
1 garlic clove, sliced

Start by making your 'fish' sauce. Place all the ingredients in a saucepan, add 500 ml (2 cups) of water and bring to a simmer over low heat. Simmer gently without stirring (otherwise you will break up the seaweed) for 20 minutes to develop the flavours. Remove from the heat and set aside to cool and infuse for 2 hours (or you can do this for longer if you have more time). Strain through a fine sieve, discarding the solids. Keep the sauce in the fridge for up to 1 week. (Alternatively, you can use a seafood-based fish sauce if you are not ethically compromised.)

Place the carrot in a microwave-safe bowl, splash with a little water and cover the bowl with plastic wrap. Microwave for 1 minute to soften slightly. Drain straight away as you don't want the carrot to overcook.

Meanwhile, place the vermicelli in a large heatproof bowl. Cover with boiling water and stand for 2 minutes or until tender. Drain well and return to the bowl.

Combine the chilli, sugar and 1½ tablespoons of the lime juice in a jug. Give the 'fish' sauce a shake to mix in the sediment on the bottom and add 125 ml (½ cup) to the jug. Mix until well combined.

Divide the lettuce among serving bowls and drizzle with the remaining lime juice. Add the noodles, carrot, cucumber, cabbage, bean sprouts, tomatoes and herbs and drizzle with the dressing. Sprinkle with the peanuts and serve with lime wedges on the side.

MEATY ADDITION: Shred ½ Roast chicken (see page 262) or slice 300 g Chinese barbecued pork and add to the bowls.

#3 The Aleppo herb rice salad bowl

SERVES: 4 **PREP:** 25 mins **COOKING:** 1 hour 10 mins

Here at the Matt Preston Institute of Fine Food we don't just put our licked fingers in the air when it comes to picking the titles for all the recipes in these books to see which way the wind is blowing. (And if you have seen us doing this outside the Institute we are much more likely hailing an Uber.)

Oh no, there is a full and complete program of qualitative and quantitative research behind each name, and the words 'Aleppo', 'Herb', 'Salad' and 'Bowl' tested off the chart. It says authenticity, it says community, it mentions a city and it says both exotica and freshness. For example, you'd be 70 per cent less likely to make this recipe if it was called 'Mosul Beetroot Rice Bucket'. I rest my case.

300 g (1½ cups) long-grain brown rice
875 ml (3½ cups) vegetable stock
6 baby beetroot bulbs with stems
and leaves attached
2 tablespoons honey
1 tablespoon freshly squeezed
lemon juice
1 garlic clove, crushed
1 teaspoon ground cumin
½ teaspoon sweet paprika (or Aleppo
pepper, which is available online)
6 Lebanese eggplants, halved
lengthways, flesh scored in
a crisscross
100 g (1 cup) walnut halves
260 g (1 cup) thick natural yoghurt
1 tablespoon tahini
¼ cup finely shredded mint
sea salt and freshly ground
black pepper
100 g baby spinach leaves
2 zucchini, peeled into ribbons
75 g punnet pomegranate arils (which
is what posh correct people call
those gem-like seeds)
extra-virgin olive oil, sumac and
lemon wedges, to serve

Place the rice and stock in a large saucepan and bring to the boil over high heat, then reduce the heat to a bare simmer. Cover and cook for 40 minutes or until all the stock has been absorbed. Remove from the heat and leave the rice to steam for 10 minutes. Fluff up the grains with a fork, then set aside to cool.

Preheat the oven to 180°C/160°C fan-forced. Line two large baking trays with baking paper.

Trim the stems off the beetroot, leaving a little still attached to the bulb. Reserve the stems and leaves. Wrap the bulbs in foil and place on one of the baking trays.

Whisk together the honey, lemon juice, garlic, cumin and paprika in a bowl. Put the eggplant on the remaining tray, cut-side up, and brush with a little of the honey mixture.

Place the eggplant and beetroot in the oven and roast for 20 minutes. Remove the trays from the oven, scatter the walnuts over the beetroot tray, and brush the eggplant with the remaining honey mixture. Roast for a further 10 minutes or until the walnuts are lightly toasted, the beetroot is tender and the eggplant is golden.

Meanwhile, combine the yoghurt, tahini and mint in a bowl. Season with salt and pepper.

If you can, wear kitchen gloves to peel the beetroot or you will end up with purple hands. Carefully use the foil to rub off all the skin, then cut them in half.

Divide the rice among serving bowls. Top with the eggplant, beetroot, spinach and zucchini. Place a dollop of tahini yoghurt on top and sprinkle with the walnuts and pomegranate arils. Drizzle with olive oil and sprinkle with sumac, then serve with lemon wedges.

MEATY ADDITION: Add 500 g shredded Slow-roasted lamb shoulder (see page 264) to the bowls.

#4 The #blessed bento bowl

SERVES: 4 **PREP:** 15 mins (plus 1 hour marinating) **COOKING:** 15 mins

What started as dried lunches for Japanese farmers and hunters packed into bags or old segmented seed boxes a thousand years ago have evolved into the lavish bento boxes of today. The first fancy bento boxes appeared about 450 years ago in the Azuchi-Momoyama Period (1574–1600) as a sort of picnic basket to take when you went out viewing the cherry blossoms or to a tea ceremony. The name, lifted from a slang term from an earlier dynasty, meant 'convenient'.

The bento's use broadened in the Edo Period when no journey, or trip to an interminably long performance of some kabuki maruhon-mono play, was complete without a bento box filled with rice balls, chestnuts, pickles and seafood. Bento's popularity spread further with the arrival of train travel, and special train bento called ekiben were first sold at Utsunomiya Station in Tochigi Prefecture in 1885. You'll still find a dizzy array of train foods sold at your local bullet train station, although plastic has replaced the wooden bento, and traditional travel snacks like rice balls have been largely superseded by western-influenced snacks, such as white bread sangers filled with crumbed pork schnitzel and barbecue sauce.

Bento had also waned after World War I when times were tough and only the rich could afford the luxury of a packed lunch. This prompted schools to ban them – to save the loss of face of students who were hard up – and gradually establish egalitarian school canteens.

Personally, I think this bowl would be equally at home in one of those cafeterias or in a gorgeous lacquered wooden box. It's also perfect for watching a Netflix binge marathon, which is like modern kabuki.

And it looks like an 80s bathroom suite.

Just don't replace the rice with rice balls shaped like pandas complete with nori or black bean eyes, ears and paws. No matter how tempted you are by the myriad different panda moulds for sale on the internet.

300 g silken tofu, cut into 2 cm cubes
60 ml (¼ cup) ponzu sauce (you can buy this in larger supermarkets or Asian supermarkets)
335 g (1½ cups) sushi rice, rinsed well
2 tablespoons sushi seasoning
110 g (1 cup) frozen podded edamame
150 g snow peas, trimmed, strings removed
2 nori sheets, quartered
4 baby cucumbers, thinly sliced
pickled ginger, to serve
1 spring onion, white and green parts cut into matchsticks
black sesame seeds, for sprinkling

Place the tofu in a shallow, flat-bottomed glass or ceramic dish (make sure the dish isn't too big as you want all the tofu to be slightly submerged in the sauce). Drizzle with the ponzu sauce and set aside for 1 hour to marinate. Halfway through (that's after 30 minutes, maths fans) very, very carefully turn these tender babies over.

Meanwhile, place the rice and 500 ml (2 cups) of water in a saucepan. Bring to the boil over high heat, then reduce the heat to low and simmer, covered, for 10 minutes or until all the liquid has been absorbed. Remove from the heat, then cover and leave the rice to steam for 10 minutes. Fluff up the grains with a fork and stir through the sushi seasoning, then set aside to cool to room temperature (yes, warm is also fine if your prefer your sushi rice at body temperature).

Bring a saucepan of water to the boil. Add the edamame and snow peas and cook for 1–2 minutes or until heated through. Drain. If you like, slice the snow peas diagonally in half lengthways for sexier presentation.

Place two nori quarters in each serving bowl to line half the bowl. Add the rice and top with the tofu and its marinade, edamame, snow peas, cucumber and pickled ginger. Sprinkle with the spring onion and sesame seeds and serve.

MEATY ADDITION: Add 300 g thinly sliced sashimi-grade salmon or tuna or sliced Barbecued or chargrilled whole beef fillet (see page 267) to the bowls.

#5 (She was an ...) American bowl

SERVES: 4 **PREP:** 30 mins **COOKING:** 50 mins

It's a curse but I can't read this recipe without the chorus of Tom Petty's 'American Girl' reverberating around my head. Worse than that I can even see the music ...

She was an American girl.

I know us blokes become hypochondriacs as we get older, but I suspect this is the first sign of an aneurism. Either that or I have seen John Travolta's film Phenomenon *too many times. That was the one where he was actually an angel, right?*

2 teaspoons smoked paprika
sea salt
600 g sweet potato, peeled and
    cut into 4 cm cubes
3 carrots, cut into 10 cm long batons
2 tablespoons olive oil
2 red onions, cut into thick wedges
200 g (1 cup) white quinoa, rinsed
150 g (1 cup) frozen corn kernels
2 tablespoons sesame seeds, toasted
20 g butter
2 tablespoons maple syrup
¼ teaspoon ground cinnamon
125 g (1 cup) pecan halves
⅓ cup coarsely chopped flat-leaf
    parsley
finely grated zest of 1 lemon
Kewpie mayonnaise and barbecue
    sauce, to serve

Preheat the oven to 200°C/180°C fan-forced. Line a large baking tray with baking paper.

Combine the paprika and 3 teaspoons of salt in a bowl. Place the sweet potato and carrot on the prepared tray and drizzle with half the olive oil. Sprinkle with the paprika salt. Add the onion to the tray and drizzle with the remaining oil. Roast, turning halfway through, for 50 minutes or until the sweet potato is golden and the carrot and onion are slightly charred.

Meanwhile, place the quinoa and 750 ml (3 cups) of water in a saucepan. Bring to the boil over high heat, then reduce the heat to low and simmer, covered, for 12 minutes or until all the water has been absorbed. Stir in the corn kernels, then remove from the heat. Cover and set aside to steam for 10 minutes (the corn will cook in the residual heat during this time), then fluff up the grains with a fork. Add the sesame seeds and toss to combine.

Now that everything is cooking away, line another baking tray with baking paper. Heat the butter, maple syrup and cinnamon in a frying pan over medium heat until bubbling. Cook, stirring occasionally, for 4 minutes or until thickened. Add the pecans and toss for 2 minutes until well coated. Pour over the prepared tray and set aside to cool and set.

Combine the parsley and lemon zest in a bowl and season with salt.

Divide the quinoa mixture among serving bowls and top with the roasted veggies. Scatter over the candied pecans and the parsley mixture. Serve with a dollop of mayo and a squeeze of barbecue sauce side by side.

#6 The crunchy granola Sunday bowl

SERVES: 4 **PREP:** 20 mins (plus overnight draining) **COOKING:** 1 hour 10 mins

Like Neil Diamond's famous tune, this can be eaten any day of the week, not just Sunday. #GoodTimes.

170 g (½ cup) orange marmalade,
  warmed in a microwave for
  30 seconds until runny
½ teaspoon ground cinnamon
1 kg Kent pumpkin, unpeeled,
  deseeded and cut into 2 cm
  thick wedges
2 red onions, quartered
olive oil spray
sea salt and freshly ground
  black pepper
2 bunches baby carrots, trimmed
  (use rainbow carrots if you can
  get them)
¼ teaspoon saffron threads, soaked
  in 1 tablespoon warm water
1 tablespoon olive oil
250 g (1½ cups) cracked freekeh or
  pearl barley
100 g chopped kale, massaged with
  a little olive oil

LABNE
500 g Greek-style yoghurt
1 teaspoon sea salt

MACADAMIA GRANOLA
20 g unsalted butter
50 g (½ cup) rolled oats
45 g (¼ cup) pumpkin seeds
45 g (¼ cup) macadamias, coarsely
  chopped
1 teaspoon sea salt flakes
2 tablespoons brown sugar
2 teaspoons maple syrup

To make the labne, line a sieve with two layers of muslin and place over a bowl. Mix together the yoghurt and salt, then spoon into the lined sieve. Place in the fridge overnight to drain.

To make the granola, melt the butter in a large frying pan over medium heat until foaming. Add the oats and pumpkin seeds and cook, tossing, for 5 minutes or until they start to toast. Add the macadamias and cook for 2 minutes or until toasted. Add the salt and sugar and toss for 2 minutes or until well coated and the sugar starts to dissolve – it will still be a little grainy, but this is fine. Add the maple syrup and cook, tossing, for 2–3 minutes or until well coated. Transfer to a tray to cool.

Preheat the oven to 220°C/200°C fan-forced. Line two baking trays with baking paper.

Combine the warmed marmalade and cinnamon in a bowl. Place the pumpkin on one of the prepared trays and brush with half the marmalade. Add the onion and spray with olive oil. Season with salt and pepper and roast for 15 minutes.

While the pumpkin and onion are roasting, place the carrots on the remaining tray. Drizzle with the saffron water and season with salt and pepper.

Remove the pumpkin from the oven and brush with the remaining marmalade. Return to the oven, along with the tray of carrots, and roast for a further 30 minutes. Leave the pumpkin in the oven and remove the carrots. Drizzle the carrots with the olive oil and toss, then return to the oven and roast both trays for another 10 minutes or until the pumpkin is caramelised and the carrots are golden.

While all your veggies are roasting, place the freekeh or pearl barley and 875 ml (3½ cups) of water in a large saucepan. Bring to the boil over high heat, then reduce the heat to low and simmer for 25 minutes or until all the water has been absorbed. Fluff up the grains with a fork.

Divide the freekeh or pearl barley among serving bowls. Top with the pumpkin, onion, carrots and kale. Spoon a dollop of labne on top and sprinkle with the granola.

 TIP: You can also sprinkle this granola on balls of ice-cream with chocolate sauce to make a crunchy granola sundae.

MEATY ADDITION: Add 1 x quantity sliced Roast pork fillet (see page 272) or 4 Barbecued or chargrilled lamb skewers (see page 265) to the bowls.

#7 The Japanese #blessed bowl of virtue

SERVES: 4 PREP: 20 mins (plus 30 mins marinating) COOKING: 10 mins

We all like to feel good about ourselves, and can I just take this opportunity to say how good you are looking? Have you done something to your hair? Maybe it's all this vego food you're interested in eating. Sure, positive reinforcement is one thing but the other is to encourage positive reinforcement from your food as well. Here's a bowl that makes you feel better about yourself just by reading the recipe.

300 g firm tofu, halved lengthways, then cut crossways into 1 cm thick slices
125 ml (½ cup) soy sauce or tamari
3 cm knob of ginger, peeled and finely grated
½ bunch coriander, leaves picked, stalks finely chopped
1 teaspoon chilli flakes
2 tablespoons peanut oil
1 bunch broccolini, stems halved lengthways
270 g soba noodles
1 bunch radishes, very thinly shaved (use a mandoline if you have one)
80 g (½ cup) smoked almonds, coarsely chopped

NEW YORK DRESSING
85 g (⅓ cup) Kewpie mayonnaise
¼ teaspoon liquid smoke, or to taste
4 drops of Maggi seasoning

Combine the tofu, tamari, ginger, coriander stalk and chilli flakes in a glass or ceramic bowl. Place in the fridge, turning the tofu occasionally, for 30 minutes to marinate.

Heat the peanut oil in a large non-stick frying pan over medium–high heat. Add the broccolini and cook, tossing, for 5 minutes or until bright green and slightly charred. Transfer to a plate and cover to keep warm. Using tongs, carefully transfer the tofu slices to the pan (reserve the marinade). Cook for 2 minutes each side or until golden. Add the marinade, then immediately remove from the heat, as you want it to heat through without evaporating too much.

Cook the noodles following the packet instructions. Drain and refresh under cold running water.

To make the dressing, mix together the mayo, liquid smoke and Maggi seasoning in a bowl. Cover and place in the fridge until required.

Divide the noodles among serving bowls. Top with the broccolini, radish and then the tofu with a drizzle of the sauce left in the pan. Add a fat dollop of the New York dressing and sprinkle with the almonds and coriander leaves.

MEATY ADDITION: Replace the tofu with 300 g thinly sliced chicken breast fillets, marinate and cook, following the recipe.

#BLESSED
HUMMUS BOWLS

It is strange in an era where the US has become increasingly suspicious of anything Arab that hummus sales have exploded. The US hummus market has soared from $5 million in 1996 to $725 million in 2016, with one in four US homes having a version of this traditional chickpea dip in their fridge. Not bad for a dip whose recipe was first recorded in Cairo in the 13th century, albeit without tahini and garlic. In part this explosion has been due to a further broadening of ingredients, from the sensible, such as beetroot or pumpkin, to the ridiculous (chocolate hummus anyone?). Here we paddle furiously to catch the huge hummus wave before it crashes on our shores.

Smokey sweet potato hummus

SERVES: 6
PREP: 15 mins
COOKING: 35 mins

400 g sweet potato, peeled and cut into 1.5 cm pieces
125 ml (½ cup) olive oil, plus extra to serve
2 teaspoons smoked paprika, plus extra for dusting
sea salt and freshly ground black pepper
400 g can chickpeas, rinsed and drained
2 tablespoons tahini
2 garlic cloves, crushed
2 tablespoons freshly squeezed lemon juice
2 ice cubes
finely chopped toasted walnuts, for sprinkling
baked pita bread, to serve

Preheat the oven to 180°C/160°C fan-forced. Line a baking tray with baking paper.

Place the sweet potato on the prepared tray, drizzle with 1 tablespoon of the olive oil and sprinkle with the paprika. Toss until the sweet potato is well coated and season with salt and pepper. Roast for 35 minutes or until the sweet potato is tender.

Reserve one-third of the sweet potato and place the rest in a food processor. Add the chickpeas, tahini, garlic, lemon juice and ice cubes. Blitz until smooth, scraping down the side occasionally. With the motor running, gradually add the remaining oil and blitz until creamy.

Spoon the hummus into a bowl. Use the back of a spoon to make an indent in the centre, then fill with the reserved sweet potato. Sprinkle with the walnuts and extra paprika and drizzle with extra oil. Serve with baked pita breads.

Roast onion (aka French onion) hummus

SERVES: 6
PREP: 15 mins
COOKING: 1 hour

2 large onions, quartered
6 garlic cloves, unpeeled
80 ml (⅓ cup) extra-virgin olive oil, plus extra to serve
3 thyme sprigs, leaves picked
1 tablespoon apple cider vinegar
400 g can chickpeas, rinsed and drained
65 g (¼ cup) sour cream
2 tablespoons tahini
1 tablespoon freshly squeezed lemon juice
2 ice cubes
sea salt and freshly ground black pepper
crinkle cut potato chips, to serve

Preheat the oven to 180°C/160°C fan-forced. Line a baking tray with baking paper.

Place the onion and garlic on the prepared tray, drizzle with 1 tablespoon of the olive oil and sprinkle with the thyme. Roast for 40 minutes. Drizzle the vinegar over the onion and roast for a further 20 minutes or until the onion is tender and slightly burnt around the edges.

Squeeze the garlic cloves out of their skins and into a food processor. Add the chickpeas, sour cream, tahini, lemon juice and ice cubes. Blitz until smooth, scraping down the side occasionally. With the motor running, gradually add the remaining oil and blitz until creamy. Reserve two of the onion quarters and add the remaining quarters to the processor and blitz until well combined. Season and transfer to a serving bowl.

Roughly chop the reserved onion quarters and sprinkle over the hummus. Drizzle with a little extra oil and serve with chips.

Green hummus

SERVES: 4
PREP: 10 mins

400 g can chickpeas, rinsed and drained (if you like,
    buy another can, then drain and serve a handful
    of chickpeas in the middle of the hummus)
50 g baby spinach leaves
1 garlic clove, crushed
½ cup flat-leaf parsley leaves
¼ cup basil leaves
2 tablespoons snipped chives, plus extra to serve
1 teaspoon ground cumin
1 tablespoon freshly squeezed lemon juice
2 ice cubes
60 ml (¼ cup) olive oil, plus extra to serve
sea salt and freshly ground black pepper
a whole lotta green veggies, to serve

Place the chickpeas, spinach, garlic, parsley, basil, chives, cumin,
lemon juice and ice cubes in a food processor and blitz until
smooth, scraping down the side occasionally. With the motor
running, gradually add the olive oil and blitz until creamy. Season
to taste with salt and pepper.

Spoon the hummus into a bowl. Use the back of a spoon to
make an indent in the centre, then drizzle with extra oil and
sprinkle with extra chives, a little salt and chickpeas (if using).
Serve with green veggies.

Chickpea hummus with pickled red cabbage

SERVES: 6

PREP: 15 mins (plus 2 hours pickling)

2 × 400 g cans chickpeas, rinsed and drained
6 garlic cloves, crushed
95 g (⅓ cup) tahini
2 teaspoons ground cumin
2 tablespoons freshly squeezed lemon juice
3 ice cubes
125 ml (½ cup) olive oil
sea salt
Greek-style yoghurt, to serve

PICKLED RED CABBAGE
125 ml (½ cup) apple cider vinegar
   or red wine vinegar
2 garlic cloves, thinly sliced
2 fresh or dried bay leaves
2 teaspoons caster sugar
1 teaspoon caraway seeds
1 teaspoon sea salt
¼ red cabbage, finely shredded
   on a mandoline

To make the pickled cabbage, combine the vinegar, garlic, bay leaves, sugar, caraway seeds and salt in a large glass or ceramic bowl. Stir until the sugar has dissolved, then add the cabbage and toss until well combined. Set aside to pickle for 2 hours, stirring every 30 minutes.

Meanwhile, place the chickpeas, garlic, tahini, cumin, lemon juice and ice cubes in a food processor and blitz until smooth, scraping down the side occasionally. With the motor running, gradually add the olive oil and blitz until creamy. Season to taste with salt.

Spoon the hummus into the centre of a serving plate and swirl the yoghurt in the centre. Use a fork to lift the cabbage out of the pickling liquid and place around the edge of the hummus.

Barbecue

In Australia we love our barbecues, and there's no reason why plant-based cooking shouldn't embrace them, too. In fact, the roasty, toasty flavours the grill brings can help lift even the most unassuming vegetable into superstar status, whether it's charred broccolini with a sunflower seed hummus or my lettuce tacos with haloumi, corn and avocado. I'll also let you in on a little secret – the cheesy papusas that open this chapter and, perhaps more surprisingly, the grilled snowpea sandwich are my favourites here.

Oozy, melty, cheesy pupusas – emigrated

MAKES: 8 PREP: 30 mins COOKING: 1 hour 10 mins

Last year I had a wonderful weekend up at Sydney's Parklands Food Fest. It's a true community event and I came away with more information on different foods and ingredients than I left behind at my demo. This recipe is inspired by a couple of Salvadoran cooks who joined me on stage to cook pupusas – even though my first attempt at cooking them their way was clumsy in the extreme, they still tasted great. Rest assured, the more you make these pupusas, the quicker and prettier they get.

Implements for making pupusas dating back thousands of years have been found at archaeological excavations in the El Salvador countryside. Those original dumplings were vegetarian and filled with squash, flowers, buds and mushrooms. The addition of meat was attributed to Franciscan friar Bernardino De Sahagún, who lived among the people for over 50 years, translating the psalms and gospels into the local Nahuatl language but also, more unusually, cataloguing the history of the Spanish conquest from the Tenochtitlan-Tlatelolco point of view. This earned him the mantle of the world's first anthropologist.

350 g Kent pumpkin, unpeeled, deseeded and cut into thick wedges
60 ml (¼ cup) olive oil
½ teaspoon chilli flakes
sea salt
300 g (2 cups) masa flour
140 g (1⅓ cups) coarsely grated mozzarella

GARLIC YOGHURT SAUCE
260 g (1 cup) thick natural yoghurt
1 garlic clove, crushed
1 tablespoon freshly squeezed lemon juice
sea salt and freshly ground black pepper, to taste

Preheat the oven to 200°C/180°C fan-forced. Line a large baking tray with baking paper.

Place the pumpkin on the prepared tray. Drizzle with 1 tablespoon of the olive oil, then sprinkle with the chilli flakes and season with salt. Bake for 1 hour, turning over halfway through, until the pumpkin is golden and caramelised around the edges. Set aside to cool. Scoop out the flesh with a spoon and roughly mash. Discard the skin.

Whisk 1 tablespoon of the remaining oil and 125 ml (½ cup) of water in a bowl.

Place the flour and 1 teaspoon of salt in a large bowl, add 500 ml (2 cups) of water and mix with your hands until a soft dough forms. Dip your hands in the oil and water mixture, grab about ⅓ cup of the dough and shape into a ball, then flatten into a thin disc. If the dough is cracking or crumbly, add a little more water.

Place a tablespoon of mozzarella in the centre of the disc. Top with 2 teaspoons of the mashed pumpkin and flatten slightly, then top with another tablespoon of mozzarella. Fold in half and press the edges together to seal. Flatten to about 1 cm thick, making sure the edges don't crack. Repeat with the remaining dough, pumpkin mixture and mozzarella to make eight pupusas in total.

To make the garlic yoghurt sauce, combine all the ingredients in a bowl.

Preheat a barbecue flat plate on medium–high. Add the remaining oil, then the pupusas and use an egg flip to press and flatten them a little more. Cook for 2–3 minutes each side or until golden brown. Serve with the yoghurt sauce and some freshly cracked black pepper.

 TIP: Do play with different fillings, like pulled pork for the carnivores or refried beans. Either way, serve them with a traditional curtido. This is a bit like a light Central American sauerkraut that can be a tart cabbage slaw made with white cabbage, oregano, thinly sliced onion, threads of carrot, salt and lime juice.

MEATY ADDITION: Reduce the pumpkin to 150 g and add 100 g finely chopped Roast chicken (see page 262) or Slow-roasted pork shoulder (see page 270) to the filling.

Mexican sweet potato street salad

SERVES: 6 **PREP:** 20 mins **COOKING:** 35 mins

OK, I admit it. I have an obsession with sweet corn. Partnering it with sweet potatoes, sweet maple syrup, onions and capsicum whose sweetness has been amplified by time on the grill means we need to bring some sour and salt to the party. So don't be shy with your seasoning! That's the way to get this fiesta started ...

2 corn cobs, husks on
3 sweet potatoes (about 1 kg), peeled, halved crossways, then cut lengthways into thin wedges
2 tablespoons olive oil
sea salt and freshly ground black pepper
1 green capsicum, quartered
2 red onions, thinly sliced into rings
2 tablespoons maple syrup
70 g (½ cup) pecan halves (optional)
½ bunch coriander, leaves picked
lime wedges, to serve

CHIPOTLE MAYO
125 g (½ cup) your favourite good-quality mayonnaise, whether that's vegan or vegetarian
1–3 teaspoons finely chopped chipotles in adobo sauce (deseeded if you prefer less heat)
finely grated zest and juice of ½ lime

Preheat a barbecue grill and flatplate with a lid on high to get it really cranking.

Pull back the corn husks and remove any stringy silks. Pull the husks back over the corn and dampen the cobs with water.

Toss the sweet potato and half the olive oil in a bowl. Season well.

Place the corn on the hot grill and the sweet potato on the flat plate. Put the lid down and cook, turning halfway through, for 15 minutes or until just cooked through.

Meanwhile, to make the chipotle mayo, combine all the ingredients in a small bowl. Keep adding chipotle until it reaches the flavour and heat you want.

Remove the corn from the grill but continue to cook the sweet potato, turning occasionally. Using a tea towel, carefully pull back and remove the husks (take care not to burn yourself). Remove any silks still attached, then return the corn to the grill.

Add the capsicum to the grill and the onion to the flat plate and drizzle with the remaining oil. Continue to cook all the veggies with the lid up, turning occasionally, for a further 10–12 minutes or until the onion is golden and the other vegetables are nicely charred.

Transfer the corn, capsicum and sweet potato to a tray. Drizzle the onion left on the flat plate with the maple syrup and cook for 3–5 minutes, until caramelised and sticky. Transfer to a bowl.

Use a large knife to cut the corn from the cobs, then cut the capsicum into thick strips.

Arrange the sweet potato, corn and capsicum on a serving plate and season with salt. Dollop on the chipotle mayo, then top with the maple syrup onion, pecan halves (if using) and coriander leaves. Serve with lime wedges.

MEATY ADDITION: Serve with Barbecued or chargrilled chicken skewers (see page 260) or Barbecued or chargrilled pork cutlets (see page 271) as part of a shared meal.

Barbecued carrots & toasted crunchy brown rice with green mole

SERVES: 4 PREP: 30 mins COOKING: 1 hour 30 mins

'Whoa', I hear you chorus in unison. Aren't moles – those short-sighted tunnellers that pockmark English lawns – animals?

Surely, like avocados and other fruit and veg that require the unpaid labour of insects to pollinate them, moles can't have been taken off the list of banned things by the vegan pope? (BTW, if there isn't one there should be.)

Nope, this is an Oaxacan-inspired mole sauce and not a fricassee of a mole's little legs stripped bare of their black velvet pants, like tiny versions of the ones I wore when I picked up a couple of Logies a long time ago in a galaxy far, far away. I looked like Darth Vader had dropped the cape and helmet to become a Vegas lounge act, but I digress …

300 g (1½ cups) short-grain brown rice
sea salt and freshly ground black pepper
8 thick large carrots, halved lengthways
2 tablespoons olive oil
20 g butter
coriander leaves, to serve

GREEN MOLE SAUCE
40 g (¼ cup) slivered almonds
45 g (¼ cup) pumpkin seeds
2 tablespoons sesame seeds
250 ml (1 cup) vegetable stock
400 g canned tomatillos, drained (or chopped green tomatoes, or the least ripe tomatoes you can find)
35 g (¾ cup) baby spinach leaves
½ green capsicum, roughly chopped
2 jalapeno chillies (or 3 long green chillies), deseeded and roughly chopped
2 garlic cloves
½ bunch coriander, leaves picked
¼ cup oregano leaves
1½ teaspoons ground cumin
1 teaspoon sea salt

Place the rice and 580 ml of water in a large saucepan and add a good pinch of salt. Bring to the boil, then immediately drop the heat to a bare simmer. Cover and cook for 40 minutes or until the water is absorbed. Remove from the heat and set aside with the lid on to steam for 10 minutes. Fluff up the grains with a fork.

Meanwhile, preheat a barbecue flat plate with a lid on medium–high. Place the carrot in a bowl and add the oil. Season well with salt and pepper and toss until well combined. Reduce the heat on the barbecue to medium, then turn off the burners in the middle of the barbecue leaving the outside burners going (this is called indirect cooking). Place the carrot in the centre of the plate where the burners have been turned off. Close the barbecue and cook, turning the carrots over halfway, for 1 hour or until tender and charred around the edges.

While the rice and carrot are cooking, make the mole sauce. Toast the almonds, pumpkin seeds and sesame seeds in a saucepan over medium heat, stirring often, for 3–5 minutes or until golden. Transfer to a high-powered blender. Add the stock and blitz until well combined. Add the remaining ingredients and blitz until smooth. Pour back into the saucepan and place over medium–low heat. Cook, stirring constantly to prevent the sauce from catching, for 8–10 minutes or until thickened.

Melt the butter in a large frying pan over medium heat until foaming. Add the rice and press it down to form a pancake. Cook, without touching it, for 20–30 minutes. You need the rice to stick together and get all golden and crisp on the base so you can turn it out in one piece.

Place a plate over the frying pan, then carefully and quickly invert the pan to get the crispy rice cake onto the plate. Top with the carrot and spoon over the green mole sauce. Top with loads of coriander leaves, a sprinkling of salt and serve.

MEATY ADDITION: Serve with Baked white fish fillets (see page 274) as part of a shared meal.

Lettuce taco

SERVES: 4–6 PREP: 30 mins COOKING: 30 mins

If taco was a verb the title of these tacos would be an order ... Let us taco!

3 avocados, roughly chopped
½ bunch coriander, leaves and stalks
  finely chopped
1 lime, halved
60 g butter, at room temperature
1 teaspoon ground coriander
3 corn cobs in their husks
4 roma tomatoes, halved
olive oil spray
½ teaspoon smoked paprika
sea salt and freshly ground
  black pepper
2 red capsicums, quartered
4 jalapeno chillies
1 small red onion, cut into 1 cm
  thick rings
12 fresh bay leaves
650 g haloumi, cut into 12 × 1.5 cm
  thick slabs
24 large butter lettuce leaves, washed

Place the avocado in a bowl and mash with a fork until almost smooth. Stir in the chopped coriander and squeeze in the juice from one of the lime halves. Place in the fridge to chill.

Preheat a barbecue with a lid on high to get it really cranking.

Combine the butter and ground coriander in a bowl. Pull back the corn husks and remove and discard any stringy silks. Spread the coriander butter over the corn, then pull the husks back over and dampen the cobs with water.

Place the corn on the hot grill. Put the lid down and cook, turning halfway, for 15 minutes or until just cooked though.

Meanwhile, place the tomatoes on a plate or tray. Spray the cut surface with olive oil, then sprinkle with the paprika and season with salt.

Remove the corn from the grill and, using a tea towel, very carefully pull back and remove the husks and any silks still attached. (Take care not to burn yourself.) Return the corn to the grill and add the capsicum and jalapenos. Place the onion and tomatoes, cut-side down, on the flat plate. Cook all the veggies with the lid up, turning occasionally, for a further 10 minutes or until everything is nicely charred.

Place the corn on a chopping board and cut the kernels from the cobs. Tip into a bowl. Roughly chop the capsicum and add to the corn, then squeeze over the remaining lime half and season well.

Halve and deseed the jalapenos and place in a food processor. Add the tomatoes and onion and blitz until well combined. Season well. Get everyone to sit down, ready to assemble their own tacos.

Place a bay leaf on a slab of haloumi, then add to the barbecue flat plate, leaf-side down. Repeat with the remaining bay leaves and haloumi. Cook for 2 minutes each side or until golden.

Pair up the lettuce leaves so that one sits inside another, then fill with the smashed avocado. Top with the corn mixture, haloumi slabs and a dollop of charred jalapeno salsa. Remind people to remove the bay leaves before they eat!

 TIP: There are a number of other ways you could 'lettuce taco'. How about cutting baby cos lettuces into wedges, brushing with olive oil and grilling them on the barbecue to soften and catch a little at the edges. Dress with lemon, more oil and your favourite hard cheese, finely grated. Wrap each wedge in a tortilla with a splodge of the Smokey almond mayo on page 228 or the Chipotle mayo on page 38.

Barbecued haloumi with grilled peaches & green couscous

SERVES: 4 **PREP:** 15 mins (plus 30 mins soaking) **COOKING:** 15 mins

I love the way that haloumi can show you so many faces in the kitchen: golden and squeaky, milky and soft, or grated and mixed with dill or mint for a buttery hand-pie filling. Here, the saltiness of the haloumi enjoys the sweet embrace of juicy peach as it tans on skewers.

280 g (1½ cups) couscous
375 ml (1½ cups) vegetable stock
20 g butter, chopped
6 peaches, halved, stones removed, each peach cut into 6 wedges
500 g haloumi, cut into 2–3 cm cubes
2 tablespoons olive oil
sea salt and freshly ground black pepper
60 g baby rocket leaves, coarsely chopped
75 g (½ cup) pistachio kernels, coarsely chopped
½ cup shredded mint leaves
pomegranate arils (that's the ruby-like seeds to you and me), to serve (optional)

HOT HONEY DRESSING
2 tablespoons olive oil
2 tablespoons lemon juice
2 teaspoons harissa or sriracha chilli sauce
1 tablespoon honey
sea salt and freshly ground black pepper

Soak 12 bamboo skewers in cold water for 30 minutes to stop them burning during cooking. (Alternatively you can use metal skewers.)

Use this time to get your couscous done. Place the couscous in a heatproof bowl. Pour the stock into a saucepan and bring to the boil over medium heat. Pour it over the couscous and set aside for 5 minutes or until all the liquid has been absorbed. Add the butter and let it melt, then fluff up the grains with a fork.

Preheat a barbecue grill with a lid on medium–high.

Thread the peach wedges and haloumi cubes alternately onto the skewers. Place on a tray.

Drizzle the olive oil over the skewers and season well with salt and pepper (you won't need too much salt as the haloumi is already quite salty). Place the skewers on the grill and close the barbecue. Cook for 3–4 minutes each side or until the haloumi is golden and the peach is charred and tender. Transfer to a plate.

Meanwhile, to make the hot honey dressing, place all the ingredients in a small saucepan and stir over low heat until combined and warmed through.

Add the rocket, pistachio and mint to the couscous and toss until well combined. Season with salt and pepper and transfer to a serving platter.

Top the couscous with the skewers and drizzle with the dressing. Sprinkle with pomegranate arils, if desired, and eat immediately.

MEATY ADDITION: Halve 18 prosciutto slices lengthways and wrap each one around a peach wedge before threading onto the skewers. Alternatively, serve with Barbecued or chargrilled whole beef fillet (see page 267) as part of a shared meal.

The new burger with the lot

SERVES: 4 **PREP:** 20 mins (plus 30 mins chilling) **COOKING:** 20 mins

I have a photo on my phone of the most disgusting vegan burger I've ever tasted. It was made with black beans, beetroot and malcontent. It made my more vegan sister also very unhappy, because she had bought it for many dollars at a supermarket. This beetroot burger patty is waaaaaay better! So the rule here is 'make, don't buy'.

60 ml (¼ cup) apple cider vinegar
2 teaspoons caster sugar
1 teaspoon sea salt
1 Lebanese cucumber, halved, deseeded and thinly sliced diagonally
½ green apple, cored and cut into matchsticks
1 large celery stalk, cut into matchsticks
200 g soft creamy feta
130 g (½ cup) Greek-style yoghurt
freshly ground black pepper
2 tablespoons olive oil
4 grainy bread rolls, sliced in half
8 butter lettuce leaves
1 avocado, mashed and seasoned with sea salt and freshly ground black pepper

BEETROOT PATTIES
1 tablespoon olive oil
1 small onion, finely chopped
1 beetroot bulb, coarsely grated
1 garlic clove, crushed
150 g (1 cup) cooked red quinoa
50 g (½ cup) rolled oats
60 g (½ cup) walnuts, finely chopped
1 tablespoon finely chopped dill
finely grated zest of ½ lemon
1 egg
sea salt and freshly ground black pepper

To make the beetroot patties, heat the oil in a frying pan over medium–high heat. Add the onion and cook, stirring, for 5 minutes or until softened. Add the beetroot and garlic and cook for 5 minutes or until the beetroot has softened. Transfer to a bowl and set aside to cool slightly.

Add the quinoa, oats, walnuts, dill, lemon zest and egg to the beetroot mixture. Season well with salt and pepper and mix until well combined. Shape into four 2 cm thick patties. Place on a plate, cover with plastic wrap and chill in the fridge for 30 minutes.

Meanwhile, place the vinegar, sugar and salt in a bowl and stir until the sugar and salt have dissolved. Add the cucumber, apple and celery and toss until well combined. Set aside to pickle for 20 minutes.

Place the feta in a small bowl and mash with a fork until smooth and creamy. Add the yoghurt and mix until smooth and well combined. Season with pepper.

Preheat a barbecue grill and flat plate on medium–high. Heat the oil on the flat plate, add the patties and cook for 3–4 minutes each side or until golden. Transfer to a tray and cover with foil. Set aside to firm up slightly while you barbie the rolls.

Place the cut side of the rolls on the barbecue grill and cook for 1–2 minutes or until toasted.

Spread the toasted base of each roll with the whipped feta and top with two lettuce leaves and a patty. Using tongs or a fork, drain the pickled cucumber mixture and place on top. Dollop on the smashed avocado and finish with the remaining roll halves.

Cauliflower steaks with red hummus

SERVES: 4 **PREP:** 15 mins **COOKING:** 10 mins

I don't really understand the attraction of fake meat that bleeds. Who is it going to attract? For me, part of the attraction of plant-based dishes is precisely that they don't bleed. It's probably something to do with carnivore guilt. Still, for that section of society here's a steak that comes swimming in something sort of red that doesn't involve a laboratory Petri dish.

2 teaspoons cumin seeds
juice of 1 lemon
60 ml (¼ cup) olive oil
sea salt and freshly ground
    black pepper
35 g (⅓ cup) currants
finely grated zest of ½ lemon
2 small heads cauliflower
⅓ cup flat-leaf parsley leaves

RED HUMMUS (AKA MUHAMMARA)
150 g roasted red capsicum (from
    a jar is fine)
60 g (½ cup) walnuts, toasted
400 g can chickpeas, rinsed
    and drained
2 garlic cloves, crushed
1 tablespoon tahini
1 tablespoon harissa
2 teaspoons ground cumin
2 tablespoons freshly squeezed
    lemon juice
2 small ice cubes
2 tablespoons olive oil
sea salt and freshly ground
    black pepper

Preheat a barbecue flat plate with a lid on medium–high.

Combine the cumin seeds, 2 tablespoons of the lemon juice and 2 tablespoons of the olive oil in a bowl. Season well.

While your barbecue heats up, combine the currants, lemon zest, remaining lemon juice and remaining oil in a bowl. Season with salt and set aside so the currants plump up a bit.

Cut each cauliflower into 1.5 cm thick steaks, leaving the base intact (you will get about three steaks from each cauliflower). Save any leftover cauliflower for making rice to go with the Sri Lankan beetroot and cashew curry on page 236.

Brush the cauliflower steaks with the cumin mixture and place on the barbecue flat plate. Close the lid and cook for 5 minutes or until golden and nicely charred. Turn over and cook for another 5 minutes or until the cauliflower is tender and golden.

Meanwhile, make the red hummus. Blitz the capsicum and walnuts in a food processor until almost smooth. Remove half and place in a bowl. Add the chickpeas, garlic, tahini, harissa, cumin, lemon juice and ice cubes to the processor and blitz until almost smooth. With the motor running, add the oil in a thin, steady stream until smooth and well combined. Season with salt and pepper.

Add the parsley to the currants and toss together well.

Spread the hummus over serving plates. Top with the reserved capsicum and walnut purée followed by the cauliflower steaks. Sprinkle with the currant mixture and serve.

MEATY ADDITION: Reduce the cauliflower to 1 and serve with 4 Barbecued white fish fillets (see page 275) or 4 Barbecued or chargrilled chicken breast fillets (see page 260).

The upskilling toastie with homemade vegan cheese

SERVES: 4 **PREP:** 15 mins (plus overnight soaking and 4 hours chilling) **COOKING:** 1 hour

We live in an age when there is an obsession to learn more, know more. Whether that's a language, an obscure sport to consume your weekends, or a culinary skill, such as making sourdough bread, roasting your own green coffee beans or making your own salami or cheese.

This recipe will fulfil your desire to improve yourself because who doesn't want to learn how to make vegan 'cheese'?

Hello? Are you still there? Good, as I fear that I heard a lot of pages turning after that last sentence.

In addition to homemade 'pepperfake' cheese, this dish contains some very fine fried onions that go just as well with steak, burgers or grilled chicken breast for all you carnivores out there.

2 onions, thinly sliced into rings
60 ml (¼ cup) olive oil
sea salt and freshly ground
   black pepper
1 red capsicum, thinly sliced
1 green capsicum, thinly sliced
8 thick slices white bread
your favourite vegan spread, for
   spreading
barbecue sauce or Tamarind &
   chipotle ketchup (see page 217),
   for spreading

'PEPPERFAKE' CHEESE
80 g (½ cup) raw cashews
boiling water
2 teaspoons agar agar powder
375 ml (1½ cups) almond milk
1 teaspoon olive oil
2 jalapeno chillies, deseeded and
   finely chopped
1 long red chilli, deseeded and
   finely chopped
1 teaspoon finely chopped rosemary
2 tablespoons nutritional yeast
1 tablespoon tapioca flour
1 teaspoon sea salt
½ teaspoon onion powder
½ teaspoon garlic powder
1 teaspoon apple cider vinegar

Before you start making your cheese, line a 500 ml (2 cup) rectangular glass or ceramic dish with plastic wrap. Place the cashews in a heatproof bowl, cover with boiling water and leave to soak overnight.

The next day, combine the agar agar and 250 ml (1 cup) of the almond milk in a saucepan over medium–high heat and bring to the boil. Reduce the heat to low and cook, stirring, for 3–4 minutes or until the agar agar is dissolved. Set aside to cool.

Heat the oil in a small frying pan over medium heat. Add the jalapeno, red chilli and rosemary and cook, stirring, for 2 minutes or until tender but not brown. Set aside.

Drain the cashews and place in a high-powered blender with the nutritional yeast, tapioca flour, salt, onion powder, garlic powder, vinegar and remaining almond milk and blitz until smooth.

Stir the cashew mixture and jalapeno mixture into the agar milk until well combined. Pour into the prepared dish and place in the fridge for 4 hours or until firm.

Preheat a barbecue flat plate to medium. Add the onion and 2 tablespoons of the olive oil and season with at least 1 teaspoon of salt. Cook, turning occasionally, for 20 minutes. Move the onion to one side of the plate and add the red and green capsicum and remaining oil to the other side. Cook for 10 minutes or until the capsicum has softened and the onion is dark golden and hopefully a little burnt around the edges – these are the good crispy bits! Transfer to a bowl.

Meanwhile, unmould your 'cheese' and cut it into 1.5 cm thick slices.

Preheat the oven to 180°C/160°C fan-forced.

Spread the bread slices with vegan spread. Sandwich pairs of the bread slices together so the spread is on the inside. Top each stack with the cheese slices, onion, capsicum and sauce or ketchup. Slide the top layer of bread off the bottom layer and onto the barbecue flat plate – the spread side should hit the plate and sizzle. Top with the remaining bread slice, spread-side up, and cook for 2–3 minutes each side or until the bread is golden and crisp. Transfer to a baking tray.

Pop the toasties in the oven and cook for 15 minutes or until the cheese has softened. Cut in half and serve.

Corn in a cup

SERVES: 8 **PREP:** 20 mins **COOKING:** 10 mins

Sweet corn is a loved street food, from the roadsides of empty winding hill tracks in Sri Lanka to the clogged city streets of Mexico, but they are always served on the cob. Not so in Kuala Lumpur where one of the tastiest junk food snacks is 'corn in a cup' – no tedious tooth-work or dressings ending up on your chin here, as you eat it with a spoon. I was immediately enamoured and love the idea of making a cup of corn loaded with lots of different flavour bombs.

80 g butter, at room temperature
I kg frozen corn kernels, just thawed

MISO–ALMOND BUTTER
100 g (⅓ cup) almond butter, at room temperature
2 tablespoons white miso paste

SUGAR-CRUSTED CHILLI COCONUT
55 g (I cup) flaked coconut
55 g (¼ cup) brown sugar
½ teaspoon sea salt flakes
I teaspoon sriracha chilli sauce

CHILLI & TOMATO SALAD
250 g cherry tomatoes, quartered or halved if small
2 long green chillies, stalks removed and seeds knocked out with a wooden spoon, thinly sliced
2 tablespoons coarsely chopped coriander
sea salt and freshly ground black pepper

TO SERVE
sour cream
coarsely chopped smoked almonds
coarsely grated jalapeno cheese or crumbled feta
lime wedges

Start by making your miso–almond butter. Place the almond butter, miso and 2 tablespoons of hot water in a bowl and mix well (you want it to be the consistency of double cream). Add a little more water if you like it thinner.

To make the sugar-crusted chilli coconut, place the coconut, sugar and salt in a frying pan over medium heat and cook for 3–5 minutes or until the sugar has dissolved and the coconut is toasted. (Once the sugar starts to melt, make sure you stir constantly as it can burn quickly.) Add the sriracha and cook, tossing, for I minute or until well combined. Transfer to a serving bowl.

Now throw your chilli and tomato salad ingredients together in a bowl.

Preheat a barbecue flat plate on medium–high or a large frying pan over medium–high heat. Add half the butter, then the corn and cook, tossing, for 2–3 minutes or until nice and charred (don't panic if the corn pops a little). Spoon into a serving bowl. Dollop the remaining butter on top to slowly melt through.

Spoon the corn into cups and serve with all the toppings or make your own combinations.

 My favourite combos are:
- Miso–almond butter and chilli and tomato salad
- Sour cream, smoked almonds and jalapeno cheese
- Sour cream, crumbled feta and chilli and tomato salad
- Sugar-crusted chilli coconut, sour cream and lime wedges
- Miso–almond butter and sugar-crusted chilli coconut.

MEATY ADDITION: Serve 4 roughly chopped Barbecued or chargrilled chicken thigh fillets (see page 261) or shredded Slow-roasted pork shoulder (see page 270) as an option for your toppings.

Grilled snow pea sandwiches with ricotta butter & lemon

SERVES: 4 **PREP:** 10 mins **COOKING:** 10 mins

Looking for an alternative to the summer mountains of sweet chilli and sour cream, salt and vinegar and even black truffle chips, I stumbled upon something veg that the kids would eat in equal quantities – buttered blanched snow peas with salt flakes. It became 2019's edamame or kale chips for us. And they are even better with ricotta in a bread roll … this is the new frontier, baby. It's scary but it's good.

250 g fresh ricotta
150 g butter, at room temperature
finely grated zest of 1 lemon
2 tablespoons finely chopped mint
sea salt and freshly ground
    black pepper
250 g snow peas, trimmed, strings
    removed
olive oil spray
4 long bread rolls
150 g (2 cups) finely shredded iceberg
    lettuce
55 g (⅓ cup) salted roasted cashews,
    coarsely chopped

Press the ricotta between two layers of the most absorbent paper towel you can find to remove as much liquid as possible. Place in a bowl and add the butter, lemon zest and mint. Season well with salt and pepper. Use electric beaters to beat until smooth and well combined. Cover and place in the fridge until required.

Preheat a barbecue grill on high. While your barbie heats up, get a bowl of iced water ready and bring a small saucepan of water to the boil. Cook half the snow peas for 2 minutes or until they turn bright green and tender crisp. Plunge straight into the iced water to stop the cooking process and keep them nice and crisp. Drain.

Spray the remaining snow peas with olive oil and season with salt and pepper. Barbecue on one side only for 2–3 minutes or until charred on the underside and bright green on top.

Cut the bread rolls in half without cutting all the way through. Open them up slightly and barbecue on the grill, cut-side down, for 1–2 minutes or until lightly toasted. Thickly spread one side of the cut surfaces with the ricotta butter. Fill with the lettuce and both types of snow peas, neatly arranged in triple-decked rows. Sprinkle with the chopped cashews, season well and serve.

MEATY ADDITION: Replace the cashews with Crispy pork crackling (see page 268).

Barbecued broccolini with sunflower seed hummus & lemon salt

SERVES: 4 **PREP:** 15 mins (plus 4 hours soaking) **COOKING:** 5 mins

Respect to Dave Verheul at Embla for introducing the world to his magnificent wood-roasted broccolini that pairs the singed florets with a sunflower seed miso. This is a shoddy cheat's version that captures some of that pleasure but without all the effort or the need to fly to Melbourne.

1 tablespoon sea salt flakes
finely grated zest of 1 lemon
3 bunches broccolini, thicker stems
  halved lengthways
2 tablespoons olive oil, plus extra
  to serve
freshly ground black pepper
lemon wedges, to serve

SUNFLOWER SEED HUMMUS
150 g (1 cup) sunflower seeds
95 g (⅓ cup) tahini
3 garlic cloves, crushed
1 teaspoon smoked paprika
60 ml (¼ cup) freshly squeezed
  lemon juice
125 ml (½ cup) olive oil

To make the sunflower seed hummus, place the sunflower seeds in a bowl and cover with plenty of cold water. Cover and set aside for at least 4 hours or overnight to soak. Drain.

Next, blitz the sunflower seeds, tahini, garlic, paprika and lemon juice in a food processor until almost smooth, scraping down the side regularly. With the motor running, gradually add the oil and 125 ml (½ cup) of water in a thin steady stream until the hummus reaches a spreadable consistency.

Combine the salt and lemon zest in a bowl.

Preheat a barbecue flat plate on medium–high. Place the broccolini in a bowl and drizzle with the olive oil. Season well with salt and pepper and toss until well combined. Barbecue, turning occasionally, for 3–4 minutes or until cooked and nicely charred at the edges and tips.

Divide the hummus among serving plates and top with the broccolini. Drizzle with extra oil, sprinkle with the lemon salt and serve with lemon wedges.

MEATY ADDITION: Serve with Barbecued or chargrilled beef steaks (see page 266) or Roast pork belly (see page 273) as part of a shared meal.

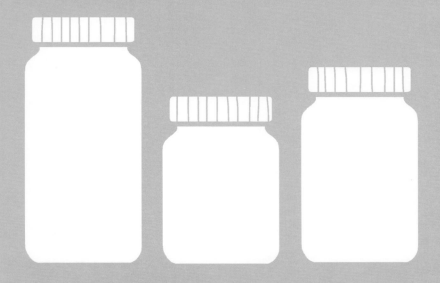

Pasta, noodles & rice

I love this section, as it's full of stuff that makes up my menu at home during the week.
From the simplest of arrabiatas, a carbonara built around leek not bacon and a mushroom
stroganoff, to easy potstickers, a quick and tasty ramen and a very special fried rice (that
is, I can assure our carnivorous friends, very special, even if it does leave out the spam).

Do give the beetroot orecchiette and the spinach pici with green beans a go,
as well as the green lasagne – it's actually a lot less labour intensive than a
traditional lasagne and it tastes freakin' awesome.

Arrabiata – the odd angry sauce

SERVES: 4 **PREP:** 10 mins **COOKING:** 15 mins

The Italians love to rush – perhaps that's why they invented the Ferrari, the Ducati, the Lamborghini, the Maserati and the Bugati. What I have yet to determine is what motivates this need for speed. I suspect it leaves more time for snoozing in the sun after a long leisurely lunch under the vines, perambulating along the seafront in a pastel linen suit at dusk, or just sitting in an ancient square lingering for hours over a tiny cup of coffee, arguing over the relative merits of the squad for the World Cup and/or mistakes made with the squad for the last World Cup. Perhaps that's why this pasta dish is so quick to make.

Ooh, and don't forget to boil a kettle before you start! It will save you valuable minutes waiting for water to boil for all the pastas in this chapter.

500 g spaghetti
80 ml (⅓ cup) extra-virgin olive oil
1 large red onion, finely chopped
1–2 teaspoons chilli flakes
2 × 400 g cans cherry tomatoes
  (if you can find them, otherwise
  any other canned toms will do)
1 lemon with 2 pinky-sized strips
  of lemon peel removed
sea salt
pinch of caster sugar (optional)
4 long red chillies
handful of cherry tomatoes
150 g pecorino or parmesan, finely
  grated

Bring a large saucepan of well-salted water to the boil over high heat. Add the spaghetti and stir in a glass of cold water to separate the pasta and stop it sticking. Return to the boil, then reduce the heat and simmer for 1 minute less than it says on the packet or until just al dente. Drain.

Meanwhile, heat 2 tablespoons of the olive oil in a deep frying pan over medium–high heat, add the onion and cook, stirring occasionally, for 4–5 minutes or until softened and translucent. Stir in 1 teaspoon of the chilli flakes, then add the canned tomatoes and lemon peel. Cut the lemon into quarters and squeeze the juice from one quarter into the pan. Bring to the boil, then reduce the heat and simmer until the pasta is ready. Taste the sauce and season with salt, more lemon juice and a little sugar, if needed.

Meanwhile, cut the chillies into 1 cm thick slices, removing the seeds and veins inside. Warm the remaining oil in a small frying pan over low heat, add the chilli and cherry tomatoes and cook for 2–3 minutes or until slightly softened and heated through.

Taste the sauce and add more chilli flakes and salt if needed, then toss with the spaghetti. Scatter with some of the chilli slices and finish with a good sprinkling of pecorino or parmesan. Serve with the remaining chilli slices on the side.

 TIP: The sauce in this recipe will give a fresh, bright arrabiata. For a more savoury, intense sauce, remove the lemon peel and continue to cook for 40 minutes or until the oil starts rendering out.

Leek carbonara with strozzapreti (aka priest strangler pasta)

SERVES: 4 PREP: 15 mins COOKING: 20 mins

Cooking leeks in the microwave is one of my favourite kitchen speed hacks as it delivers deliciously creamy and unadulterated leekiness. It's also perfect for this speedy take on carbonara that allows Peppa and her friends to stay safely in the sty. I can be VERY boring and explain how carbonara was originally more of an American dish than an Italian one, but I'll stop now …

FOOD NERD FACT: Strozzapreti, meaning priest strangler, was given its name by Italian peasants as a biting political comment on the greed of some of the Italian clergy.

2 litres vegetable stock
400 g strozzapreti, casarecce, or any
  mid-length curled-edge pasta
1 tablespoon olive oil
1 onion, quartered and sliced
1 teaspoon brown sugar
4 decent-sized leeks, well washed,
  root end trimmed but not cut off
6 eggs (using just the yolks will make
  it richer but I'd only do that if I had
  a yen to make a pavlova)
150 g parmesan, finely grated
sea salt and freshly ground
  black pepper
1 whole nutmeg

Bring the stock to the boil in a large saucepan. Add the pasta and cook for 1 minute less than it says on the packet or until just al dente.

Meanwhile, heat the olive oil in a frying pan over high heat, add the onion and cook, tossing occasionally, for 8–10 minutes or until the onion is a little burnt at the edges. Sprinkle over the sugar, toss and return to the heat to burn and caramelise the onion a little more. Set aside until needed.

Place two leeks in a flat-bottomed microwave-safe dish (a pie plate works well) and microwave on high for 5 minutes. Leaving the ends sealed allows them to steam beautifully in their own juices. Repeat with the other two leeks.

Whisk together the eggs, parmesan and lots of black pepper in a bowl.

Carefully split the hot leeks in half lengthways and remove their soft cooked middles, leaving the tough outer leaves behind. Slice the middles crossways into four pieces, then roughly cut them lengthways into ribbons. Grate over a little nutmeg and cover to keep warm.

Roughly drain the pasta over a bowl in the sink, reserving 250 ml (1 cup) of the cooking liquid. Return the pasta to the pan. We don't mind if a little of the stock sticks with the pasta as it's going to help make the sauce satiny when you toss it with the egg and cheese.

Now call everyone to the table – this dish is time sensitive!

Pour the egg mixture over the hot pasta and stir to coat. Splash in a little of the reserved cooking liquid. Place the lid on the pan and stand for a minute or so, jiggling it occasionally. We want the sauce to cook in the residual heat of the pan and pasta but we *don't* want the egg to set.

After a minute give it a check and stir through the leek. Taste and season with salt, some grated nutmeg and more pepper, if needed. Sprinkle with the fried and slightly burnt onion and serve.

MEATY ADDITION: Sprinkle the top with 200 g chopped Crispy bacon (see page 268) or Crispy prosciutto shards (see page 269).

Easy potstickers

MAKES: 22 PREP: 30 mins COOKING: 25 mins

Child labour is somewhat frowned upon in these progressive times but call it 'educational life-skilling' and you'll be applauded for it. That's the idea with these dumplings. Get the kids or your guests to make their own dumplings and lionise the best without disheartening the fat-thumbed boobs whose potstickers look like they've been squidged together after getting in the way of an out-of-control runaway front-end loader. Just give them a 'participation award'. Everyone will know what that means!

60 ml (¼ cup) peanut oil
120 g shiitake mushrooms, finely chopped
60 g (1 cup) finely chopped wombok
3 cm knob of ginger, peeled and finely grated
2 garlic cloves, crushed
½ bunch coriander, stalks and leaves separated and finely chopped
60 g canned water chestnuts, drained and finely chopped
2 spring onions, white and green parts finely chopped, plus extra sliced to serve
1 tablespoon soy sauce or tamari
1 tablespoon Shaoxing rice wine
1 teaspoon sesame oil
ground white pepper
cornflour, for dusting
22 gow gee wrappers

BLACK VINEGAR DIPPING SAUCE
60 ml (¼ cup) black vinegar
2 tablespoons mushroom soy sauce or tamari
1 teaspoon chilli flakes

Heat 1 tablespoon of the peanut oil in a wok or large frying pan over medium–high heat. Add the mushroom and wombok and cook, stirring occasionally, for 5 minutes or until softened. Add the ginger, garlic and coriander stalk and stir-fry for 1 minute. Add the water chestnut, spring onion, soy sauce or tamari, Shaoxing rice wine, sesame oil and coriander leaves and toss until well combined. Transfer to a heatproof bowl and season with white pepper.

Lightly sprinkle a tray with cornflour. Place one gow gee wrapper on a clean work surface and put 2 level teaspoons of the mushroom mixture in the middle. Brush the edge with water, then fold over to enclose the filling, pinching pleats along the edge to seal as you go. Place on the floured tray. Repeat with the remaining wrappers and filling to make 22 dumplings all up.

Heat 1 tablespoon of the remaining peanut oil in a frying pan over medium heat. Add half the dumplings and cook for 2–3 minutes or until the bases are golden brown. Pour 80 ml (⅓ cup) of water into the pan, then cover and steam for 5 minutes or until the dumplings are cooked through. Transfer the dumplings to a serving plate and cover with foil to keep warm. Repeat with the remaining peanut oil and dumplings.

To make the dipping sauce, combine all the ingredients in a small bowl.

Sprinkle the extra spring onion over the potstickers and serve with the dipping sauce.

MEATY ADDITION: Stir 120 g Pan-fried chicken mince (see page 266) into the mushroom mixture and use 10 more gow gee wrappers.

Mapo dofu comes to town

SERVES: 4 **PREP:** 15 mins **COOKING:** 35 mins

It's 8708 km from China's Sichuan Province to my house but I reckon it's worth this soft custardy tofu making that journey if it ends up in my dinner bowl, along with golden fried wheat noodles bought from my local supermarket. I know it's not traditional but it works so well! The crispy wok-caught edges of the fried noodles echo the crisp, toasty texture of the crispy lentils. Respect to talented MC alum Karlie Verkerk who developed the original mapo dofu recipe for my last cookbook, which forms the heart of this new urban version.

110 g (½ cup) dried black lentils
120 ml vegetable oil
7 garlic cloves, 4 thinly sliced,
    3 crushed
1 tablespoon Sichuan peppercorns,
    toasted and ground with a mortar
    and pestle
500 g hokkien noodles
boiling water
1 teaspoon sesame oil
6 spring onions, white part finely
    chopped, green part thinly sliced
1 tablespoon cornflour
4 large shiitake mushrooms,
    finely chopped
3 cm knob of ginger, peeled and
    finely grated
2 tablespoons fermented chilli
    bean paste, such as doubanjiang
    (or gochujang or sriracha
    chilli sauce)
1 tablespoon light soy sauce
2 teaspoons chilli flakes (optional)
1 teaspoon caster sugar
600 g firm silken tofu, cut into
    2 cm cubes
1½ tablespoons Chinese-style chilli oil
    (such as chiu chow)
1 long red chilli, deseeded and
    thinly sliced

Cook the lentils in a large saucepan of boiling water for 30 minutes or until soft. Drain well.

Meanwhile, heat half the vegetable oil in a small frying pan over low heat, add the sliced garlic and fry for 2–3 minutes or until golden (don't let it burn or it will be bitter). Remove and drain on paper towel, then set aside.

Heat 1 tablespoon of the remaining oil in a large deep frying pan over medium–high heat. Fry the cooked lentils, stirring occasionally, for 4–5 minutes or until crispy. Add half the Sichuan pepper and stir to combine. Transfer to a bowl and set aside.

Place the noodles in a heatproof bowl, cover with boiling water and set aside for 5 minutes to separate the noodles. Drain well. Heat half the remaining oil in a frying pan over high heat, add the noodles and cook, tossing, for 8–10 minutes or until they start to catch a little. Add the sesame oil and green part of the spring onion and toss until well combined. Transfer to a bowl.

Combine the cornflour and 375 ml (1½ cups) of water in a bowl or jug until smooth.

Meanwhile, heat the remaining oil in the same frying pan over medium heat. Add the mushroom and cook, stirring occasionally, for 3 minutes or until soft and starting to brown. Add the crushed garlic, ginger and white part of the spring onion and cook for a further 2 minutes. Add the chilli bean paste, soy sauce, chilli flakes (if using), sugar and remaining Sichuan pepper and toss to combine. Reduce the heat to low, stir in the cornflour mixture and cook for 3 minutes or until the sauce has thickened.

Add the tofu to the mushroom mixture, being careful not to break up the cubes. Remove from the heat and use a spatula to gently spoon the mushroom mixture over the tofu. Set aside for 2 minutes or until the tofu is warmed through.

Wrap nests of noodles among serving bowls, then fill the centre with the tofu mixture. Drizzle the chilli oil over the tofu (not the noodles) and top with the crispy lentils, chilli and fried garlic slices. Serve immediately.

MEATY ADDITION: Replace the mushrooms with 250 g pork or chicken mince.

Mushroom stroganoff with parsley-flecked noodles

SERVES: 4 **PREP:** 15 mins **COOKING:** 50 mins

Seriously, what's not to love? All the joy of a creamy stroganoff but none of the dead animal! You won't miss it, I promise.

And those parsley-flecked noodles are 'hella' tasty ... or so I was told by another dad who was trying to appear down AF with the kids. I asked him if AF meant 'As if' ...

60 ml (¼ cup) olive oil
800 g mixed mushrooms (such as chestnut, button, Swiss brown and portobello), sliced
1 onion, thinly sliced
2 garlic cloves, crushed
2 teaspoons sweet paprika
2 tablespoons tomato paste
375 ml (1½ cups) vegetable stock
1 tablespoon mushroom soy sauce or tamari
125 g (½ cup) creme fraiche or sour cream
400 g pappardelle or fettuccine
knob of butter
½ cup finely chopped flat-leaf parsley (pick out the smaller leaves and save them for serving)
sea salt

Heat 1 tablespoon of the olive oil in a large non-stick frying pan over high heat. Working in batches, add enough mushrooms to cover the base of the pan without overcrowding (this will stop them from sweating and allow them to become nice and golden). Cook, tossing, for 4–5 minutes, until golden, then transfer to a bowl. Repeat with the remaining mushrooms, adding a little more oil as needed.

Heat the remaining oil in the pan over medium heat. Add the onion and cook, stirring, for 4–5 minutes or until soft. Add the garlic and paprika and cook for 30 seconds or until aromatic. Stir in the tomato paste and cook, stirring, for 1 minute or until it darkens slightly.

Add the stock and soy sauce or tamari to the pan, and bring to the boil. Simmer rapidly for 15 minutes or until the liquid reduces by half. Stir in the mushrooms and creme fraiche or sour cream, then reduce the heat to medium–low and simmer gently for 10 minutes or until the mushrooms are well coated in the sauce.

Meanwhile, bring a large saucepan of salted water to the boil. Cook the pasta for 1 minute less than it says on the packet or until al dente. Drain and return to the hot pan with the knob of butter, then toss through the chopped parsley.

Spoon the pasta into a large serving bowl and top with the stroganoff. Scatter with the baby parsley leaves, sprinkle with a little salt and serve.

MEATY ADDITION: Replace half the mushrooms with 2 sliced beef scotch fillet steaks and cook in the same way as the mushrooms.

Simple spinach pici with green beans

SERVES: 4 **PREP:** 20 mins (plus 30 mins chilling) **COOKING:** 15 mins

I love the way the beans and pici look so similar, especially when obscured under a finely grated drift of your favourite parmesan. I use the words 'your favourite' cos I reckon you are old enough to decide for yourself whether you want a traditional hard cheese or one made without animal rennet.

200 g baby spinach leaves

300 g (2 cups) '00' flour or plain flour, plus extra if needed and for dusting

300 g green beans, trimmed and halved crossways

2 tablespoons olive oil

3 garlic cloves, finely chopped

150 g your favourite parmesan or pecorino, finely grated

freshly ground black pepper

1 whole nutmeg

Blitz the spinach in a food processor or blender until pureed. Tip into the bowl of an electric mixer fitted with the dough hook attachment, add the flour and mix until well combined and the gluten in the flour has been activated (you'll know this has happened when the dough feels a little bouncy and elastic). Add more flour if it still feels sticky. Wrap in plastic wrap and rest in the fridge for at least 30 minutes.

Bring a large saucepan of salted water to the boil over high heat, add the green beans and blanch for 1 minute. Remove the beans with a slotted spoon and set aside but keep the water boiling.

Line a baking tray with baking paper. Roll the dough into a couple of long, skinny, flattened sausages about as thick as your thumb (but much, much longer) and cut into 1 cm thick pieces. Flour your work bench. Roll each piece away from you across the floured bench, using the heel of your hand to apply pressure, to create long, skinny shapes strikingly similar to the green beans. Place on the prepared tray.

Add the spinach pici to the boiling salted water. They will sink, so carefully jiggle the pan to stop them sticking to the bottom and adjust the heat so the water is barely simmering. Using a slotted spoon, remove the pici when they float to the surface – this means they are cooked. Reserve the cooking water.

Heat the olive oil in a large frying pan (large enough to hold the beans and pici) over medium heat and throw in the garlic. Cook for 1–2 minutes or until softened. Add the beans and pici, along with a splash of the reserved pasta water. Toss to emulsify the oils and juices into a thin sauce.

Divide among shallow bowls and top with loads of parmesan or pecorino, black pepper and a fine grating of nutmeg.

 TIPS: Add your favourite fresh herbs (flat-leaf parsley, mint, tarragon, oregano etc.) and some fresh ricotta, or a couple of poached eggs, to make it a more substantial meal.

You can cook the beans and pici together in the same pan if you are confident with your timings.

Green lasagne with spinach bechamel & all the colours of the Italian flag

SERVES: 6–8 PREP: 30 mins COOKING: 1 hour 45 mins

This is the simplest of dishes, cleverly designed to camouflage vegetables in every layer. And in spite of various attempts to trick it up (adding mushrooms, haloumi, silverbeet etc), we have come to the conclusion that this simplest version is impossible to improve upon.

It's essentially the recipe I demo'd during a **MasterChef MasterClass**, *only in that version I fried the zucchini in olive oil to tan it up. However, baking it instead will save you about 20 minutes of prep time, and results in a lasagne that is almost as tasty, but less about the golden zucchini and more about the bright tomato sauce.*

1 kg zucchini, cut lengthways into
  1 cm thick slices
olive oil spray
sea salt and freshly ground
  black pepper
1 tablespoon olive oil
3 large carrots, finely chopped
3 large celery stalks, finely chopped
1 large onion, finely chopped
4 garlic cloves, crushed
2 tablespoons tomato paste
700 g bottle passata
400 g can diced tomatoes
1 large vegetable stock cube
4 fresh or dried bay leaves
6 large fresh lasagne sheets
100 g (1 cup) coarsely grated
  mozzarella
50 g (½ cup) finely grated parmesan

SPINACH BECHAMEL

250 g packet chopped frozen
  spinach, thawed and excess liquid
  squeezed out
500 ml (2 cups) full-cream milk
70 g butter
60 g plain flour
¼ teaspoon ground or freshly
  grated nutmeg
sea salt and freshly ground
  black pepper

Preheat the oven to 210°C/190°C fan-forced. Line two large baking trays with baking paper.

Place the zucchini slices on the prepared trays in a single layer. Spray with olive oil and season well with salt and pepper. Bake for 20–25 minutes or until tender and lightly golden.

Meanwhile, heat the olive oil in a large saucepan over medium heat. Add the carrot, celery and onion and cook, stirring, for 10 minutes or until soft. Add the garlic and cook, stirring, for 1 minute or until aromatic. Add the tomato paste and cook, stirring, for 2–3 minutes or until well combined. Add the passata, diced tomatoes, stock cube, bay leaves and 150 ml of water. Simmer, stirring often, for 40 minutes or until the mixture has thickened. Season with salt and pepper.

It's time to make your spinach bechamel. Place the spinach and milk in a high-powered blender and blitz until very smooth and the milk is a deep green colour. (Alternatively, use a stick blender.) Melt the butter in a saucepan over medium heat until foaming. Add the flour and cook, stirring, for 1–2 minutes or until the mixture bubbles and starts to colour. Remove from the heat. Gradually whisk in the spinach milk until smooth. It will look quite thick at this stage but we need to cook it so it thickens even more. Stir over medium heat for 5 minutes or until the sauce is very thick and comes away from the side of the pan when stirred. Season generously with the nutmeg and salt and pepper to taste.

Remove the baked zucchini from the oven and reduce the temperature to 180°C/160°C fan-forced.

Reserve 250 ml (1 cup) of the tomato mixture and set aside. Spread another 250 ml (1 cup) over the base of a 5 cm deep, 30 cm × 23 cm baking dish. Top with one-third of the lasagne sheets, trimming to fit. Top with half the remaining tomato mixture and half the zucchini, layering across the dish and slightly overlapping. Top with another layer of lasagne sheets, the remaining tomato mixture and the remaining zucchini. Top with a final layer of lasagne sheets and spoon over the reserved tomato mixture. Spread the spinach bechamel over the top. Combine the mozzarella and parmesan in a bowl, then sprinkle them evenly over the bechamel. Bake for 30–40 minutes or until golden and tender.

 TIP: If you have time to fry your zucchini, heat a little olive oil in a frying pan over medium heat. Cook the slices in batches for 3–4 minutes each side, until golden.

Sunflower seed risotto

SERVES: 4 **PREP:** 20 mins (plus overnight soaking) **COOKING:** 40 mins

There is no little controversy over whether a risotto can be made with anything other than rice. But when you travel to Copenhagen and find a Messina-born chef making risotto with sunflower seeds because rice doesn't grow in Scandinavia you have to respect his logic. The restaurant was Relae, and the chef was Christian Puglisi. My version is different but is definitely inspired by Christian's original.

500 g sunflower seeds
750 ml (3 cups) vegetable stock
2 tablespoons extra-virgin olive oil
50 g unsalted butter or coconut
  butter, chopped
1 onion, finely chopped
2 garlic cloves, crushed
125 ml (½ cup) white wine
60 g (¾ cup) finely grated parmesan
  (or use 30 g nutritional yeast)
300 g broad beans, blanched and
  podded
200 g frozen peas
2 celery stalks, finely chopped
sea salt and freshly ground
  black pepper
1 teaspoon thyme leaves
nasturtium leaves, to serve, if you
  have them (and if you don't, take
  this as a cue to plant some as they
  grow like weeds and have the same
  peppery bite as rocket, but they
  won't bolt on you)
1 lemon

Place the sunflower seeds in a bowl of cold water and leave to soak overnight. Drain and rinse under cold water until the water runs clear.

Pour the stock into a large saucepan and bring to the boil over medium heat. Reduce the heat and keep at a low simmer.

Blitz one-quarter of the sunflower seeds and 60 ml (¼ cup) of the stock in a food processor until smooth.

Heat the olive oil and half the butter in a large deep frying pan over medium heat. Add the onion and cook, stirring, for 3–4 minutes, until softened. Add the garlic and cook for 1–2 minutes, until aromatic. Add the remaining sunflower seeds and toss to coat. Pour the wine into the pan and cook, stirring, for 2–3 minutes or until reduced by at least half. Add the stock and cook, stirring occasionally, for 25 minutes or until most of the liquid has been absorbed and the sunflower seeds have softened.

Stir in the sunflower seed puree and 50 g of the parmesan (or 25 g of the nutritional yeast).

Melt the remaining butter in a frying pan over medium–high heat. Add the broad beans, peas and celery and cook, stirring occasionally, for 2–3 minutes or until softened. Season and remove from the heat.

Divide the risotto among serving plates. Top with the broad bean mixture, thyme leaves, nasturtium leaves (if using) and remaining parmesan (or nutritional yeast). Finely grate over a little lemon zest, then cut the lemon into wedges and serve alongside the risotto.

MEATY ADDITION: Shred 2 Poached chicken breast fillets (see page 261) and toss through the broad bean mixture.

Mushroom Ned Ned noodles

SERVES: 4 **PREP:** 20 mins **COOKING:** 15 mins

Could it be that the Sichuan dish Dan Dan Noodles is named after bushranger Ned Kelly's less famous brother who died at the siege of Glenrowan?

After all, the gang had spent plenty of time along Woolshed Valley with the Chinese miners, smoking opium and generally playing up. So isn't it likely that they'd name a hard-hitting, heavyweight vegan version of this dish after Ned, who won the unofficial heavyweight championship of Victoria in a 20-round bareknuckle boxing fight with Isaiah 'Wild' Wright at Beechworth in August 1874?

If, somehow, they didn't, then I am sure they would approve and I feel justified in re-imagining history.

1 tablespoon peanut oil

400 g portobello mushrooms, finely chopped

2 spring onions, white and green parts separated and thinly sliced

1 tablespoon finely grated ginger

1 tablespoon light soy sauce

1 tablespoon Shaoxing rice wine

400 g your favourite wheat noodles (such as ramen or udon)

1 bunch gai larn, cut lengthways into thirds, any thicker stems cut into 1 cm thick batons

80 g (½ cup) roasted unsalted peanuts, very coarsely chopped, leaving some whole

sesame seeds, to sprinkle

SICHUAN CHILLI SAUCE

1 tablespoon Sichuan peppercorns

90 g (⅓ cup) smooth peanut butter (unsweetened)

2 garlic cloves, crushed

2 tablespoons Chinese-style chilli oil (such as chiu chow), plus a little extra for drizzling (optional)

60 ml (¼ cup) light soy sauce

2 tablespoons black vinegar

2 teaspoons sesame oil

2 teaspoons caster sugar

To make the Sichuan chilli sauce, toast the Sichuan peppercorns in a small frying pan over medium heat for 1 minute or until aromatic. Tip into a mortar and grind with the pestle until finely crushed, then transfer to a bowl. Add the remaining ingredients and whisk until well combined.

Heat the peanut oil in a wok or large frying pan over high heat, add the mushroom and cook, tossing, for 5–8 minutes or until dry and golden. Add the white part of the spring onion, the ginger, soy sauce and Shaoxing rice wine and stir to combine. Remove from the heat and set aside.

Bring a large saucepan of water to the boil. Add the noodles and cook, stirring occasionally, for 2 minutes to separate them. Add the gai larn and cook for a further 1 minute. Drain, reserving 80 ml (⅓ cup) of the cooking liquid.

Add the hot cooking liquid to the chilli sauce to loosen it, then divide among serving bowls. Top with the noodles and the mushroom mixture followed by the gai larn. Sprinkle with the peanuts, green part of the spring onion and a few sesame seeds. Drizzle over some extra chilli oil if you like it hotter.

MEATY ADDITION: Halve the mushrooms to 200 g and add 200 g Pan-fried beef mince (see page 266) to the mushroom mixture.

Burnt butter spaghettini

SERVES: 4 PREP: 10 mins COOKING: 15 mins

This is an obvious homage to one of my all-time favourite dishes – Alex Herbert's prawn gnocchi with burnt butter – but with a twist in the form of crunchy roasted burnt butter and hazelnut crumbs. These play the role of a more familiar crunchy breadcrumb crumble, or 'pangrattato'. Oh and no prawns unless you want to add them, you racy pescatarian, you!

170 g unsalted butter
170 g skim milk powder
2 teaspoons caster sugar
½ teaspoon sea salt
400 g spaghettini
60 ml (¼ cup) vermouth or white wine
finely grated zest and juice of 1 lemon
50 g skinless blanched hazelnuts (see TIPS)
freshly ground black pepper
lemon thyme, thyme, dill, bronze fennel, fennel tops, wild fennel or even just finely chopped flat-leaf parsley, to serve

Preheat the oven to 200°C/180°C fan-forced. Line a baking tray with baking paper.

Start by making some crumbs. Melt 65 g of the butter in a small saucepan. Transfer to a bowl, then add 150 g of the skim milk powder and toss to combine. Spread out in a thin layer on the prepared tray and sprinkle with the sugar and salt. Bake for 8 minutes or until light golden, rotating the tray and stirring the crumbs halfway through to ensure even toasting. Remove and set aside to allow the crumbs to cool a little.

Cook the spaghettini in a saucepan of boiling salted water for 1 minute less than it says on the packet or until just al dente. Drain and return to the pan.

Meanwhile, melt the remaining butter in a large frying pan over high heat. Stir in the remaining skim milk powder and cook for 2 minutes or until a little golden and the butter is smelling nutty. Add the vermouth or wine and cook, stirring, for 2–3 minutes to deglaze the pan and reduce the liquid by half. Season with a squeeze of lemon juice and salt (if needed). Throw in the drained pasta and toss to emulsify, then whack up the heat as you want to burn some of the pasta a little bit.

Blitz or crush the hazelnuts in a food processor, then add to the golden 'burnt butter' crumbs.

Divide the pasta among shallow serving bowls and top with the burnt butter hazelnut crumbs, lemon zest, a good grinding of black pepper and the fresh herb of your choice.

 TIPS: Some will tell you this is just as delicious with a spaghetti made from ribbons of lightly blanched zucchini. I think they are exaggerating a little but it'll do if you can't find any of that gluten-free pasta you like.

If you need to remove the skins from the hazelnuts, spread them out on a separate baking tray and bake for 5 minutes while you bake the skim milk powder crumbs. Rub the skins off in a tea towel.

MEATY ADDITION: Toss 600 g Pan-fried prawns (see page 275) through the pasta.

Simple beetroot orecchiette with hazelnuts, sorrel & curds

SERVES: 4 **PREP:** 20 mins (plus 30 mins chilling) **COOKING:** 1 hour 5 mins

Making vegetable pasta with the kids is a perfect Sunday activity – just like making playdough, except you can eat it.

250 g beetroot bulbs

350 g (2⅓ cups) '00' flour or plain flour, plus extra if needed and for dusting

2 egg yolks

sea salt

extra-virgin olive oil, for drizzling

50 g (⅓ cup) skinless blanched hazelnuts (see TIPS on page 105), toasted and coarsely chopped

150 g ashed goat's cheese, crumbled

finely grated zest and juice of 1 lemon

6 thyme sprigs, leaves picked

100 g red-vein sorrel leaves

Preheat the oven to 200°C/180°C fan-forced.

Wrap each beetroot bulb in foil and place in a roasting tin. Roast for 1 hour or until tender when pierced with a skewer. Leave to cool slightly, then remove the foil. Put on some kitchen gloves to stop your hands turning pink and peel the beetroot.

Blitz the beetroot in a food processer until pureed. Transfer to a bowl, add the flour, egg yolks and 1 teaspoon of sea salt and mix until combined. Turn out onto a well-floured work surface and knead until smooth and elastic, adding a little more flour if needed. Wrap in plastic wrap and rest in the fridge for 30 minutes.

Line a baking tray with baking paper. Divide the dough into four portions, then roll each portion into a long thin sausage on a well-floured work surface. Cut into 1 cm thick pieces and pinch each piece with your (floured) thumb and finger about one-fifth of the way down to create an ear shape that is thinner at the bottom where you've applied pressure and has a rounded fat lip at the top. Place on the prepared tray.

Bring a large saucepan of salted water to the boil over high heat. Add the orecchiette and cook for 2 minutes or until they float to the surface. Drain, then drizzle with a little olive oil to coat so they don't stick together.

Divide the orecchiette among serving bowls and top with the hazelnuts, goat's cheese, lemon zest and juice, thyme leaves and sorrel. Finish with a little more oil and a good pinch of salt.

Papal gnocchi

SERVES: 4 as a starter or 2 as a greedy dinner **PREP:** 30 mins **COOKING:** 10 mins

Vatican City in Rome isn't really part of Italy but that doesn't mean it can't have its own pasta. The yellow and white colours I've chosen reference the papal flag, the time in the oven represents the threat of the eternal fires of hell, and the coverage of grated gruyere is a nod to the protection of the Swiss guards. The choice of pasta itself is driven by the old Catholic church's obsession with relics like the bones of saints and slivers of the true cross ('gnocchi' comes from the Italian for 'a knot in wood' and the German word for 'bone'). My own eternal soul is hoping that this sucking up will get me over the issue of an earlier recipe (see page 88), which uses a pasta that translates as 'priest strangler'.

2 tablespoons olive oil, plus extra
   for drizzling
1 yellow capsicum, thinly sliced
250 g yellow cherry tomatoes
4 spring onions, white part
   thinly sliced
500 g fresh ricotta, sliced and pressed
   between sheets of paper towel to
   suck out excess moisture
50 g (⅓ cup) plain flour, plus extra
   if needed
120 g gruyere, smoked cheddar or
   parmesan, finely grated
sea salt and freshly ground
   black pepper
150 g bocconcini, drained and halved

Preheat the oven to 160°C/140°C fan-forced. Drizzle a little oil into a baking tin and place in the oven to warm up.

Bring a large saucepan of salted water to the boil over high heat. Reduce the heat and keep at a simmer.

Meanwhile, heat the oil in a large frying pan over medium–high heat. Add the capsicum, tomatoes and spring onion and cook, stirring occasionally, for 2–3 minutes or until softened and starting to catch. Remove from the heat and set aside.

Place the ricotta and flour in a large glass or ceramic bowl. Gently mix until combined. Stir in 50 g of the grated cheese and a pinch of salt. If it needs more flour to bind, add it little by little until the dough comes together.

Divide the dough into four portions. On a sheet of baking paper roll each portion into a long 2 cm thick sausage. Carefully cut each sausage into 1–2 cm pieces without tearing the paper (the paper will help you carry the gnocchi to the pan).

Spread the seared capsicum mixture over the base of the hot baking tin and dot with the bocconcini. Return the tin to the oven and turn the oven off.

Working in three batches, cook the gnocchi in the saucepan of simmering water. It will only take about a minute to cook, so be on your toes. Using a slotted spoon, remove the gnocchi as soon as they float to the surface, then gently shake them dry. When you finish each batch, remove the tin from the oven and arrange the gnocchi over the capsicum mixture and bocconcini. Sprinkle over a quarter of the remaining grated cheese and return the tin to the oven.

When the last batch of gnocchi goes into the pan, preheat the grill on high.

Arrange the last layer of gnocchi in the tin and sprinkle over the remaining grated cheese. Place under the grill for 2–3 minutes or until melted and golden.

Serve from the baking tin at the table. No garnish – just plenty of black pepper.

Singapore noodles

SERVES: 4 **PREP:** 15 mins **COOKING:** 10 mins

This is one of those great fusion dishes that says as much about the cultural and ethnic make-up of Singapore as many guidebooks. Singapore is a great melting pot of Indian, Arabic and Chinese ideas, and this dish is but one example. Stuffed roti, or murtabak, might be another if you are searching for some proof to support this claim.

150 g rice vermicelli noodles
boiling water
1 tablespoon peanut oil
1 onion, cut into thin wedges
1 red capsicum, cut into thin strips
200 g green beans, trimmed and
　halved lengthways
120 g snow peas, trimmed, strings
　removed and halved diagonally
　lengthways
1 tablespoon Madras curry powder
2 garlic cloves, crushed
1 teaspoon caster sugar
100 g bean sprouts
1 tablespoon soy sauce or tamari
2 spring onions, white and green parts
　thinly sliced diagonally

Place the noodles in a heatproof bowl. Cover with boiling water and set aside for 5 minutes or until just tender. Drain well.

Heat the peanut oil in a wok or large frying pan over high heat. Add the onion, capsicum, beans and snow peas and stir-fry for 5 minutes. Add the curry powder and garlic and stir-fry for 30 seconds or until fragrant. Add the sugar and 2 tablespoons of water and toss until well combined.

Add the noodles, bean sprouts and soy sauce or tamari to the wok or pan and use two wooden spoons to toss until everything is well combined. Sprinkle with the spring onion and serve.

MEATY ADDITION: Toss in 16 Pan-fried prawns (see page 275) just after the vegetables are cooked.

Cheat's puttanesca with orecchiette

SERVES: 4 PREP: 20 mins COOKING: 15 mins

The classic pasta sauce from Ischia off the coast of Naples is wonderfully flexible, working equally well with everything from slow-cooked lamb or chicken to kale and seafood, such as mussels. This is perhaps surprising, given its robust, salty flavours. Less surprising is how well it goes with this robust ear-shaped pasta, which originated in Apulia (just over the Apennines from Napoli) and spread across southern Italy. While the ancient Etruscans who lived near Rome might take the title as Italy's pasta pioneers, it was in Naples that pastas were first commercially made for trade. So there!

500 g orecchiette
80 ml (⅓ cup) extra-virgin olive oil
4 pale celery stalks, finely chopped,
    pale green leaves reserved
1 bunch flat-leaf parsley, leaves
    picked, stalks finely chopped
1 large onion, finely chopped
4 garlic cloves, crushed
125 ml (½ cup) dry white wine or,
    better still, vermouth
2 × 400 g cans crushed tomatoes
150 g pitted black olives, drained
    (to be on the safe side, check they
    are all pitted before adding them
    to the sauce)
3 long red chillies, chopped into
    1 cm thick rings
110 g capers in brine, rinsed
    and drained
finely grated zest and juice of 1 lemon
sea salt, if needed
pinch of caster sugar, if needed

Cook the orecchiette in a saucepan of boiling salted water for 1 minute less than it says on the packet or until just al dente.

Meanwhile, heat half the olive oil in a large saucepan over high heat, add the celery stalk, parsley stalk and onion and cook, stirring, for 3–4 minutes or until the onion is translucent. Add the garlic and cook, stirring, for 1 minute or until aromatic. Pour in the wine or vermouth and cook, scraping up any bits caught on the base of the pan. Add the tomatoes, olives, half the chilli and half the capers and bring to the boil.

While the sauce and pasta are cooking, dry the remaining capers on paper towel. Heat the remaining oil in a small frying pan over medium–high heat, add the capers and fry for 1–2 minutes, until they are crispy. Drain on a plate lined with paper towel.

Roughly chop the parsley leaves.

Squeeze the juice of half the lemon (or more if needed) into the puttanesca sauce and adjust the seasoning with salt and a little sugar if needed (remember the capers and olives will add lots of salt).

Drain the orecchiette and toss it in the puttanesca sauce to emulsify. Divide among bowls and sprinkle with the crispy capers, lemon zest, celery leaves, chopped parsley leaves and remaining chilli.

MEATY ADDITION: Add 25 g anchovy fillets (the best and pinkest you can find) with the garlic.

Pumpkin & sage cannelloni

SERVES: 6 **PREP:** 30 mins **COOKING:** 1 hour 50 mins

This is the story of a love triangle but with a happy ending. You see, pumpkin loves sage and nutmeg equally. The trouble is, if you flavour your pasta filling with both, like the most uncomfortable three-way, it leaves a nasty taste in your mouth.

But I've found that if you marry the pumpkin with the nutmeg and then let it have a little sage action on the side when the sage has moved in next door with the tomato sauce, somehow this works out well for all concerned.

*I think this is the basic concept that **Married At First Sight** has been trying to nail for a few seasons now.*

P.S. If you are worried about how the tomato sauce feels about all of this, please don't. It's having too much fun between those silky sheets of lasagne with the salty feta and fresh ricotta to be bothered, but thanks for caring.

1.5 kg butternut pumpkin, unpeeled, deseeded and cut into 1.5 cm thick slices
60 ml (¼ cup) olive oil
sea salt and freshly ground black pepper
1 onion, finely chopped
3 garlic cloves, crushed
3 × 400 g cans diced tomatoes
1 tablespoon finely chopped sage
2 strips lemon peel
500 g fresh ricotta
½ teaspoon ground or freshly grated nutmeg
40 g (½ cup) coarsely grated parmesan
7 fresh lasagne sheets, halved crossways
200 g Greek feta, sliced
baby rocket leaves, to serve
1 head radicchio, leaves shredded, to serve (optional)

Preheat the oven to 180°C/160°C fan-forced. Line a baking tray with baking paper.

Place the pumpkin on the prepared tray and drizzle with 2 tablespoons of the olive oil. Season with plenty of salt and pepper. Roast for 1 hour or until tender, then remove and set aside for 5 minutes to cool slightly. Use a spoon to scoop the pumpkin flesh away from the skin and place in a bowl. Discard the skin.

Meanwhile, cook up your tomato mixture. Heat the remaining oil in a large frying pan over medium heat. Add the onion and cook, stirring, for 5 minutes or until soft. Add the garlic and cook, stirring, for 30 seconds or until aromatic. Add the diced tomatoes, sage and lemon peel and season with salt. Simmer for 15 minutes or until the sauce has thickened slightly. Remove the lemon peel. Spread half the tomato mixture over the base of a 29 cm × 25 cm baking dish.

Add the ricotta, nutmeg and half the parmesan to the pumpkin and mix until combined.

Divide the pumpkin mixture among the lasagne sheets, placing it in a line in the centre following the short edge. Roll up the sheets to enclose the filling.

Place the rolls, seam-side down, on top of the tomato mixture in the dish and spoon over the remaining tomato mixture. Top with the sliced feta and sprinkle with the remaining parmesan. Bake for 50 minutes or until golden. Sprinkle with rocket leaves and serve with shredded radicchio on the side, if you like.

 TIP: If you prefer to use dried tubes of cannelloni, make the tomato sauce wetter by adding 150 ml of vegetable stock with the canned tomatoes. You'll need this extra liquid to cook the pasta.

Cheat's ramen with udon

SERVES: 4 **PREP:** 10 mins **COOKING:** 20 mins

Here is a vegan ramen that doesn't skimp on the umami hit of a great ramen served in Shibuya or Shimokitazawa. #GoodTimes. I could tell you a long and rambling story about our search for the best ramen when GC, GM and I were in Tokyo for MasterChef but that might make us sound like wankers and I wouldn't do that to the boys. BTW, ironically, the best ramen we had was somewhere no one has ever heard of. Perhaps because it has a name that not one of us can remember.

1.5 litres vegetable stock
2 cm knob of ginger, peeled and thinly sliced
3 garlic cloves, thinly sliced
12 small dried shiitake mushrooms
2 spring onions, white and green parts separated and thinly sliced
80 g (¼ cup) white miso paste
2 tablespoons soy sauce or tamari
2 tablespoons mirin or mirin seasoning
300 g fresh udon noodles
115 g packet baby corn, halved lengthways and rinsed
1 bunch baby bok choy, halved lengthways
60 g fried tofu puffs, sliced
sesame oil and togarashi spice mix, to serve
1 nori sheet, thinly shredded with scissors, to serve

Place the stock, ginger, garlic, shiitake mushrooms and white part of the spring onion in a large saucepan over high heat and bring to the boil. Reduce the heat to low and simmer for 10 minutes to allow the flavours to develop. Use tongs to remove all the flavourings except the mushrooms.

Add the miso, soy sauce or tamari, mirin and 375 ml (1½ cups) of water to the stock mixture and bring to a simmer over low heat. Add the udon noodles and corn and cook for 5 minutes or until the noodles are almost ready. Add the bok choy and cook for 2 minutes or until the stems are just tender and the noodles are cooked through.

Divide the noodles among serving bowls. Use those tongs to transfer the bok choy to the bowls, along with the mushrooms and corn. Ladle over the hot stock mixture. Top with the fried tofu and drizzle with sesame oil. Sprinkle with the togarashi and nori and serve.

MEATY ADDITION: Replace the tofu with 2 thinly sliced Poached chicken breast fillets (see page 261).

The new view from Old Smoky with poor man's parmesan

SERVES: 4 **PREP:** 45 mins (plus 1 hour chilling) **COOKING:** 45 mins

Meatballs with pasta is a very American thing. So much so that the Appalachian Mountains folk tune 'On Top of Old Smoky', which was a hit for The Weavers in 1951, was converted into a heart-rending tale about a wandering meatball by Tom Glazer in his 1963 hit 'On Top of Spaghetti'. Glazer was folk songwriting royalty for the likes of pre-electric Bob Dylan, Burl Ives and Pete Seeger. In a strange turn of events, Glazer's other big songwriting credit was 'Because All Men Are Brothers', which was recorded by Peter, Paul and Mary as well as – wait for it – The Weavers. But I digress ...

As these are veggie balls, rather than meatballs, maybe our Italian readers will be more comfortable eating them with pasta (Italians eat their meatballs with crusty bread). Given that many of these American folk balladeers sang about living in poverty, I'm sure they would have been equally at home writing songs about pangrattato breadcrumbs, the Italian 'cucina povera' substitute for expensive parmesan as a topping for a cheap pasta dinner.

400 g spaghetti
2 tablespoons olive oil

ZUCCHINI BALLS

2 small zucchini, coarsely grated
400 g can borlotti or cannellini beans,
    rinsed and drained
½ red onion, coarsely grated
2 garlic cloves, crushed
105 g (1½ cups) fresh breadcrumbs
    (made from day-old bread)
½ cup coarsely chopped herbs (such
    as flat-leaf parsley and basil)
1 teaspoon dried oregano
2 tablespoons plain flour
1 teaspoon soy sauce or tamari
finely grated zest of ½ lemon
sea salt and freshly ground
    black pepper, to taste

NAPOLI SAUCE

60 ml (¼ cup) extra-virgin olive oil
4 garlic cloves, thickly sliced
2 × 400 g cans diced Italian tomatoes
1 teaspoon sea salt

POOR MAN'S PARMESAN

2 tablespoons olive oil
70 g (1 cup) fresh breadcrumbs
    (made from day-old bread)
2 teaspoons nutritional yeast
¼ teaspoon smoked paprika

To make the zucchini balls, place the grated zucchini in a colander lined with paper towel and top with another layer of paper towel. Press down with a wooden spoon or the heel of your hand to drain off the excess water. Repeat this step with the borlotti or cannellini beans. Transfer the zucchini and beans to a food processor, add the remaining ingredients and blitz until well combined.

Using slightly wet hands, roll heaped tablespoons of the zucchini mixture into balls (you should have enough to make about 22 balls). Transfer to a tray lined with baking paper and place in the fridge for 1 hour to firm up.

While your zucchini balls chill, get your Napoli sauce ready. Heat the olive oil in a saucepan over low heat, add the garlic and cook for 1–2 minutes or until starting to change colour. Use a slotted spoon to remove and discard the garlic. Add the diced tomatoes, then increase the heat to medium and simmer gently for 20 minutes. Season well with salt.

Now let's make the poor man's parmesan. Heat the oil in a large frying pan over medium–high heat, add the breadcrumbs and cook, tossing, for 5 minutes or until light golden. Sprinkle with the yeast and paprika and toss to combine. Transfer to a bowl, then wipe out the pan as we are about to use it again.

Bring a large saucepan of salted water to the boil. Cook the pasta for 2 minutes less than it says on the packet or until just al dente. Drain and return to the pan.

Meanwhile, heat half the olive oil in a non-stick frying pan over medium heat. Add half the zucchini balls and cook, turning, for 3–4 minutes or until golden. Transfer to a plate. Repeat with the remaining olive oil and zucchini balls. Return all the balls to the pan.

Add the Napoli sauce and carefully turn the zucchini balls so they are well coated. Cook for 1–2 minutes or until everything is heated through.

Divide the pasta among serving bowls, top with the zucchini balls and sauce, then finish with a good sprinkling of poor man's parmesan.

Creamy pumpkin & leek risotto

SERVES: 4 **PREP:** 15 mins **COOKING:** 40 mins

'Creamy' used to be a word reserved for the world of animal milkers but now there are some really good creamy vegan cheeses out there that will give you the same joy without the (albeit historical) risk of smallpox to some poor milkmaid. You could also take a leaf out of the sunflower seed risotto on page 100 and soak a couple of cups of cashews overnight, then drain and blitz them to add creaminess if you wanted to cut down on the cheese.

1 litre (4 cups) salt-reduced
   vegetable stock
1 tablespoon soy sauce or tamari
40 g butter or a vegan alternative
1 tablespoon olive oil
540 g butternut pumpkin, peeled,
   deseeded and cut into 2 cm chunks
sea salt and freshly ground
   black pepper
1 leek, halved lengthways, thinly
   sliced crossways
2 garlic cloves, crushed
330 g (1½ cups) arborio rice (or any
   fancy risotto rice, such as carnaroli
   or the king, vialone nano)
125 ml (½ cup) dry white wine
40 g (½ cup) shredded parmesan, plus
   extra to serve (or nutritional yeast
   if parmesan doesn't live up to your
   ethical stance)
75 g (¼ cup) mascarpone (or a soft
   vegan marinated feta), plus a little
   extra to serve
¼ cup shredded basil, plus extra
   leaves to serve

Pour the stock and soy sauce or tamari into a saucepan and bring just to the boil over high heat. Reduce the heat to low and hold at a very gentle simmer.

Heat the butter and half the olive oil in a large heavy-based saucepan over medium–high heat. Add the pumpkin and season with salt and pepper, then cover and cook, stirring once or twice, for 6–8 minutes or until starting to soften. Transfer to a bowl.

Heat the remaining oil in the same pan over medium heat. Add the leek and garlic and cook, stirring, for 5 minutes or until soft and translucent (do not brown). Add the rice and cook, stirring, for 2–3 minutes or until the grains appear slightly glassy. Toasting the grains like this ensures the rice cooks evenly.

Add the wine to the pan and cook, stirring, until most of the liquid has been absorbed. The rice should move in the pan like wet sand. Now return the pumpkin to the pan, along with about 125 ml (½ cup) of the hot stock and stir until the liquid has been absorbed.

Continue adding the stock to the pan in batches, making sure it has been absorbed before adding the next. After about 20 minutes the rice should be tender yet firm to the bite.

Remove the risotto from the heat. Stir in the parmesan and mascarpone with gusto, and then the basil. Season to taste and divide among shallow serving bowls. Finish with a few dollops of extra mascarpone and a scattering of basil leaves and extra parmesan.

MEATY ADDITION: Coarsely chop 100 g sliced pancetta and add to the leek base mixture at the start.

Vegan bolognese

SERVES: 6–8 **PREP:** 40 mins **COOKING:** 1 hour 10 mins

Ask yourself, why do you love spag bol? Now, let me take a stab: it's the way the rich sauce coats the strands of pasta, isn't it? Well that's the pleasure of this bolognese, too! But with the added bonus of lentils and diced fennel, which makes it even more texturally interesting.

1 litre (4 cups) vegetable stock
10 g dried porcini mushrooms
20 g dried shiitake mushrooms
2 tablespoons olive oil
2 carrots, finely chopped
1 onion, finely chopped
1 baby fennel bulb, finely chopped
3 garlic cloves, crushed
3 thyme sprigs, plus extra leaves
   to serve
2 fresh or dried bay leaves
sea salt and freshly ground
   black pepper
320 g (about 4) portobello
   mushrooms, finely chopped
400 g cup mushrooms, finely chopped
2 tablespoons tomato paste
700 g bottle passata
200 g (1 cup) dried Puy lentils, rinsed
   and drained
650 g wholemeal or spelt penne, or
   pasta of your choice
Poor man's parmesan (see page 118)
   or vegan parmesan, to serve

Warm the stock, porcini and shiitake mushrooms in a saucepan over medium heat. Remove from the heat and set aside to infuse while you make the next step.

Heat half the olive oil in a large saucepan over medium heat. Add the carrot, onion and fennel and cook, stirring, for 8 minutes or until soft. Add the garlic, thyme and bay leaves and season with salt. Cook, stirring, for 1 minute or until aromatic. Transfer to a heatproof bowl.

Use a slotted spoon to remove the porcini and shiitake mushrooms from the stock. Place on a chopping board and finely chop. Reserve the stock.

Heat the remaining olive oil in the pan, add the portobello and cup mushrooms and cook, stirring, for 8–10 minutes or until all the liquid has evaporated. Add the tomato paste and cook, stirring, for 2 minutes. Return the carrot mixture to the pan, then add the passata, shiitake and porcini mushrooms, reserved stock and three-quarters of the lentils and bring to a simmer. Reduce the heat to low and cook, partially covered and stirring often, for 20 minutes. Add the remaining lentils and cook for 20 minutes or until just tender. Season with salt and pepper.

Meanwhile, cook the pasta in plenty of salted boiling water for 2 minutes less than it says on the packet or until just al dente. Drain.

Divide the pasta among serving bowls and top with the lentil bolognese. Finish with a generous sprinkling of poor man's parmesan or vegan parmesan — yes you can use real Italian Parmigiana Reggiano assuming no judgy types are watching … not that you see many of those around here — and a few thyme leaves.

MEATY ADDITION: Add finely chopped pancetta to the carrot mixture or, for a meatier version, replace the cup mushrooms with 400 g Pan-fried pork and veal mince (see page 266).

Very special fried rice – hold the spam

SERVES: 4 PREP: 15 mins (plus 2 hours marinating) COOKING: 20 mins

ME: I really think we should add some frozen peas and pan-fried frozen corn to this. And how about a few cubes of fried carrot?

MICHELLE (playing the role of Heimdall, guardian of the gateway to the recipe Bifröst): No, the title of this book is not 'Bogan Vegan'.

ME: Maybe it should be!

MICHELLE: So Loki, you reveal yourself finally …

Everyone looks excitedly down the page to see if Chris Hemsworth is about to appear as Thor.

2 tablespoons peanut oil
1 bunch broccolini, cut into thin stems
200 g brussels sprouts, leaves separated
3 spring onions, white and green parts sliced diagonally
6 cm knob of ginger, peeled and cut into thin strips
2 × 250 g packets microwave brown rice, heated, or 550 g (3 cups) cooked brown rice, both cooled overnight in the fridge
2 tablespoons soy sauce or tamari
2 teaspoons sesame oil
1 tablespoon sesame seeds, toasted (optional)

STICKY TERIYAKI TOFU
80 ml (⅓ cup) teriyaki marinade
3 cm knob of ginger, peeled and finely grated
3 teaspoons sriracha chilli sauce or your favourite chilli sauce
80 ml (⅓ cup) honey
400 g firm tofu, cut into 2 cm cubes

For the sticky teriyaki tofu, combine the teriyaki marinade, ginger, sriracha and 60 ml (¼ cup) of the honey in a large bowl. Add the tofu and toss to combine. Cover and marinate in the fridge for 2 hours, tossing occasionally.

Heat half the peanut oil in a wok or large frying pan over high heat until just smoking. Using a slotted spoon or tongs, add half the tofu and cook, tossing gently, for 3–4 minutes, until golden. Transfer to a bowl. Repeat with the remaining tofu. Add any marinade left in the bowl and the remaining honey to the wok or pan and cook, stirring, for 1–2 minutes or until the mixture boils and thickens. Pour over the tofu and toss until well coated. Cover to keep warm and set aside.

Give the wok or pan a little rinse and wipe but don't be overly fussy as we are using it again now.

Heat the remaining peanut oil in the wok or pan over high heat. Add the broccolini and cook, tossing, for 2–3 minutes or until starting to turn bright green and slightly charred around the edges. Add the brussels sprout leaves, spring onion and ginger and toss for 2 minutes or until the brussels sprouts are starting to wilt. Add the rice and half the soy sauce or tamari and toss for a further 2 minutes or until heated through and well combined.

Transfer the rice to a serving bowl or platter and drizzle over the sesame oil and remaining soy sauce or tamari. Top with the tofu and sprinkle with the sesame seeds (if using).

MEATY ADDITION: Toss 120 g (about 4) sliced Fried lap cheong (see page 268) through the rice with the vegetables.

Our mac 'n' cheese with chunky garlic bread topping

SERVES: 4 PREP: 15 mins COOKING: 45 mins

Who doesn't love garlic bread with their pasta? So why not combine these two favourites into one dish? That's the sort of thinking that should see a certain prize committee in Oslo sitting up and taking notice.

Failing that I'll settle for the World Food Prize for 2019 … Sure, last year's winners Dr Lawrence Haddad and Dr David Nabarro's complementary global leadership in elevating maternal and child undernutrition within food security issues was most laudable, but it was no mac 'n' cheese with a garlic bread topping!

250 g macaroni
20 g butter
2 golden shallots, finely chopped
    (yes, you could use that ½ red
    onion sitting forlornly in the
    fridge instead)
1½ tablespoons plain flour
375 ml (1½ cups) milk
100 g (1 cup) coarsely grated
    vintage cheddar
sea salt and freshly ground
    black pepper
200 g baby roma or grape tomatoes
180 g cherry bocconcini, drained well

GARLIC BREADCRUMBS
100 g soy and linseed sourdough
    bread, cut into 1 cm pieces
¼ cup very finely chopped
    flat-leaf parsley
3 garlic cloves, crushed
60 g butter, melted

Preheat the oven to 200°C/180°C fan-forced.

Cook the macaroni in a saucepan of boiling salted water for 2 minutes less than it says on the packet or until just al dente. Drain and return to the pan.

While the pasta cooks, melt the butter in a saucepan over medium heat. Add the shallot and cook, stirring, for 3 minutes or until soft. Stir in the flour for 1 minute or until the mixture bubbles. Remove the pan from the heat and gradually whisk in the milk until smooth. Return to medium heat and simmer, stirring, for 2 minutes or until the mixture boils and thickens. Stir in the cheddar until melted and combined, then season with salt and pepper.

Pour the sauce over the pasta and toss together.

Cut six of the tomatoes in half and set aside. Add the remaining whole tomatoes to the pasta mixture and stir to combine. Spoon into a medium baking dish. Arrange the reserved halved tomatoes on top, cut-side down. Scatter over the cherry bocconcini and gently press them down.

To make the garlic breadcrumbs, combine all the ingredients in a bowl.

Scatter the breadcrumbs over the macaroni mixture, allowing some of the tomatoes and bocconcini to show through. Bake for 30 minutes or until the top is golden and crisp.

 TIP: I'm warming to the idea of a pasta bake with a garlic bread crust. Layer slices of bread on top, overlapping like potatoes on a Lancashire hotpot, then brush with garlic butter as it cooks.

MEATY ADDITION: Toss 6 (about 150 g) chopped rashers Crispy bacon (see page 268) to the creamy pasta prior to baking.

Carrot alfredo with cashews two ways

SERVES: 4 PREP: 15 mins (plus 1 hour soaking) COOKING: 10 mins

Cashews are the fanciest of all nuts – apart from those ostentatious macadamias and hard-to-get-at pistachios. Here they shine in a vegan version of fettuccine Alfredo, another Italian dish that is far more common overseas than back in the old country.

Like carbonara here, and bolognese in the UK, fettuccine Alfredo is the king of *Sh-Italian pasta in the US. This creamy-sauced dish was popularised by the king and queen of Silent-era Hollywood, the swashbuckling Douglas Fairbanks Jnr and America's sweetheart Mary Pickford (think the Brangelina or Kimye of their day). They claimed they ate it every night on their honeymoon in Rome, and boasted that the flamboyant chef Alfredo di Lelio would toss the pasta at their table, accompanied by an orchestra!

I've made it gluten free and vegan because that's so Hollywood 2020.

*Sh-Italian is a word coined for those dishes that are often immediately identified as Italian, but don't actually have any concrete or remaining links with Italy, yet they still exist outside the country. Spaghetti bolognese is the most loved of all of these.

150 g raw cashews
boiling water
400 g carrots, spiralised
¼ bunch flat-leaf parsley, leaves
   picked, stalks chopped
sea salt
1 tablespoon olive oil
2 garlic cloves, crushed
2 teaspoons Dijon mustard (see TIP)
finely grated zest of 1 lemon and
   the juice of ½ lemon
50 g salted roasted cashews, crushed

Tip the cashews into a heatproof bowl and pour over boiling water. Set aside for 1 hour to soften.

Place the carrot in a microwave-safe bowl. Microwave on high for 4 minutes or until slightly softened. Pat dry with paper towel.

Drain the cashews, then place in a food processor or blender. Add the chopped parsley stalks and a splash of warm water and blitz to the consistency of thick cream. Season to taste with salt.

Heat the olive oil in a large frying pan over medium heat. When it's sizzling, add the garlic and cook until lightly golden and fragrant. Throw in the carrot and cook savagely for 1 minute or until it catches and burns a little. Add the mustard and lemon juice and stir through. Pour the cashew sauce over the carrot mixture and cook, tossing, for 1 minute or until thickened and warmed through.

Serve topped with the parsley leaves, lemon zest and crushed cashews.

 TIP: Dijon mustard is a tricky beast that can be made with vinegar or verjuice, which may have used eggs in their production. If this is a problem for you, use a vegan Dijon mustard or make a paste with mustard powder and lemon juice and add, to taste.

Bakes

The oven is the Harry Potter of kitchen equipment making magic happen every time you use it. Raw carrots, for example, are transformed into gnarled, chewy orange candy, while sloppy batters turn into springy cakes. The oven is also your best friend, as it will cook stuff for you slowly and safely while you go off and do other, more enjoyable, things.

Some of my absolute favourites in this chapter include a BLT made with carrot bacon, Chinese steamed buns filled with caramel brussels sprouts, a hearty vegetable stew topped with cheesy dumplings and a totally awesome lentil shepherd's pie. Oh, and don't forget to try my decadent veg souffles with creamed leek, cheddar and jalapeno chillies.

The other BLT – 'bacon', lettuce & tomato sandwich

SERVES: 4 PREP: 10 mins COOKING: 15 mins

Much has been written about the process of creating 'carrot bacon'. Food muse Michelle Southan and I feel that pairing miso and smoked paprika gives a far more intense salty flavour and roasty rasher look than the usual addition of tahini, which can be drying and has a dominant flavour all of its own. Piled in this sandwich, the carrot bacon also brings some of the chewiness and smokiness that meat eaters relish with their bacon.

8 thick slices bread, toasted
8 oak or frilly lettuce leaves
4 small ripe tomatoes, thickly sliced

CARROT BACON
1 tablespoon olive oil
1 tablespoon soy sauce or tamari
1 tablespoon white miso paste
2 teaspoons smoked paprika
2 large carrots, peeled into ribbons

INSTANT MUSTARD MAYO
1 egg
350 ml (1 cup) grapeseed oil
1 tablespoon freshly squeezed
  lemon juice
1 teaspoon wholegrain mustard
sea salt and freshly ground
  black pepper

Preheat the oven to 170°C/150°C fan-forced. Line two large baking trays with baking paper.

To make the carrot bacon, combine the olive oil, soy sauce or tamari, miso and paprika in a bowl.

Place the carrot ribbons on the prepared trays and brush on both sides with the miso mixture. Bake for 10 minutes. Turn over and brush the carrot with any remaining miso mixture, then bake for a further 5 minutes or until slightly charred around the edges.

Meanwhile, to make the mustard mayo, carefully crack the egg into a jug, without breaking the yolk. Pour over the grapeseed oil and lemon juice. Position a stick blender carefully over the egg so the basket covers and encloses the yolk. Blend for 1–2 seconds to emulsify. Pull the blender up to incorporate all the ingredients until a thick mayonnaise forms. Stir in the mustard and season.

Spread one side of the toast slices with the mustard mayo. Top half the slices with the lettuce, tomato and carrot bacon. Top with the remaining bread slices mayo-side down.

TIPS: Make double quantities of this carrot bacon to use another time. I like to dice and add it to bacon-free carbonara (see page 88) after I've stirred the cheese and egg mixture into the hot pasta.

For a vegan BLT, ditch the mustard mayo and spike your favourite vegan mayo with nutritional yeast and mustard powder.

MEATY ADDITION: Replace the carrot with 8 rashers Crispy bacon (see page 268).

Zucchini nests with eggs, kale, capers & olives

SERVES: 6 **PREP:** 15 mins (5 mins if you buy pre-made zoodles) **COOKING:** 30 mins

Any vegan will tell you, eggs should be left in their nests. It's the same with this dish*.

*Although it goes without saying that this dish is not vegan!

250 g kale, stems removed and leaves torn into large pieces

2 tablespoons extra-virgin olive oil, plus extra to serve

150 g marinated pitted green olives, roughly chopped

4 large zucchini, shredded with a julienne peeler or use a spiraliser to make noodles

6 eggs

2 tablespoons baby capers, rinsed and drained

½ teaspoon chilli flakes

finely grated zest of ½ lemon

Preheat the oven to 180°C/160°C fan-forced.

Place the kale on a baking tray. Drizzle with the olive oil and massage into the kale until it is well coated. Spread out the kale in a single layer and scatter the olives over the top.

Divide the zucchini into six portions. Twirl each portion around your fingers to make a nest and place around the inside edge of an ovenproof frying pan or round baking dish. The nests need to be full so don't worry if there seems to be too much zucchini – it will shrink down during cooking.

Place the kale tray and zucchini nests in the oven and bake for 15 minutes. Remove the zucchini and leave the kale in the oven. Crack an egg into each zucchini nest and scatter the capers over the top. Return to the oven and bake for a further 15 minutes, removing the kale about 5 minutes before the zucchini nests are ready.

Scatter the crispy kale leaves and olives over the eggs. Drizzle with some extra olive oil and sprinkle with the chilli flakes and lemon zest. Serve straight from the pan or dish.

MEATY ADDITION: Line the inside of each zucchini nest with a slice of prosciutto or thin streaky bacon.

The other, other KFC – Korean Fried Cauliflower

SERVES: 4 as a starter **PREP:** 15 mins **COOKING:** 40 mins

*My white beard makes me look like the Colonel, so I might as well take advantage of it with this KFC dish …
It also makes me look like Dumbledore or Gandalf and this dish is really wizard too!!! Ed: Groan.*

*Whatever you do, don't get any of the sweet and spicy red sauce in your beard as it will make you look like you
have just feasted on live rabbits.*

75 g (½ cup) plain flour
70 g (½ cup) cornflour
2 teaspoons onion powder
1 teaspoon garlic powder
1 teaspoon ground ginger
1 teaspoon baking powder
1 teaspoon sea salt
125 ml (½ cup) vodka
1 head cauliflower, cut into
   large florets
sesame seeds and sliced spring onion,
   to serve

GOCHUJANG SAUCE
60 ml (¼ cup) tomato sauce
   or ketchup
55 g (¼ cup) brown sugar
2 tablespoons gochujang chilli paste
2 tablespoons soy sauce or tamari
1 tablespoon rice wine vinegar

Preheat the oven to 230°C/210°C fan-forced. Line a baking tray with baking paper.

Combine the flour, cornflour, onion powder, garlic powder, ginger, baking powder and salt in a bowl. Gradually whisk in the vodka and 80 ml (⅓ cup) of water. Add the cauliflower and toss to coat. Use tongs to transfer the cauliflower to the prepared tray, draining off any excess batter as you go. Bake for 20–30 minutes, until golden and crisp.

Meanwhile, to make the gochujang sauce, place all the ingredients in a saucepan and stir over medium heat for 2 minutes or until the sugar has dissolved. Bring to the boil, then remove from the heat.

Place the cauliflower in a large bowl. Pour over half the sauce, tossing as you go so all the florets are well coated. Return to the baking tray and bake for a further 10 minutes or until tender.

Place the cauliflower on a serving plate and drizzle over some of the remaining sauce. Pour the rest into a serving bowl, sprinkle sesame seeds and sliced spring onion over the cauliflower and serve.

MEATY ADDITION: Replace half the cauliflower with 700 g chicken wingettes or drumettes. Place the chicken and cauliflower on separate trays when baking.

Decadent vego souffles with creamed leek, cheddar & jalapeno

SERVES: 6 **PREP:** 20 mins **COOKING:** 30 mins

Like breakfast vol-au-vents, DIY barber smocks that catch the hair you cut, and the desk hammock that hangs under your desk for your feet to rest in, these decadent vego souffles are actually 'a thing'. But I would say these satiny souffles are worth more than all the other three combined.

80 g butter, plus well-softened butter for greasing
finely grated parmesan, for dusting
3 leeks, trimmed and cut into 5 mm thick rounds
60 ml (¼ cup) thickened cream
5 jalapeno chillies, deseeded and finely chopped (you could also use long green chillies)
70 g pickled jalapeno chillies, finely chopped
2 tablespoons jalapeno brine (from the jar)
2 teaspoons plain flour
80 g (1 cup) coarsely grated vintage cheddar
2 eggs yolks
7 egg whites
1 teaspoon caster sugar

Preheat the oven to 200°C/180°C fan-forced. Line the base of a small roasting tin with a folded tea towel.

Grease six 250 ml (1 cup) ramekins with the well-softened butter and finish by drawing upward strokes up the side of each ramekin. These tramlines of fat will help the souffles rise. Place in the fridge for 10 minutes to chill. Brush the ramekins upwards with softened butter again to reinforce these tramlines. Add the parmesan and rotate the ramekins to coat the inside, shaking off any excess. Place in the fridge.

Heat half the butter in a large saucepan over medium heat until foaming and add the leek. Cover and cook, stirring occasionally, for 10 minutes or until very soft. Add the cream and cook, stirring, until well combined. Divide the leek mixture among the ramekins, then place them back in the fridge.

Place the fresh chilli, pickled jalapeno and pickling brine in a jug and blitz with a stick blender until almost smooth.

Melt the remaining butter in the same pan over medium heat. Add the flour and cook, stirring, until it forms a paste. Gradually stir in the jalapeno mixture until well combined. Add the cheddar and cook until melted and the mixture forms a thick paste. Remove from the heat and quickly whisk in the egg yolks until well combined. Cover and keep warm.

Bring a kettle to the boil.

Using an electric mixer fitted with the whisk attachment, whisk the egg whites and sugar in a clean, dry bowl until stiff peaks form. Be careful not to overbeat. Fold one-third of the egg white into the cheddar mixture, then add the remaining egg white in two more batches.

Divide the egg mixture among the chilled ramekins. Run your fingernail or the blunt tip of a knife around the inside rim of each dish and place in the lined roasting tin. Pour boiling water into the tin until the water reaches halfway up the side of the ramekins. Bake for 10–12 minutes or until puffed and golden. Serve immediately.

MEATY ADDITION: Add 6 chopped rashers Crispy bacon (see page 268) or Crispy prosciutto shards (see page 269) to the leek mixture.

Dadaist sausage rolls for Barry Humphries

MAKES: 24 **PREP:** 30 mins **COOKING:** 45 mins

I once spent an hour talking to Barry Humphries on the radio and realised that from his early Dadaist performance pieces (such as 'the Russian salad inflight conundrum' and 'the tramp looking in the dustbin for something to eat who produces a fancy dinner complete with napery and lit candelabra') to his first London stage performance as a pie maker in Sweeney Todd, his whole oeuvre can be viewed through the prism of food.

With this in mind – and respecting that Dame Edna is now seeking to enter the realms of celebrity chef in the Martha Stewart/Nigella Lawson mould – I present a Dadaist sausage roll, absurd in that it contains no sausage meat. What makes it even more absurd is that the vast majority of sausage meat contains more fat and filler than actual meat.

But then, like a joke, art is never improved by explanation. It is far better to make a batch of these sausage rolls and see where Sir Les Patterson stands on the whole pie versus sausage roll debate that gripped pollies of his era (as seen when Bob Carr slammed sausage rolls to win the New South Wales election).

1 tablespoon olive oil
1 small red onion, finely chopped
2 garlic cloves, crushed
2 whole star anise
1 tablespoon soy sauce or tamari
250 g cottage cheese
1 carrot, coarsely grated
1 zucchini, coarsely grated and
    squeezed to remove excess
    moisture
20 g (½ cup) panko breadcrumbs
60 g (½ cup) pecans or walnuts,
    finely chopped
2 eggs
sea salt and freshly ground
    black pepper
3 sheets puff pastry, just thawed
1 tablespoon sesame seeds
tomato sauce or relish, to serve

Heat the olive oil in a frying pan over medium heat. Add the onion, garlic and star anise and cook, stirring frequently, for 5 minutes or until soft. Add the soy sauce or tamari and cook, stirring, for 2 minutes or until the liquid is almost absorbed. Set aside to cool and discard the star anise.

Preheat the oven to 200°C/180°C fan-forced. Line two baking trays with baking paper.

Combine the onion mixture, cottage cheese, carrot, zucchini, breadcrumbs, nuts and one egg in a bowl and season well.

Beat the remaining egg in a bowl. Cut the pastry sheets in half. Place one-sixth of the veggie mixture lengthways along the centre of each piece of pastry. Brush one long edge with the beaten egg, then fold over to enclose the filling, pressing to seal. Cut each roll crossways into four pieces.

Place the sausage rolls, seam-side down, on the prepared trays. Brush the pastry with the beaten egg, then use a small sharp knife to pierce the tops a few times to allow steam to escape. Sprinkle with the sesame seeds and bake for 35 minutes or until golden and cooked through. Serve with tomato sauce or relish.

MEATY ADDITION: Add 4 finely chopped slices of prosciutto to the cottage cheese mixture.

The creamiest coddled egg

SERVES: 6 **PREP:** 15 mins **COOKING:** 55 mins

I love me an eggs Florentine, so here it is, sort of. Perhaps better described as coddled eggs crossed with the signature dish of one of the more unusual fast food successes of the last decade, LA's egg-focused, and questionably named, Eggslut. The combination of soft, oozy egg cooked slowly in a water bath with rich satiny mash and silky spinach is about as comforting as a dish can get. It's like a dummy for adults. So go on, suck on this.

700 g sebago potatoes, peeled and quartered
sea salt and freshly ground black pepper
40 g unsalted butter, plus extra for greasing
1 small garlic clove, crushed
185 ml (¾ cup) pouring cream, plus 2 tablespoons extra
60 g baby spinach leaves
70 g coarsely grated gruyere, plus extra for sprinkling
100 g (1 cup) coarsely grated mozzarella
boiling water
6 eggs, at room temperature
snipped chives, to serve

Preheat the oven to 190°C/170°C fan-forced.

Cook the potato in a large saucepan of salted boiling water for 15 minutes or until tender. Drain, then return the potato to the pan and partially cover for 5 minutes to allow it to steam. Press the potato through a potato ricer or mash with a masher until very smooth (or you can press through a sieve if you still have a few lumps). Season well with salt and pepper.

Melt the butter in a small frying pan over medium heat, add the garlic and cook for 1 minute or until soft but not brown.

Add the garlic butter, cream and spinach to the potato. Place over medium heat and cook, stirring constantly, for 3–4 minutes or until the spinach has wilted. Add the cheeses and cook, stirring, for 2–3 minutes or until melted.

Butter six 250 ml (1 cup) ovenproof dishes and place them in a large roasting tin.

Divide the hot potato mixture among the dishes and smooth the surface. Pour boiling water into the roasting tin until it comes one-third of the way up the sides of the dishes. Transfer to the oven and bake for 15 minutes. Remove the tin and crack an egg into each dish. Cover the tin with foil and bake for 15 minutes or until the whites are just set. Remove the foil and sprinkle a little extra grated gruyere over the eggs. Return the tin to the oven and cook until the cheese is golden, but the yolks are still runny. Scatter over the chives, season with pepper and serve.

MEATY ADDITION: Serve topped with 6 smoked salmon slices or 1 x quantity Spicy chorizo coins (see page 269).

PUFF PASTRY HAND PIES

Hand pies are so hot right now …
… but then that's easily the best way to eat them.

Creamy artichoke & fennel hand pies

MAKES: 12
PREP: 15 mins
COOKING: 20 mins

1 baby fennel bulb, trimmed and finely chopped
280 g jarred marinated artichoke hearts, drained and finely chopped (if you buy them loose at the deli you'll need 180 g drained artichokes)
40 g (½ cup) shredded parmesan
125 g (½ cup) whole-egg mayonnaise
finely grated zest of ¼ lemon
sea salt and freshly ground black pepper
3 sheets puff pastry, just thawed
1 egg, lightly beaten and sieved

Preheat the oven to 220°C/200°C fan-forced. Line two baking trays with baking paper.

Combine the fennel, artichoke, parmesan, mayonnaise and lemon zest in a bowl and season with salt and pepper.

Cut the pastry sheets into quarters. Place 2 tablespoons of the artichoke mixture in the centre of each pastry square. Fold the corners into the centre of each square, overlapping in the centre to join. Place on the prepared trays, then brush the pastry with the egg. Bake for 20 minutes or until golden.

Caprese hand pies

MAKES: 20
PREP: 15 mins
COOKING: 20 mins

5 sheets puff pastry, just thawed
3 fresh mozzarella balls, cut into 1 cm thick slices and drained on paper towel
20 cherry tomatoes, each cut into 3 slices
1 egg, lightly beaten and sieved

PEPPERY BASIL PESTO

40 g baby rocket leaves
½ cup basil leaves
2 small garlic cloves, crushed
60 g (¾ cup) shredded parmesan
45 g (¼ cup) pine nuts, toasted
80 ml (⅓ cup) olive oil

Preheat the oven to 220°C/200°C fan-forced. Line two baking trays with baking paper.

To make the pesto, blitz the rocket, basil, garlic, parmesan and pine nuts in a food processor until finely chopped. With the motor running, gradually add the olive oil in a thin, steady stream until well combined.

Using an 11 cm cutter, cut out 20 circles of puff pastry. Place a teaspoon of pesto in the centre of each pastry circle, then a slice of mozzarella and 3 tomato slices. Brush the edge of the dough with a little water, then fold the dough over onto itself into a half-moon shape. Pinch and pleat the edge with your fingers to seal and place on the prepared trays. Brush the pastry with the egg and bake for 20 minutes or until golden.

Serve the pies with an extra dollop of pesto on top or pop the leftovers in a jar in the fridge where it will keep for up to 1 week.

Samosa hand pies

MAKES: 12
PREP: 20 mins (plus cooling)
COOKING: 35 mins

600 g sebago potatoes, peeled and coarsely chopped
20 g butter
2 long green chillies, deseeded and finely chopped
2 teaspoons cumin seeds
2 teaspoons mustard seeds
1 teaspoon ground turmeric
¼ teaspoon chilli powder
40 g (¼ cup) frozen baby peas, thawed
sea salt
2 tablespoons coarsely chopped coriander
3 sheets frozen puff pastry, just thawed
1 egg, lightly beaten and sieved
mango chutney, to serve

Bring a large saucepan of water to the boil. Add the potato and
cook for 10 minutes or until just tender. Drain and cool slightly,
then cut into 1.5 cm pieces.

Preheat the oven to 220°C/200°C fan-forced. Line two baking
trays with baking paper.

Melt the butter in a frying pan over medium–high heat. Add
the green chilli, cumin seeds, mustard seeds, turmeric and chilli
powder and cook, stirring, for 1–2 minutes or until aromatic
and the chilli has softened slightly. Add the potato and peas and
toss until well combined. Season well with salt, then remove
from the heat and set aside to cool. Stir in the coriander.

Cut the pastry sheets into quarters. Place 2 tablespoons
of the potato mixture in the centre of each pastry
square. Fold the pastry over the filling to make a
triangle and crimp the edges with the back of a fork
to seal. Place on the prepared trays, then brush the
pastry with the egg. Bake for 20 minutes or until
golden. Serve with mango chutney.

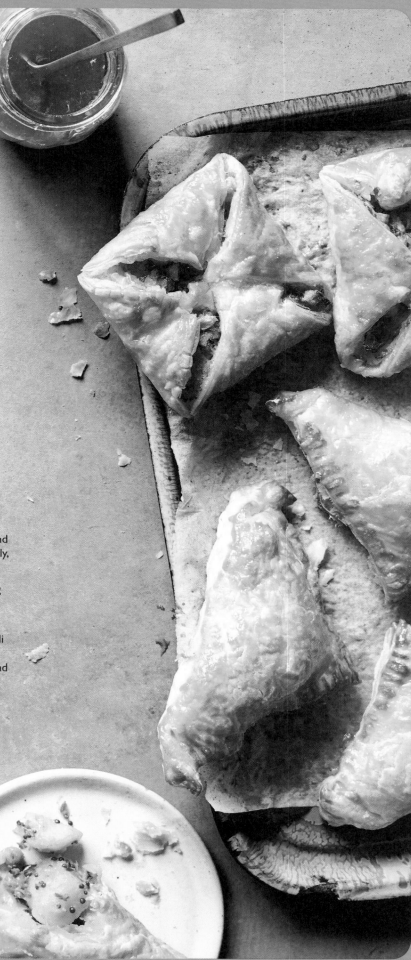

Decadent brie, leek & almond honey pie

SERVES: 6 as a starter **PREP:** 10 mins **COOKING:** 25 mins

This dish is the very definiton of D.F.V food (see page 9), which I'm dubbing as the latest food craze right here, right now. Welcome to D.F.V food! It's decadent, sweet and salty; like all the best junk food.

20 g butter
1 leek, trimmed and thinly sliced
    into rounds
1 teaspoon thyme leaves
1 sheet frozen puff pastry, just thawed
200 g whole wheel double brie
1 egg yolk, lightly beaten and sieved
60 ml (¼ cup) honey
25 g (¼ cup) flaked almonds, toasted
sea salt

TO SERVE
thinly sliced sourdough
red grapes

Preheat the oven to 220°C/200°C fan-forced. Line a baking tray with baking paper.

Melt the butter in a frying pan over medium heat. Add the leek and thyme and cook, stirring, for 5 minutes or until softened. Set aside to cool.

Place the cooled leek mixture in the centre of the pastry and top with the wheel of brie. Fold up the sides of the pastry to enclose the filling, then place seam-side down on the prepared tray. Brush the pastry with the egg yolk and bake for 20 minutes or until puffed and golden.

Meanwhile, heat the honey in a small saucepan over low heat. Stir in the almonds.

Place the pie on a serving plate, then pour over the almond honey and season with salt. Serve with some thinly sliced sourdough and red grapes on the side. Dig in while the cheese is nice and oozy.

 TIP: For a twist, replace the honey with cranberry sauce and stir until melted. Stir in coarsely chopped hazelnuts instead of almonds, then drizzle over the pie.

Zucchini slice version 5.0

SERVES: 6–8 **PREP:** 20 mins **COOKING:** 25 mins

Just like you can never underestimate the foolishness of teenage boys or the turning circle of a road train, you should never underestimate the number of zucchini slice recipes Australia needs every summer before it stops driving it up to the top on the online search list. Here's another one.

I'd love to say it's better than every other zucchini slice recipe that has come before it … but I won't. A bit like each generation of teenage boys really. But it looks and, dare I say, smells waaaay better!

5 eggs
150 g (1 cup) self-raising flour
2 zucchini, coarsely grated
80 g (½ cup) frozen baby peas
80 g (1 cup) coarsely grated cheddar
(one that you don't have an intense
political disagreement with)
60 ml (¼ cup) olive oil
1 tablespoon coarsely chopped
dill fronds
sea salt and freshly ground
black pepper
1 bunch asparagus, trimmed
100 g Greek feta, broken into chunks
(likewise, one that shares your own
dairy or non-dairy values)

TANGY HERB SALAD
1 bunch basil, leaves picked
1 bunch chives, snipped into
2 cm lengths
1 cup dill fronds
70 g (⅔ cup) flaked almonds, toasted
2 tablespoons olive oil
juice of ½ lemon
sea salt and freshly ground
black pepper

Preheat the oven to 170°C/150°C fan-forced. Grease and line a 30 cm × 20 cm slice tin with baking paper.

Place the eggs in a large bowl and beat with a fork until combined. Add the flour and beat until smooth. Stir in the zucchini, peas, cheddar, olive oil and dill, and season with salt and pepper.

Pour into the prepared tin and top with the asparagus and feta. Bake for 25–30 minutes or until set.

Meanwhile, make a little side salad. Place all the herbs in a bowl, add the almonds and toss to combine. Whisk together the olive oil and lemon juice in a small jug and season well. Drizzle over the herbs and toss together.

Top the slice with the herb salad and serve.

 TIP: Make this slice ahead and store in the fridge for up to 3 days, or cut into squares, wrap in plastic wrap and freeze for up to 3 months.

MEATY ADDITION: Serve with 150 g hot or cold smoked salmon.

Crunchy eggplant schnitzels

SERVES: 4 **PREP:** 20 mins (plus 30 mins chilling) **COOKING:** 30 mins

There's nothing that can't be made better by crumbing. So says one of the great culinary thinkers of this century, Mr Dave O'Neil. He is right of course but add a zigzag of Japanese mayonnaise and smokey barbecue sauce and things get even better. Perhaps if he'd known that gem as well he might have polled more than 2.3 per cent of the vote when he stood for the federal seat of Gellibrand in the 2007 election.

75 g (½ cup) plain flour
300 g panko breadcrumbs
160 g (1 cup) sesame seeds
80 g (¼ cup) white miso paste
1 egg
2 × 500 g eggplants, cut lengthways into 1.5 cm thick slices
grapeseed oil, for shallow-frying
350 g white cabbage, very finely shredded (use a mandoline, if you have one)
⅓ cup finely chopped flat-leaf parsley
1 tablespoon freshly squeezed lemon juice
sea salt and freshly ground black pepper
Kewpie mayonnaise, tonkatsu or barbecue sauce and lemon wedges, to serve

Tip the flour onto a plate and combine the breadcrumbs and sesame seeds on a second plate. Whisk together the miso and egg in a bowl.

Press both sides of the eggplant slices into the flour to coat. Working with one piece at a time, brush one side of the eggplant with the miso mixture, then press it miso-side down into the breadcrumb mixture to coat. Repeat with the other side. Transfer to a tray. When you have coated all the eggplant, place in the fridge for 30 minutes to set.

Preheat the oven to 180°C/160°C fan-forced. Line a baking tray with baking paper.

Pour enough grapeseed oil into a large frying pan to come 1 cm up the side and heat over medium–high heat. Add the eggplant in batches and cook for 2–3 minutes each side or until golden, adding a little extra oil as needed. Drain on paper towel.

Place all the eggplant slices on the prepared tray and bake for 10 minutes or until tender.

Meanwhile, combine the cabbage, parsley and lemon juice in a bowl. Season well with salt and pepper.

Divide the cabbage salad among serving plates and place the schnitzels alongside. Drizzle with mayo and tonkatsu or barbecue sauce and serve with lemon wedges.

MEATY ADDITION: Replace half the eggplant with 4 uncrumbed chicken schnitzel fillets, follow the recipe above and then bake on a separate tray.

Cheesy whole roasted cauliflower

SERVES: 4–6 PREP: 10 mins COOKING: 1 hour

I love cauliflower cheese but the problem for me is that it just doesn't have enough pasta in it. Here's the solution, which also comes with charry bits of cauilflower florets, which are extra creamy from roasting. I would hazard that this does more for the happiness of life on this planet than a barely passable recipe for mealy worm stew. Ethical vegans, rather than vague-uns who don't mind a little animal exploitation every now and then (assuming no one gets hurt), should use their favourite vegan cheese and butter substitute here.

1 head cauliflower, large outer
  leaves removed
½ bunch flat-leaf parsley, leaves
  picked and stalks finely chopped
1 garlic clove, crushed
80 g butter, at room temperature
sea salt and freshly ground
  black pepper
80 g (1 cup) coarsely grated
  gruyere, firm blue cheese or
  vegan melty cheese
250 g elbow pasta
1 tablespoon milk powder

Preheat the oven to 220°C/200°C fan-forced.

Place the whole cauliflower in a large microwave-safe bowl. Cover and microwave on high for 8–12 minutes (depending on size) until tender. Place in a flameproof roasting tin and set aside to cool slightly.

Mix together the parsley stalk, garlic and half the butter in a bowl. Rub all over the cauliflower and into the florets, and season with salt. Roast for 20–25 minutes or until lightly golden. Remove the cauliflower from the oven and place the cheese on top. Pile it high and in between the florets, but do this carefully as it will be hot. Roast for a further 15 minutes or until the cheese is melted and golden.

While your cauli roasts, cook the pasta in a saucepan of boiling salted water for 1 minute less than it says on the packet or until just al dente. Drain.

Remove the cauliflower from the tin and transfer to a large serving bowl. Cover loosely with baking paper, then foil (this stops the cheese sticking to the foil).

Add the remaining butter to the roasting tin and melt over medium–high heat. Add the milk powder and cook, tossing, for 2 minutes or until toasty. Add the pasta and cook for 5–8 minutes or until the pasta is just starting to crisp up a bit. Season very well with salt and pepper.

Spoon the pasta around the cauliflower and sprinkle with loads of parsley leaves.

MEATY ADDITION: Toss 6 chopped rashers Crispy bacon (see page 268) through the cooked pasta.

Michelle's vineyard three-cheese galette

SERVES: 6 **PREP:** 30 mins (plus 30 mins resting) **COOKING:** 30 mins

The simplest of all tarts. Free form and literally just pulled together. And so very understanding if you don't have time to make the pastry yourself – even though this pastry is almost easier than opening a packet and separating the frozen sheets. If you do go with bought pastry, just sprinkle the inside liberally with grated parmesan and push it in before filling.

250 g fresh ricotta
150 g goat's cheese
2 spring onions, white and green
    parts thinly sliced
finely grated zest of ½ lemon
sea salt and freshly ground
    black pepper
150 g brussels sprouts, very thinly
    sliced (use a mandoline if you
    have one)
150 g seedless red grapes
6 thyme sprigs
45 g (⅓ cup) walnuts, coarsely
    chopped

PARMESAN PASTRY
225 g (1½ cups) plain flour, plus
    extra for dusting
150 g unsalted butter, chilled and
    chopped
20 g (¼ cup) finely grated parmesan
1 egg yolk
1 tablespoon chilled water

To make the pastry, blitz the flour, butter and parmesan in a food processor until the mixture resembles fine breadcrumbs. Add the egg yolk and water and process until the dough just comes together. Turn out onto a lightly floured surface and gently press into a disc. Cover with plastic wrap and place in the fridge to rest for 30 minutes.

Place the ricotta, goat's cheese, spring onion and lemon zest in a bowl and mix until smooth. Season well with salt and pepper.

Preheat the oven to 200°C/180°C fan-forced.

Turn out the pastry onto a large piece of baking paper and use a lightly floured rolling pin to roll it out to a 32 cm round. Keeping the pastry on the paper, slide it onto a baking tray.

Spoon the ricotta mixture into the centre of the pastry, leaving a 4 cm border. Top with the brussels sprout, grapes and thyme. Fold the pastry edge up and over the filling, pleating it roughly as you go. Bake for 20 minutes. Sprinkle with the walnuts and bake for a further 10 minutes or until the grapes are plump and juicy, and the walnuts are golden.

 TIP: Serve with the Twofer salad (see page 37).

Vegetarian mushroom moussaka

SERVES: 8 **PREP:** 30 mins (plus 30 mins cooling) **COOKING:** 1 hour 40 mins

The vegetarian lasagne in last year's Yummy Easy Quick *volume was rightfully popular but that was made with lentils rather than the delicious mushrooms that feature here. Personally, I like this version better but don't tell the lentils as they are sensitive little souls.*

1 kg desiree potatoes, peeled
3 eggplants
80 ml (⅓ cup) extra-virgin olive oil,
  plus extra for brushing
sea salt and freshly ground
  black pepper
600 g Swiss brown mushrooms,
  thinly sliced
1 onion, coarsely chopped
6 garlic cloves, finely chopped
4 thyme sprigs
½ teaspoon ground cinnamon
½ teaspoon ground allspice
60 ml (¼ cup) red wine
500 g (2 cups) passata
150 g cavolo nero (or use kale or
  silverbeet leaves), thicker stalks
  removed, leaves shredded

BECHAMEL
900 ml milk
½ teaspoon ground nutmeg
2 fresh or dried bay leaves
110 g butter
115 g (¾ cup) plain flour
90 g kefalotyri, parmesan or pecorino,
  coarsely grated
2 teaspoons sea salt
ground white pepper
3 eggs, lightly beaten

Preheat the oven to 210°C/190°C fan-forced.

Place the potatoes in a saucepan of cold salted water. Bring to the boil and cook for 15–20 minutes or until just cooked – you should be able to pierce them with a skewer but they shouldn't fall apart. Drain and leave to cool slightly, then cut into 5 mm thick slices (or as thin as you can without breaking them). Set aside.

Meanwhile, cut the eggplants lengthways into 5 mm thick slices. Brush both sides generously with olive oil and place on a few baking trays. Sprinkle with salt and bake for 25–30 minutes or until soft and golden. Alternatively, you could cook the slices on a chargrill pan or barbecue grill.

Heat 1 tablespoon of the remaining oil in a large frying pan over medium–high heat. Add one-third of the mushroom and cook, stirring, for 3–4 minutes or until golden. Transfer to a bowl. Repeat in two more batches with the remaining mushroom and a little more oil.

Heat the remaining oil in the frying pan over medium–high heat. Add the onion and cook, stirring occasionally, for 4–5 minutes or until soft. Add the garlic, thyme, cinnamon and allspice and cook for 1 minute or until aromatic. Increase the heat to high and pour in the red wine. Let it bubble away for a few minutes until reduced slightly. Return the mushroom to the pan, then add the passata and bring to the boil. Simmer for 5 minutes or until thickened. Stir in the cavolo nero and cook, stirring, for 2–3 minutes or until wilted. Season to taste.

Lightly grease a 6 cm deep, 30 cm × 25 cm baking dish with oil. Spoon half the mushroom mixture into the dish and arrange half the potato on top, followed by half the eggplant. Repeat the layers with the remaining mushroom mixture, potato and eggplant.

Time to make the bechamel. Make sure you have all the ingredients ready to go and don't wander off. Pour the milk into a saucepan, add the nutmeg and bay leaves and warm the milk without boiling over low heat. Strain through a fine sieve into a heatproof jug. Discard the bay leaves.

Wipe out the pan, then add the butter and melt over low heat. Gradually add the flour and stir for a couple of minutes until it comes together. Add the milk a little at a time, whisking well after each addition and ensuring it is well incorporated before adding the next. Add the cheese and whisk for a further 2–3 minutes or until the sauce has thickened. Add the salt and season to taste with white pepper. Remove from the heat, then add the eggs and whisk in thoroughly.

Pour the bechamel over the final eggplant layer to form a thick blanket. Bake for 45 minutes or until the top is a deep golden colour. Remove from the oven and set aside for 30 minutes before slicing.

MEATY ADDITION: Replace the mushrooms with 500 g lamb mince.

Roasted red cabbage with dates & Vietnamese mint

SERVES: 6 as a side **PREP:** 10 mins (plus 10 mins cooling) **COOKING:** 1 hour 10 mins

There was period when everyone, from the Town Mouse restaurant in Melbourne to TV's Mr Calombaris and Adelaide's nice Mr Welgemoed, was obsessed with roasted cabbage. It is a beaut way of treating this rather undervalued vegetable, especially if you bring the sweetness of dates to the party. Dates also have a weird affinity with Vietnamese mint so that's gate-crashing here, too. Try this unlikely success story to see why!

1.2 kg whole red cabbage
8 Medjool dates, pitted and coarsely chopped
100 g chilled butter, cut into 1 cm cubes
sea salt and freshly ground black pepper
60 g (½ cup) walnuts, coarsely chopped
½ cup Vietnamese mint leaves

Grab that cabbage and cut at an angle around the base of the core to remove and then discard it. Place the cabbage, cored-side up, in a large microwave-safe bowl. Add 1 tablespoon of water to the bowl and place 1 tablespoon of water in the core hole. Cover with plastic wrap and microwave on high for 20–30 minutes or until tender. Carefully remove the plastic and set the cabbage aside for 10 minutes or so to cool slightly.

Preheat the oven to 180°C/160°C fan-forced.

With the cored side facing up, use a large knife to remove the top 3 cm of the cabbage. You should be able to see all the layers inside the cabbage so it can open like a flower.

Place the cabbage cut-side up in a roasting tin. Place the date in between all the layers of cabbage – you may need to use your fingers to open them slightly and push the date in. Repeat this process with 60 g of the butter cubes, then season well with salt and pepper. Roast for 20 minutes. Sprinkle with the walnuts and dot with the remaining butter. Roast for a further 15 minutes or until the cabbage is lightly charred around the edge and the walnuts are golden.

Place the cabbage on a serving platter and sprinkle with the Vietnamese mint. Cut into wedges and serve.

MEATY ADDITION: Serve with Barbecued or chargrilled lamb or chicken skewers (see pages 265 or 260) as part of a shared meal.

The devil's miaow
(with addictive caramel brussels)

MAKES: 14 PREP: 30 mins (plus 1 hour proving) COOKING: 50 mins

We've had the cat's whiskers so why not the devil's miaow?

These bao buns are the stuff that sticky, salty temptation is made of. They read like a crime scene gone wrong – Chinese-steamed buns with caramel brussels sprouts – but they taste like you wouldn't notice signing a fabricated confession in a roach-infested gaol-cell just to have another one.

This dish is particularly D.F.V! (see page 9).

600 g brussels sprouts, halved, or
    quartered if large, trimmed
olive oil spray
sea salt and freshly ground
    black pepper
100 g caster sugar
80 ml (⅓ cup) light soy sauce
2 whole star anise
2 cm knob of ginger, peeled and cut
    into matchsticks
1 tablespoon rice wine vinegar
60 g (⅓ cup) pumpkin seeds, toasted
juice of 1 lime
200 g white cabbage, finely shredded
Kewpie mayonnaise and finely
    chopped green chilli, to serve

STEAMED BUNS
1½ teaspoons dry instant yeast
250 ml (1 cup) warmed milk
2 tablespoons melted coconut oil
2 tablespoons caster sugar
1½ teaspoons baking powder
375 g (2½ cups) plain flour, plus extra
    if needed and for dusting

Start by making your buns. Combine the yeast and milk in a bowl and stand for 2 minutes until frothy, then stir in the coconut oil. Place the sugar, baking powder and flour in a food processor. With the motor running, slowly add the yeast mixture until a dough comes together. Turn out onto a floured surface and knead for 5 minutes, adding extra flour if necessary. You want the dough to be smooth and elastic. Place the dough in a greased bowl, cover with a clean tea towel and rest in a warm place for 30 minutes or until doubled in size.

Turn out the dough onto a floured surface and divide equally into 14 balls. Use a rolling pin to roll each ball into a 10 cm long oval, then fold to form a semi-circle. Tuck a small square of baking paper into the fold to stop the dough sticking. Cover with a damp clean tea towel and set aside in a warm place for 30 minutes.

Preheat the oven to 180°C/160°C fan-forced. Line a large baking tray with baking paper.

Place the sprouts on the prepared tray in a single layer, spray with olive oil and season with salt and pepper. Roast for 20–25 minutes or until the sprouts are soft in the centre but caught and a little burny at the edges.

While the sprouts are roasting, get your buns ready. Fill a wok or large saucepan one-third full of water and bring to the boil over high heat. Place four buns in a bamboo steamer lined with baking paper, making sure they are not touching, then place the steamer over the wok or pan. Cover and steam for 12 minutes or until the buns are cooked through. Remove and set aside to cool slightly. Repeat with the remaining buns.

Meanwhile, get onto your caramel sauce. Place the sugar and soy sauce in a small saucepan and stir over low heat until the sugar has dissolved. Increase the heat to medium–high and bring to the boil. Add the star anise, ginger and vinegar and simmer for 6 minutes or until syrupy. Take the pan off the heat and carefully remove and discard the star anise. Add the pumpkin seeds, then drizzle the caramel sauce over the roasted sprouts and toss to coat.

Massage the lime juice into the cabbage in a bowl. Season with salt and pepper.

Fill the buns with the cabbage and top with the caramel-coated sprouts. Drizzle with mayo and sprinkle with chilli.

MEATY ADDITION: Sprinkle the filling in the buns with Crispy pork crackling (see page 272).

Red capsicum, black olive & caramelised onion pissaladiere

SERVES: 4 PREP: 15 mins COOKING: 1 hour

I am a huge fan of frozen puff pastry. Just make sure you buy one made with butter rather than cheap palm oil. No one likes the accusatory way those tragic homeless baby orangutans in the ads can look at you.

I'd like to claim that my version of this Nicoise take on pizza is inspired by those pleading black eyes (that's them glistening black olives) and that the soft orange and browns of the onion, capsicum and pastry echo the colour of 'the old man of the forest's' distinctive colour scheme but I'd be lying. Still, it makes you think …

20 g butter
2 tablespoons olive oil
4 onions, halved and thinly sliced
½ teaspoon dried thyme
1 sheet frozen puff pastry, just thawed
80 g roasted red capsicum (from a jar is fine), cut lengthways into long thin strips
24 pitted black olives
1 egg, lightly beaten

Heat the butter and olive oil in a large frying pan over low heat. Add the onion and thyme and cook, stirring occasionally, for 40 minutes or until the onion is brown and caramelised. Set aside to cool slightly.

Preheat the oven to 220°C/200°C fan-forced. Place a baking tray in the oven.

Place the pastry on a piece of baking paper. Use a knife to score a 1.5 cm border around the edges, but don't cut all the way through. Spread the onion mixture over the pastry inside the border.

Arrange the strips of capsicum in a diamond-shaped lattice over the onion, then place an olive in the centre of each diamond. Brush the edge of the pastry with egg. Use the paper to help slide the tart onto the hot tray and bake for 10–15 minutes or until the pastry is crisp.

MEATY ADDITION: Replace the red capsicum strips with 24 anchovy fillets.

Empanadas for the old lady in San Telmo market who supports River

MAKES: 26 PREP: 45 mins (plus 2 hours resting) COOKING: 25 mins

---

Certain cities have made a lasting impression on me … Seoul, Mumbai, Amsterdam, Dhaka, Lima and certainly Buenos Aires. In quiet moments I can still walk the streets of the old San Telmo area of BA in my mind and find the chipped sea-green interior of the old empanada shop next to the market where I had empanadas that were a textbook explanation for why these pastries are so revered. The counter was stacked with golden crescents of pastry, still warm from the oven. The walls were dotted with faded old pictures of legendary River players; footballers in baggy shorts and that famous red-sashed shirt that gave the soccer team the nickname of La Banda (or 'the stripe'). They are also known as The Millionaires, I suspect as a direct taunt to their fierce rivals, the proudly working-class Boca Juniors, who have never won quite as many championships and who were left behind when River deserted their original home in La Boca in 1923 and moved uptown to the swanky suburb of Recoleta.

These empanadas, too, are distinctly uptown.

300 g can corn kernels, drained

250 g coarsely grated mozzarella or other vegetarian melty cheese

2 spring onions, white and green parts thinly sliced

3 jalapeno chillies, deseeded and finely chopped

2 teaspoons sea salt

freshly ground black pepper

2 egg yolks, lightly beaten and sieved

50 g roasted red capsicum (from a jar is fine), cut into 5 mm thick strips and dried on paper towel

EMPANADA DOUGH

450 g (3 cups) plain flour, plus extra for dusting

1 teaspoon sea salt

150 g chilled butter, chopped

1 egg

Start by making your dough. Place the flour, salt and butter in a food processor and process until the mixture resembles fine breadcrumbs. Add the egg and 125 ml (½ cup) of cold water and process until the dough comes together (add a little extra water if your dough is a bit dry). Turn out the dough onto a well-floured surface and gently press into a ball. Cover with plastic wrap and place in the fridge to rest for 2 hours.

Preheat the oven to 190°C/170°C fan-forced. Line a baking tray with baking paper.

Combine the corn, cheese, spring onion and jalapeno in a bowl. Season with the salt and pepper.

Divide the dough in half. On a lightly floured surface, roll out one portion of dough until about 3 mm thick (this is important so keep rolling). Cut out discs using an 11 cm round cutter.

Holding a disc in the palm of your hand and over the filling bowl to catch any runaway corn kernels, place 1 heaped tablespoon of the filling in the centre. Brush the edge of the dough with a little water, then fold the dough over onto itself into a half-moon shape. Pinch and pleat the edge with your fingers to seal and place on the prepared tray. Bring the scraps of pastry together to use later and repeat the process with the remaining portion of dough. If there is enough leftover pastry, re-roll all the scraps to make a few extra empanadas.

Brush the empanadas with the egg yolk. Drape a capsicum strip over each empanada and gently press into the dough. Bake for 25 minutes or until golden.

PIZZA

Pizza is the greatest food known to humankind but ever since heading out with a coeliac friend for a pizza frenzy and seeing how abused her pizza was I've been thinking about how we can bring better pizza pleasure to everyone. And even how we can bypass the traditional dough base to incorporate even more veggies. I'm delighted to say that during the testing that followed even cereal-loving Dr Wheat approved of the vegetable bases that resulted, and while they don't offer the puffiness of the traditional Neapolitan-style base they do provide both crispness and flavour! And that is no small thing.

Fresh tomato, lemon & olive pizza

I am regularly asked when this obsession with cauliflower being the answer to every gluten-free question will end. My response is always, 'Ask the cauliflower as it has all the answers!'

MAKES: 1 pizza
PREP: 15 mins
COOKING: 40 mins

½ lemon, thinly sliced
2 teaspoons sea salt
130 g (1¼ cups) coarsely grated mozzarella
4 small heirloom tomatoes, sliced
80 g (½ cup) pitted green olives

CAULIFLOWER PIZZA CRUST
650 g cauliflower, florets roughly chopped
70 g shredded parmesan
2 tablespoons coarsely chopped basil
2 eggs
sea salt and freshly
    ground black pepper

To make the crust, process the cauliflower in a food processor until finely chopped. Transfer to a microwave-safe bowl, then cover and microwave on high for 5 minutes or until tender. Set aside for 5 minutes to cool slightly. Place in a large piece of muslin and tie the edges to enclose, then squeeze out as much liquid as possible. Transfer to a bowl, add the remaining ingredients and mix until well combined.

Preheat the oven to 220°C/200°C fan-forced. Line a pizza tray or baking tray with baking paper.

Press the cauliflower mixture firmly onto the tray to form a 25 cm disc. Bake for 20 minutes or until a little golden and the edges start to crisp up.

Meanwhile, combine the lemon slices and salt in a bowl.

Sprinkle 100 g (1 cup) of the mozzarella over the base, leaving a 2 cm border. Top with the tomato and olives, then sprinkle with the remaining mozzarella. Bake for 15 minutes or until the cheese is melted and golden. Scatter with the salted lemon slices and serve.

Margherita pizza

This gluten-free base makes the most of the adaptability of broccoli, which becomes particularly delicious when paired in the Calabrian manner with chilli and capers, or possibly even anchovies (if you don't mind a little deviation from the vegetarian way every now and then).

MAKES: 1 pizza
PREP: 15 mins
COOKING: 30 mins

270 g jarred marinated semi-dried tomatoes, reserving
   60 ml (¼ cup) oil from the jar
1 long red chilli, cut into 1 cm thick slices (deseed
   if you prefer less heat)
1 tablespoon rinsed and drained capers
10 large basil leaves, plus extra small leaves to serve
sea salt and freshly ground black pepper
7 bocconcini, halved, drained on paper towel
2 tablespoons shredded parmesan

BROCCOLI CRUST
450 g broccoli, florets roughly chopped
20 g shredded parmesan
40 g coarsely grated mozzarella
1 teaspoon dried oregano
2 eggs
sea salt and freshly ground black pepper

To make the crust, process the broccoli in a food processor until finely chopped. Transfer to a microwave-safe bowl, then cover and microwave on high for 5 minutes or until tender. Set aside for 5 minutes to cool slightly. Place in a large piece of muslin and tie the edges to enclose, then squeeze out as much liquid as possible. Transfer to a bowl, add the remaining ingredients and mix until well combined.

Preheat the oven to 220°C/200°C fan-forced. Line a pizza tray or baking tray with baking paper.

Press the broccoli mixture firmly onto the prepared tray to form a 25 cm disc. Bake for 12 minutes or until a little golden and the edges start to crisp up.

Meanwhile, heat the reserved semi-dried tomato oil in a small saucepan over medium–low heat. Add the chilli and cook for 2 minutes or until softened. Stir in the capers and set aside.

Place the large basil leaves and half the semi-dried tomatoes in a small food processor and process until a smooth paste forms. Season with salt and pepper. Chop the remaining tomatoes and stir into the paste.

Spread the tomato mixture over the broccoli base, leaving a 1 cm border. Top with the bocconcini and sprinkle with the parmesan. Bake for 10 minutes or until the cheese is melted and golden. Drizzle with the chilli–caper oil, top with the small basil leaves and serve.

TIP: Alternatively, you can drizzle this pizza with the Basil and parmesan oil on page 184.

The new Hawaiian (aka smoked cheddar & pineapple)

Sam Panopoulos of the Satellite Restaurant in Ontario invented the Hawaiian pizza in 1962. A Greek chef in Canada ... how Hawaiian is that?!

MAKES: 2 pizzas
PREP: 20 mins (plus 30 mins resting)
COOKING: 40 mins

180 g (⅔ cup) passata
sea salt and freshly ground black pepper
150 g (1½ cups) coarsely grated mozzarella
120 g (1½ cups) coarsely grated smoked cheddar
1 x quantity uncooked Carrot bacon (see page 133)
½ pineapple, peeled, cored and thinly sliced (canned is OK too)

PUMPKIN CRUST

560 g (3½ cups) spelt flour, plus extra for dusting
2 teaspoons dry instant yeast
1 teaspoon caster sugar
½ teaspoon sea salt
220 g (1 cup) mashed pumpkin (from about 320 g chopped pumpkin, steamed)
1 tablespoon olive oil, plus extra for greasing

To make the pumpkin crust, combine the flour, yeast, sugar and salt in a large bowl. Make a well in the centre and add the pumpkin, oil and 80 ml (⅓ cup) of warm water. Stir to combine, then use your hands to bring the dough together. (If it is a bit dry, add more water, 1 tablespoon at a time, until the dough comes together and is a little sticky.) Turn out the dough onto a well-floured surface and knead for 10 minutes or until smooth and elastic.

Place the dough in a bowl greased with oil and turn around a little to coat. Cover with a damp tea towel and set aside in a warm place for 30 minutes or until doubled in size. Punch down the dough with your fist, then knead for 30 seconds or until the dough is back to its original size. Divide the dough in half and cover one portion with a damp tea towel.

Preheat the oven to 230°C/210°C fan-forced. Place a pizza tray or large baking tray in the oven to heat up.

Flour a sheet of baking paper and press out one portion of dough to a 30 cm disc. Spread with half the passata and season with salt and pepper. Toss the cheeses together and sprinkle about 1 cup over the passata. Top with half the uncooked carrot bacon and pineapple, and sprinkle with ½ cup of the remaining cheese.

Use the paper to slide the base onto the hot tray. Bake for 20 minutes or until golden and crisp. Repeat with the remaining dough and toppings to make a second pizza.

Potato, rosemary & taleggio pizza

Cruelly dubbed my 'disco pizza' by some of my detractors, this is another example of how every corner of a pizza party can have some vegetable action.

MAKES: 2 pizzas
PREP: 20 mins (plus 30 mins resting)
COOKING: 40 mins

2 tablespoons olive oil
2 garlic cloves, crushed
600 g coliban potatoes, thinly sliced
200 g taleggio, well chilled, sliced
sea salt and freshly ground black pepper
4 rosemary sprigs, leaves picked

BEETROOT CRUST

450 g (3 cups) plain bread flour, plus extra for dusting
2 teaspoons dry instant yeast
1 tablespoon caster sugar
½ teaspoon sea salt
3 small cooked beetroot bulbs (or 250 g packet
   pre-cooked beetroot bulbs), drained well and
   coarsely grated
1 tablespoon olive oil, plus extra for greasing

To make the beetroot crust, combine the flour, yeast, sugar and salt in a large bowl. Make a well in the centre and add the beetroot, olive oil and 80 ml (⅓ cup) of warm water. Stir to combine, then use your hands to bring the dough together. (If it is a bit dry, add more water, 1 tablespoon at a time, until the dough comes together and is a little sticky.) Turn out the dough onto a well-floured surface and knead for 10 minutes or until smooth and elastic.

Place the dough in a bowl greased with oil and turn around a little to coat. Cover with a damp tea towel and set aside in a warm place for 30 minutes or until doubled in size. Punch down the dough with your fist, then knead for 30 seconds or until the dough is back to its original size. Divide the dough in half and cover one portion with a damp tea towel.

Preheat the oven to 230°C/210°C fan-forced. Place a pizza tray or large baking tray in the oven to heat up.

Combine the olive oil and garlic in a bowl.

Flour a sheet of baking paper and press out one portion of dough to a 30 cm disc. Spread with half the garlic oil. Place an overlapping layer of potato near the edge of the dough, leaving a 1 cm border. Continue into the centre of the dough, dotting evenly with the half the taleggio slices as you go. Brush the potato with more garlic oil, season with salt and pepper and sprinkle with half the rosemary.

Use the paper to slide the base onto the hot tray. Bake for 20 minutes or until golden and crisp. Repeat with the remaining dough and toppings to make a second pizza.

Magritte's 'not a meatloaf'

SERVES: 6–8 **PREP:** 30 mins (plus 10 mins standing) **COOKING:** 1 hour 10 mins

One of the fundamental rules of eating out is never to book a table at a restaurant named after a famous artist. They are invariably dreadful soulless places attached to faded four-star hotels in the duller part of town that not only have just proudly discovered the 'smear' but still hang on to the mint and fanned strawberry garnish for every dessert.

HOWEVER, let's turn a blind eye to that stipulation with this surrealist meatloaf inspired by the great Belgian artist René Magritte (a name to remember if you ever find yourself playing an infuriating game of Famous Belgians, which usually grinds to a premature halt after Eddy Merckx, Adolphe Sax, Peter Paul Rubens, Audrey Hepburn and Tintin).

The famous artist who drew a painting of a pipe with the immortal words 'This is not a pipe' scrawled on it (in one way he's right if you think about it in the light of the real title 'The Treachery of Images') was not to know that in testing this recipe we would discover that the same thing can be said about different cans of lentils.

'The Treachery of Cans of Lentils' is that some cans contain lentils that are more mushy than others, which would result in a meatloaf without the texture we require. To overcome this, the brilliant food guru Ms Southan suggested adding walnuts, so even if your lentils are treacherously mushy, you'll still get some nubbly crunch.

olive oil spray
1 tablespoon olive oil
250 g cup mushrooms, finely chopped
1 small red onion, finely chopped
2 garlic cloves, crushed
2 tablespoons tomato paste
2 × 400 g cans brown lentils, rinsed
    and drained
1 carrot, coarsely grated
140 g (1½ cups) instant rolled oats
125 g walnuts, finely chopped
½ cup finely chopped flat-leaf parsley
2 teaspoons coarsely chopped
    thyme leaves
3 eggs
sea salt and freshly ground
    black pepper

SPICY TOMATO GLAZE

125 ml (½ cup) tomato sauce
2 tablespoons brown sugar
2 tablespoons apple cider vinegar
1 tablespoon soy sauce or tamari
½ teaspoon sriracha chilli sauce

Preheat the oven to 180°C/160°C fan-forced. Spray a 20 cm × 10 cm loaf tin with olive oil and line the base and sides with baking paper.

Heat the olive oil in a large non-stick frying pan over medium heat. Add the mushroom and cook, stirring occasionally, for 5–8 minutes or until softened and any liquid has evaporated. Add the onion and garlic and cook for 5 minutes or until softened. Add the tomato paste and cook, stirring, for 2 minutes or until well combined. Set aside to cool slightly.

Add the lentils, carrot, oats, walnut, parsley, thyme and eggs to the mushroom mixture. Season well and mix until combined. Spoon the mixture into the prepared tin and smooth the surface with the back of a spoon. Bake for 20 minutes or until just set.

To make the glaze, place all the ingredients in a saucepan over low heat and stir until the sugar has dissolved. Bring to a simmer and cook, stirring, for 5 minutes or until thickened slightly.

Remove the meatloaf from the oven and spread the glaze over the top. Bake for a further 25 minutes or until golden. Remove and set aside for 10 minutes, before carefully removing from the tin and cutting into thick slices to serve.

Vegetable stew with cheesy herb dumplings

SERVES: 4–6 **PREP:** 30 mins **COOKING:** 1 hour 20 mins

Starting out as a meat-rearing production facility for the motherland is part of the reason so much Australian bush cookery relies on red meat, but really the joy of any stew is in the richness of flavour rather than the presence of meat per se. This is a stew that should feel nostalgically country, with Vegemite helping to provide the umami hit that shoulder or chuck would usually provide.

1 tablespoon olive oil
1 onion, roughly chopped
2 garlic cloves, crushed
125 ml (½ cup) white wine
500 ml (2 cups) vegetable stock
400 g can diced tomatoes
2 large carrots, thickly sliced
   diagonally
2 potatoes, peeled and
   roughly chopped
2 parsnips, peeled and
   roughly chopped
1 small swede, peeled and
   roughly chopped
2 rosemary sprigs
3 fresh or dried bay leaves
3 teaspoons Vegemite
sea salt and freshly ground
   black pepper

CHEESY HERB DUMPLINGS
300 g (2 cups) self-raising flour
80 g butter, cubed
½ cup finely chopped flat-leaf parsley
¼ cup snipped chives
120 g (1½ cups) coarsely grated
   vintage cheddar
sea salt
125 ml (½ cup) milk

Preheat the oven to 180°C/160°C fan-forced.

Heat the olive oil in a large flameproof casserole dish over medium–high heat, add the onion and cook, stirring, for 5–6 minutes or until soft. Add the garlic and cook for 30 seconds or until aromatic. Pour in the wine and simmer for 5 minutes or until the liquid has evaporated by half.

Add the stock and tomatoes and bring to a gentle simmer. Add the carrot, potato, parsnip, swede, rosemary, bay leaves and Vegemite and stir to combine. Season well, then cover and bake for 35–45 minutes, until the vegetables are just tender.

About 15 minutes before removing the casserole from the oven, start making your dumplings. Sift the flour into a large bowl, then rub in the butter with your fingertips until the mixture resembles fine breadcrumbs. Add the parsley, chives and half the cheddar, and season with salt. Make a well in the centre, then pour in the milk and mix until combined. Divide the dough into 12 equal portions and roll each portion into a ball.

Arrange the dumplings over the vegetable mixture and sprinkle with the remaining cheddar. Bake, uncovered, for 25 minutes or until the dumplings are light and fluffy and the cheese is melted and golden.

Pea, ricotta & feta filo pie

SERVES: 10–12 (or 8 hungry people) **PREP:** 30 mins (plus 10 mins standing) **COOKING:** 1 hour 5 mins

When I was a little tacker, my mum made several dishes that I particularly looked forward to (such as cabbage rolls, chicken liver risotto and roast chicken with bread sauce), but the standout for me was eggs Florentine. This Tuscan dish of eggs baked on creamy spinach with cheese is a simple supper, but here I give it a Greek spin with filo and more textural veg. With all due modesty I think we've turned it into a real showstopper.

1 tablespoon olive oil
150 g green beans, trimmed and
  cut into 1 cm coins
3 celery stalks, chopped into
  1 cm pieces
150 g (1 cup) frozen peas, thawed
45 g (¼ cup) pumpkin seeds
sea salt and freshly ground
  black pepper
600 g fresh ricotta
400 g feta, crumbled
2 eggs, lightly beaten
⅓ cup coarsely chopped mint
2 tablespoons finely chopped
  dill fronds
finely grated zest of 1 lemon
100 g butter, melted
12 sheets filo pastry
8 hard-boiled eggs, peeled

Preheat the oven to 200°C/180°C fan-forced.

Heat the olive oil in a frying pan over medium–high heat. Add the beans and celery and cook for 5 minutes or until the beans are bright green. Add the peas and pumpkin seeds and cook, stirring, for 3–5 minutes or until the pumpkin seeds are lightly toasted. Transfer the mixture to a large bowl and season well with salt and pepper.

Add the ricotta, feta, beaten egg, mint, dill and lemon zest to the veg and stir until really well combined.

Grease a 24 cm springform cake tin with a little of the butter. Place the filo on a clean work surface and cover with a dry tea towel, then a damp tea towel to stop it drying out. Brush one sheet of filo with the melted butter and fold it in half crossways. Place in the prepared tin, allowing the excess to hang over the side. Brush the filo with more butter. Repeat with the remaining filo sheets and melted butter, turning and overlapping each sheet slightly so the tin is fully lined.

Spoon half the ricotta mixture into the tin. Top with the boiled eggs, spacing them evenly apart to make a ring around the edge, then gently press them into the ricotta mixture. Top with the remaining ricotta mixture and smooth the surface.

Fold the overhanging filo back up and over the filling so it is scrunchy on top. It won't fully cover the filling so there will be a hole in the middle. Brush with the remaining butter, then bake for 45–55 minutes or until golden. Cool in the tin for 10 minutes, then release the side and cut into wedges to serve.

MEATY ADDITION: Stir 150 g finely chopped pancetta, prosciutto or even ham into the ricotta mixture.

Middle Eastern butter-roasted white cabbage wedges

SERVES: 6 PREP: 20 mins COOKING: 40 mins

I never met a wedge I didn't like.

Well, apart from the hairstyle. Those stacked-bob-with-bangs-and-all-off-the-back hairstyles that lollipop-figured Hollywood celebs like Posh used to favour and those shaved-sided 'dead-possum-collapsed-on-my-head' wedges favoured by some A-League players still give me the screamin' heebie-jeebies.

Otherwise wedges are all good. They were the first hand tools that our grunting forebears wielded, way before the wheel and the knife, and are tremendously helpful for splitting wood. And they are even better as crisp chocks of iceberg in a wedge salad, or when they are made with hot-spiced sweet potato and served with cooling sour cream.

By the by, my favourite club in my golf bag is the 60-degree Titleist wedge. It has saved me from more soul-sucking sand than a well-thrown vine in a black and white Tarzan movie.

1 small red onion, very thinly sliced
  into rings
2 tablespoons currants
zest and juice of 1 lemon
sea salt
½ savoy cabbage (about 1 kg), cut
  into 6 wedges with base intact
60 g butter, melted
1 tablespoon coriander seeds
1 tablespoon cumin seeds
2 × 400 g cans chickpeas, rinsed
  and drained
2 teaspoons sweet paprika
100 ml olive oil
2 tablespoons tahini
2 garlic cloves, peeled
flat-leaf parsley and mint leaves,
  to serve

RED WINE CARAMEL
125 ml (½ cup) red wine
100 g caster sugar

Preheat the oven to 200°C/180°C fan-forced. Line a large baking tray with baking paper.

Place the onion, currants and 1 tablespoon of the lemon juice in a bowl and season with 1 teaspoon of salt. Set aside while you make the rest of the dish.

Carefully place the cabbage wedges in a microwave-safe flat-bottomed dish and drizzle with 1 tablespoon of water. Cover with plastic wrap and microwave on high for 5 minutes or until slightly softened. Drain.

Place the cabbage wedges on the prepared tray and drizzle with the butter. Sprinkle with the coriander seeds and half the cumin seeds. Pat half the chickpeas dry with paper towel, then toss in a bowl with the paprika and 1 tablespoon of the olive oil. Season with salt. Sprinkle the chickpea mixture around the wedges and bake for 35 minutes or until the cabbage is slightly charred on the edges.

Meanwhile, place the remaining cumin seeds in a non-stick frying pan over medium heat and cook, tossing, for 2–3 minutes or until toasted and aromatic. Transfer to a food processor. Add the tahini, garlic, remaining chickpeas and 1 tablespoon of the remaining lemon juice and blitz until almost smooth. With the motor running, gradually add the remaining oil until smooth and combined.

To make your caramel, place the red wine and sugar in a small frying pan over low heat and stir until the sugar has dissolved. Increase the heat to medium–high and bring to a rapid simmer. Simmer for 5 minutes or until thickened slightly. Set aside – the caramel will thicken more as it cools.

Spread the hummus on a large serving platter. Top with the cabbage wedges, chickpeas and onion and currant mixture, then drizzle with the red wine caramel. Scatter with the lemon zest, parsley and mint and serve.

MEATY ADDITION: Serve with Barbecued butterflied lamb leg (see page 264) or Middle Eastern-inspired Roast chicken (see page 262) as part of a shared meal.

Lentil shepherd's pie with celeriac mash

SERVES: 6 PREP: 20 mins COOKING: 1 hour 10 mins

I met a magician once who explained that much of his skill was in misdirection and hopefully that's the very thing that will make your family and friends love it when you make this dish. Ideally they'll be so blown away by how delicious that mash on top is (which isn't just potato, amazingly) that they will totally forget that the rich rubbly filling underneath is actually lentils with the peas, and not mince. The instant mental association of the flavour of rosemary with the usual lamb mince should help, too.

1 tablespoon olive oil
1 onion, finely chopped
2 celery stalks, finely chopped
3 garlic cloves, crushed
400 g portobello mushrooms, roughly chopped
70 g (¼ cup) tomato paste
400 g can diced tomatoes
250 ml (1 cup) vegetable stock
2 tablespoons balsamic vinegar
1 large rosemary sprig
2 fresh or dried bay leaves
400 g can lentils, rinsed and drained
150 g (1 cup) frozen baby peas
sea salt and freshly ground
    black pepper
melted butter, for brushing

CREAMY CELERIAC MASH
½ lemon
1 large celeriac (about 700 g)
1 kg potatoes, peeled and
    roughly chopped
80 ml (⅓ cup) pouring cream
50 g butter, chopped
sea salt and freshly ground
    black pepper

Heat the olive oil in a large saucepan over medium–high heat. Add the onion and celery and cook, stirring, for 5 minutes or until softened. Add the garlic and mushroom and cook, stirring, for 5 minutes or until the mushroom has softened. Stir in the tomato paste and cook for 2 minutes.

Add the diced tomatoes, stock, vinegar, rosemary and bay leaves to the pan. Reduce the heat to medium and simmer for 15–20 minutes or until the liquid has reduced and thickened. Stir in the lentils and peas and season well.

Preheat the oven to 200°C/180°C fan-forced.

Meanwhile, make the mash. Squeeze a little lemon juice into a bowl of water. Peel the celeriac and roughly chop it, immediately dropping each piece into the acidulated water to stop it turning brown. Drain the celeriac pieces and place in a large saucepan with the potato, and cover with cold water. Bring to the boil over medium–high heat, then reduce the heat to medium–low and simmer for 15–20 minutes or until tender. Drain and return to the pan. Mash with a potato masher until smooth, then add the cream and butter and mash until combined. Season to taste.

Spoon the lentil mixture into a 2 litre ovenproof dish. Top with the mash and use a fork to rough up the surface. Brush the top with melted butter and season well. Bake for 30–35 minutes or until the mash is golden.

 TIP: If you add two finely chopped carrots with the onion and celery, you'll magically transform this into a lentil cottage pie.

MEATY ADDITION: Omit the mushrooms and add 500 g Pan-fried lamb mince (see page 266) with the lentils.

Tray bakes

I don't want to be mean, but welcome to the chapter with arguably the worst photos in the book. This isn't photographer Mark Roper's fault – as widely reported, I can confirm he is a brilliant photographer and the nicest man in the world who can do no wrong – but it's just that, like some people, tray bakes can be unphotogenic. Beauty is only skin deep, however, and the word tasty runs through all these dishes – even the clumsily named Pumpkin, potato and peanut Thai red curry tray bake that's one of my favourite dishes in the whole book.

Sumiso prairie tray bake

SERVES: 4 **PREP:** 45 mins **COOKING:** 1 hour 10 mins

Between 1880 and 1900 Japanese migration to the US increased from 148 to 24,326 as the country sought a replacement for the cheap Chinese labour that discriminatory legislation and racist riots had driven away.

While most Japanese migrants settled in Hawaii and California, a fair number headed to the Great Plains and the Canadian Prairie country as cheap labour for building the railways, mining or agricultural work, such as Nebraska's emerging sugar beet industry. Industrious and entrepreneurial, many moved on to actually own their own sugar beet farms and open stores.

However, the discrimination these first-generation Japanese settlers and their second-generation children (known as 'nisei') faced was appalling. There were unprovoked physical attacks, legal moves to disallow them to testify in court, and the unjustified confiscation of their property and land – even before internment came in during World War II. After the war, governments refused to give back the stolen land, instead threatening enforced repatriation to war-ravaged Japan, even for those born in North America.

This story is seldom told and I felt it needed a dish to commemorate it. This is a flight of fancy inspired by the thought, 'what sort of tray bake would these settlers come up with?'. Perhaps a sumiso sweetened with maple syrup from the woods to the east and soured with oranges from California?

80 g (¼ cup) white miso paste
2 tablespoons freshly squeezed
   orange juice
2 tablespoons hickory maple
   syrup (or regular maple syrup if
   unavailable), plus extra for drizzling
4 small sweet potatoes (about 250 g
   each), scrubbed and left unpeeled
sea salt and freshly ground
   black pepper
80 g (½ cup) frozen corn kernels,
   thawed
70 g (½ cup) pecan halves, coarsely
   chopped
40 g (½ cup) coarsely grated smoked
   cheddar or smoked melty cheese
shiso leaves or baby herbs, to serve
   (optional)

Preheat the oven to 180°C/160°C fan-forced. Line a large baking tray with baking paper.

Combine the miso, orange juice and maple syrup in a small bowl.

Halve the sweet potatoes lengthways and cut a crisscross pattern into the flesh area with the tip of a sharp knife. Place the halves, cut-side up, on the prepared tray (try to find a tray that will fit them all snugly in one layer). Brush them all over with half the miso mixture and season well with salt and pepper. Roast for 50 minutes or until tender.

Brush the sweet potato with the remaining miso mixture, then top with the corn and chopped pecans. Sprinkle with the cheese and roast for a further 15–20 minutes or until golden and the cheese has melted. Drizzle with extra maple syrup and sprinkle with shiso leaves or baby herbs (if using). PERFECT!

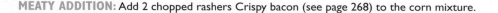

MEATY ADDITION: Add 2 chopped rashers Crispy bacon (see page 268) to the corn mixture.

Caprese 'neatball' bake

SERVES: 4–6 **PREP:** 25 mins (plus 1 hour chilling) **COOKING:** 1 hour 35 mins

Internet diagnostics are great at telling us what words, recipes and ingredients Australia is obsessed with right now. Baking these 'neatballs' with mozzarella and tomatoes is a shameless attempt to lure you with one of the most potent words for summer (along with trifle, pavlova, vego, Kardashian and punch) … and that is Caprese.

If you've read this, then the diagnostic tool has done its job. Cynical or what!

200 g Swiss brown mushrooms, roughly chopped
1 small onion, roughly chopped
13 garlic cloves, unpeeled
2 tablespoons olive oil
2 × 400 g cans cannellini beans, rinsed, drained and patted dry
½ bunch flat-leaf parsley, leaves picked
40 g (½ cup) shredded parmesan
finely grated zest of 1 lemon
1 egg
60 g (½ cup) quinoa flakes
6 roma tomatoes, halved
8 thyme sprigs
150 g (1 cup) pine nuts, coarsely chopped
olive oil spray
sea salt and freshly ground black pepper
550 g eggplant, cut into 1 cm thick rounds
6 bocconcini, drained and thickly sliced

BASIL & PARMESAN OIL
½ cup basil leaves
boiling water
125 ml (½ cup) olive oil
1 teaspoon sea salt
40 g (½ cup) finely grated parmesan

Place the mushroom and onion in a food processor. Peel three of the garlic cloves and add to the processor, then blitz until finely chopped. Transfer the mixture to a bowl and give the food processor a wipe out as we will be using it again.

Heat the olive oil in a frying pan over medium–high heat. Add the mushroom mixture and cook, stirring, for 8 minutes or until any liquid has evaporated and the onion is soft. Set aside to cool slightly.

Place the mushroom mixture, cannellini beans, parsley leaves, parmesan, lemon zest and egg in the food processor and blitz until well combined. Transfer the mixture to a bowl, add the quinoa flakes and stir until well combined. Place in the fridge for 1 hour to firm up – you want it to be rollable.

Preheat the oven to 200°C/180°C fan-forced.

Place the tomatoes, cut-side up, in a large roasting tin and scatter over the thyme and remaining unpeeled garlic cloves. Bake for 20 minutes.

Meanwhile, place the pine nuts on a plate. Roll 2 slightly heaped tablespoons of the bean mixture into a ball and then roll in the pine nuts to coat. Repeat with the remaining bean mixture and pine nuts.

Remove the tomato tin from the oven and add the meatballs. Spray with olive oil and season well with salt and pepper.

Line a baking tray with baking paper. Place the eggplant slices on the tray in a single layer, spray well with oil and season.

Place the tomato tin and the eggplant in the oven and roast for 30–35 minutes or until the eggplant is tender and starting to caramelise around the edges. Transfer the eggplant to the tomato mixture and top with the bocconcini. Bake for a further 15–20 minutes or until the cheese is melted and golden.

Meanwhile, make the basil and parmesan oil. Plunge the basil into boiling water for 1 minute or until slightly softened. Drain. Blitz the oil and salt in a blender until foaming (this should help set the green of the basil). Add the basil and blend until well combined. Transfer to a bowl and stir in the parmesan.

Drizzle the bake with the basil and parmesan oil and serve.

MEATY ADDITION: Halve the meatball mixture. Add 6 cooked Italian pork sausages (see page 270) or 12 Meaty meatballs (see page 267) just before adding the bocconcini.

One-pan Bangkok pumpkin

SERVES: 6 as a side **PREP:** 20 mins (plus cooling) **COOKING:** 50 mins

There is a bar in Bangkok that you only go to when the first pale fingers of dawn are clawing at the edges of the Thai night. It's a classic dive bar that's careened off the rails and down the small hours embankment into a gutter of twisted metal dreams. There's usually someone passed out in the overflowing ashtray at the bar and a delicate flower or two in the sort of clingy white jersey dress my mother would tut at. They sing and sway along tunelessly to the eighties VHS music tapes.

The vertical hold is dodgy on one of the old CRT TVs so it flickers. Miraculously, strobing perfectly out of time with the winking strands of jaunty fairy lights that, like metres of coiling neon bindweed, choke walls bowing in under the weight of dusty stills of long-forgotten local movie stars and career-ending polaroids of a thousand personal Hangovers that are stuck up with sticky tape aged the colour of nicotine.

The only other light is the flickering of a glass-fronted coffin guarded by an ex-wrestler who jumps from solid granite monolith to silhouette with each judder of its cheap fluoro across the frosty bottles of Chang, Archa and Leo Super. It too dances to a silent humming disco BPM all of its own.

When you wake with your Changover clawing at the blackboard walls inside your skull, this is the dish you will crave. It is the warm hug, soothing words and doona warmth that will put you back together again. Just quiet with the brittle please. We are all brittle here.

1.2 kg Kent pumpkin, unpeeled, cut into 3 cm thick wedges
2 tablespoons peanut or vegetable oil
freshly ground black pepper
½ bunch coriander, leaves picked, stalks and roots cleaned and finely chopped
2 cm knob of ginger, peeled, grated
finely grated zest and juice of 1 lime
2 tablespoons sweet chilli sauce
1 tablespoon soy sauce or tamari
1 tablespoon Vegan 'fish' sauce (see page 44)
¼ bunch Thai basil
¼ bunch mint or Vietnamese mint
lime wedges, to serve

CHILLI PEANUT BRITTLE
100 g (½ cup) caster sugar
60 ml (¼ cup) glucose syrup
120 g (¾ cup) roasted peanuts
10 g butter
1 long red chilli, deseeded, chopped
½ teaspoon sea salt
⅛ teaspoon bicarbonate of soda

Start by making your brittle. (The great part is, this will keep in an airtight container for up to 3 weeks, if you don't eat it first.) Line a large baking tray with baking paper and place on a wire rack. Combine the sugar and 80 ml (⅓ cup) of water in a saucepan over low heat and stir constantly until the sugar has dissolved. Stir in the glucose, then increase the heat to medium and bring to the boil. Boil, without stirring, until the mixture reaches 130°C on a candy thermometer. Stir in the peanuts and simmer, stirring occasionally, until the mixture reaches 155°C. Remove from the heat. Add the butter, chilli and salt, then stir in the bicarbonate of soda until well combined. Pour onto the prepared tray and spread into a thin layer with a knife. Set aside to cool completely, then cut into large shards using a sharp knife.

Preheat the oven to 200°C/180°C fan-forced. Line a baking tray with baking paper.

Place the pumpkin wedges on the prepared tray in a single layer and drizzle with half the peanut or vegetable oil. Season well and roast for 30 minutes or until tender.

Meanwhile, combine the coriander stalk and root, ginger, lime zest and juice, sweet chilli sauce, soy sauce or tamari, vegan 'fish sauce' and remaining oil in a bowl.

Remove the pumpkin from the oven and brush with the sweet chilli sauce mixture. Roast for a further 20 minutes or until the edges are nicely caramelised.

Break the brittle into small pieces. Place the pumpkin on a serving platter and crush over the brittle. Top with the basil, mint and coriander leaves and serve with loads of lime wedges.

MEATY ADDITION: Serve with Baked white fish fillets (see page 274) as part of a shared meal.

Imam bayildi – the best eggplant dish ever ... from Turkey

SERVES: 4 **PREP:** 20 mins (plus overnight draining) **COOKING:** 1 hour 10 mins

DO insert a chronically overtold tale about how this dish got its name from the way the imam literally swooned over it when he tried it. Although this is perhaps another romantic example – like the evocatively named strozzapreti (aka priest-strangler pasta, see page 88) – of how holy men too often let earthly pleasures distract them.

DON'T whatever you do, DON'T be tempted to get into some long rambling story about how, before he invaded England in 1066, adventurous Viking King Harald Hardrada had served in the mercenary imperial Varangian guard in Constantinople, rising through its ranks and not only fighting across Asia Minor, Sicily and Bulgaria but also taking responsibility for removing a despotic Byzantine ruler with a swift blow of his broad-bladed, double-edged Danish axe to the back of his neck. Note that the presence of paprika, tomatoes and capsicum mean that this dish could only have been made in Constantinople at least 600 years after Hardrada left to reclaim the thrones of Norway and Denmark.

500 g Greek-style yoghurt
4 small eggplants (about 350 g each)
olive oil spray
60 ml (¼ cup) olive oil
2 onions, halved and thinly sliced
1 large red capsicum, finely chopped
3 large garlic cloves, crushed
2 teaspoons sweet paprika
1 teaspoon ground cumin
400 g can diced tomatoes
⅓ cup finely chopped flat-leaf parsley
2 tablespoons coarsely chopped
    dill fronds
1 teaspoon caster sugar
1 teaspoon sea salt
mint leaves, to serve
freshly ground black pepper

Place the yoghurt in a muslin-lined colander set over a large bowl and leave in the fridge overnight to drain and thicken.

Preheat the oven to 200°C/180°C fan-forced. Line a roasting tin with baking paper.

Use a peeler to peel stripes down the side of each eggplant. Make a slit down the middle of each eggplant but be careful not to cut all the way through. Place in the prepared tin, cut-side down, and spray with olive oil. Bake for 30 minutes or until the skins start to shrivel.

Meanwhile, heat 1 tablespoon of the olive oil in a frying pan over medium–high heat. Add the onion and capsicum and cook, stirring, for 5 minutes or until softened. Add the garlic, paprika and cumin and cook, stirring, for 30 seconds or until aromatic. Tip in the tomatoes and cook for 5 minutes or until thickened slightly. Stir in the parsley, dill, sugar and salt.

Remove the paper from the roasting tin and turn the eggplants over so they sit cut-side up. Spoon the tomato mixture into the open slits in the eggplants. Drizzle with the remaining oil and add 60 ml (¼ cup) of water to the tin. Cover with foil and bake for 40 minutes or until the eggplant is tender. Remove the foil and set the eggplant aside to cool slightly. Dollop over the hung yoghurt, scatter a few mint leaves over the top and sprinkle with black pepper.

MEATY ADDITION: Serve with Barbecued or chargrilled lamb skewers (see page 265) as part of a shared meal.

PREPARE IN 20 MINUTES

The most mortally totally decadent tartiflette potato tray bake

SERVES: 8 **PREP:** 20 mins (plus 15 mins cooling) **COOKING:** 1 hour 35 mins

This is a winter dish so hearty that it needs some French Alps wrapped around it. A tartiflette is basically a potato gratin, but we've added silverbeet (aka Swiss chard from over the border) and camembert from Normandy to make it more of a meal.

1 tablespoon olive oil

250 g silverbeet, white stalks removed and thinly sliced, green leaves thickly shredded

1 red onion, thinly sliced into rings

385 ml (1¾ cups) pouring cream

160 ml (⅔ cup) milk

sea salt and freshly ground black pepper

2 kg sebago potatoes, peeled and thinly sliced (use a mandoline if you have one)

200 g wheel of camembert

70 g shredded parmesan

60 ml (¼ cup) extra-virgin olive oil

2 tablespoons white wine vinegar

1 teaspoon Dijon mustard

1 teaspoon caster sugar

100 g mixed salad leaves

Preheat the oven to 170°C/150°C fan-forced.

Heat the olive oil in a large frying pan over medium heat. Add the silverbeet stalk and onion and cook, stirring, for 3–4 minutes or until just softened. Add the silverbeet leaves and cook, stirring, for 2 minutes or until wilted. Set aside.

Combine the cream and milk in a jug. Season well with salt and pepper.

Arrange half the potato slices over the base of a 3 litre ovenproof dish. Sprinkle with the onion and silverbeet mixture and season with salt and pepper. Pour over half the cream mixture and top with the remaining potato slices. Pour over the remaining cream mixture and season again.

Cover with foil and place on a baking tray. Bake for 1 hour or until the potato is tender. Increase the oven temperature to 180°C/160°C fan-forced.

Cut the camembert in half and then split each piece in half horizontally so you end up with four half moons of cheese. Press these, skin-side up, into the top of your tartiflette. Sprinkle the parmesan over the exposed potato and bake, uncovered, for a further 25 minutes or until golden brown and the potato is very tender. Set aside for 15 minutes to cool slightly.

While the potato is baking, whisk together the extra-virgin olive oil, vinegar, mustard and sugar in a jug. Season well with salt and pepper. Drizzle over the salad leaves and toss until lightly coated.

Serve the bake with the guilt-reducing salad.

MEATY ADDITION: Place 200 g sliced prosciutto on top of the potatoes just before you add the parmesan.

Easy chickpea & roast carrot curry

SERVES: 4 PREP: 20 mins COOKING: 1 hour

This is the sort of curry that is studying for an engineering degree in an Aussie uni and driving for Uber at the weekends to pay for his accommodation. He would rather join the Swami Army than be a Fanatic but he still thinks Gilly was a great man. Thoroughly likeable*.

*It has been suggested that this introduction is way too blokey, and may alienate some female readers. This seems to ignore the fact that many women enjoy cricket, whether playing or watching, in all its myriad forms, and understand that the reference to Gilly refers to the great Australian wicket keeper-cum-batsman-cum-all-round great guy Adam Gilchrist.

**Another editor has raised the comment that this introduction might be perceived by some as being a textbook example of micro-rascism. The author and publisher would like to acknowledge that we in no way presume that all of our dearly loved friends from the Subcontinent study engineering ... or drive for Uber ... or even like cricket.

6 carrots, thickly sliced
60 ml (¼ cup) melted coconut oil
1 onion, cut into thick wedges
1–2 long green chillies, deseeded
  and finely chopped
1 bunch coriander, stalks and roots
  cleaned, the whole bunch chopped
2 garlic cloves, crushed
  3 cm knob of ginger, peeled and
  finely grated

1 tablespoon Indian curry powder
400 ml can coconut milk
250 ml (1 cup) vegetable stock
400 g can chickpeas, rinsed
  and drained
125 g (¾ cup) raw cashews
150 g green beans, trimmed
steamed brown basmati rice and
  lime wedges, to serve

Preheat the oven to 200°C/180°C fan-forced.

Place the carrot and 2 tablespoons of the coconut oil in a roasting tin and toss to coat. Roast, turning once, for 40 minutes.

Meanwhile, heat the remaining coconut oil in a large frying pan over medium–low heat. Add the onion, chilli and coriander stalk and root and cook, stirring regularly, for 10 minutes or until softened but not browned. Add the garlic, ginger and curry powder and cook, stirring, for 30 seconds or until aromatic. Pour in the coconut milk and stock and bring to a simmer. Simmer gently for 5 minutes, then stir in the chickpeas and remove from the heat.

Reduce the oven temperature to 180°C/160°C fan-forced. Scatter the cashews over the carrot and roast for 10 minutes or until the cashews are golden.

Add the beans to the roasting tin and pour over the chickpea mixture. Roast for a further 10 minutes or until the curry has thickened slightly. Serve with rice and lime wedges.

Sunday roast tray bake with crunchy roast potatoes

SERVES: 4 PREP: 45 mins COOKING: 1 hour 40 mins

At my house, seconds after a Sunday roast have always been more about the veg, stuffing and gravy, so why not ditch the meat altogether and go straight for this delicious combination? The amazing stuffing will make you forget all about whether you are a breast or leg person (as your pervy, middle-aged, stale white male uncle might like to say).

1 kg sebago potatoes, halved (or quartered if large)
60 ml (¼ cup) olive oil
sea salt and freshly ground black pepper
1 bunch baby carrots or 8 small carrots, trimmed and halved lengthways
2 red onions, cut into thick wedges
350 g brussels sprouts, trimmed
150 g (1 cup) frozen peas, thawed

STUFFING BALLS

1 tablespoon olive oil
1 onion, finely chopped
1 green apple, peeled, cored and coarsely grated
100 g dried cranberries, finely chopped
70 g (1 cup) fresh sourdough breadcrumbs
145 g (1 cup) hazelnuts, finely chopped
¼ cup finely chopped flat-leaf parsley
1 tablespoon finely chopped sage
finely grated zest of ½ lemon
2 eggs
sea salt and freshly ground black pepper

MUSHROOM GRAVY

50 g butter
100 g Swiss brown mushrooms, sliced
750 ml (3 cups) vegetable stock
60 ml (¼ cup) sweet sherry or muscat
2 tablespoons plain flour
½ teaspoon Vegemite

Drop the potatoes into a saucepan of cold salted water. Bring to the boil over medium heat and simmer for 5–8 minutes or until they are tender but still firm. Drain them well, then immediately return them to the pan for 1–2 minutes to steam dry, shaking occasionally to rough up the edges.

Meanwhile, to make your stuffing balls, heat the olive oil in a frying pan over medium heat, add the onion and cook, stirring, for 5 minutes or until softened. Transfer to a bowl. Add the remaining ingredients and mix until well combined. Roll into walnut-sized balls and set aside.

Now start your gravy. Melt half the butter in a saucepan over medium–high heat until foaming. Add the mushroom and cook, stirring, for 4–5 minutes or until golden. Add the stock and bring to the boil. Turn off the heat and set aside for 30 minutes to develop the flavours, then strain the stock through a fine sieve into a jug. Set aside.

Preheat the oven to 200°C/180°C fan-forced.

Heat 2 tablespoons of the olive oil in a roasting tin in the oven for 5 minutes, then carefully add the potatoes. (Adding them to the hot oil will help make them golden and crispy.) Season really well and toss, then roast for 10 minutes.

Place the carrot and red onion in a separate roasting tin (make sure it's flameproof). Drizzle over the remaining olive oil, then season well and toss to coat. After the potatoes have been in the oven for 10 minutes, add the carrot tin to the oven and roast everything for 20 minutes.

Add the stuffing balls and brussels sprouts to the carrots and onion. Return to the oven, and roast (along with the potatoes) for a further 20 minutes. Scatter the peas over the carrot mixture and roast everything for another 5 minutes. Transfer all the veggies to the potato tin and cover loosely with foil to keep warm. Don't rinse out the tin – you're going to finish the gravy in it!

Add the sherry or muscat to the roasting tin and bring to the boil over high heat. Cook, scraping the base to remove any stuck-on bits, for 2–3 minutes or until the liquid has reduced to about 1 tablespoon. Reduce the heat to medium. Add the remaining butter and stir until melted. Add the flour and cook, stirring, for 1–2 minutes or until foaming. Gradually stir in the reserved mushroom stock until well combined. Bring to the boil, then reduce the heat and simmer rapidly for 10 minutes or until the gravy has thickened. Stir in the Vegemite, then pour into a serving jug.

Pile the roast veggies and stuffing balls onto a serving platter and serve with the gravy.

MEATY ADDITION: Serve with Barbecued butterflied lamb leg (see page 264) or Barbecued or chargrilled beef steaks (see page 266) with horseradish or Dijon mustard as part of a shared meal to serve 8.

PREPARE IN
20
MINUTES

The heretic's golden cassoulet

SERVES: 4 PREP: 20 mins COOKING: 1 hour 20 mins

What would have happened if the good people of 13th century Carcassonne in south-west France had turned to the earth and not the air as their source of divinity when they turned away from the ways of the flesh? What if their heresy had been vegetarianism and not Catharism?

Would Pope Innocent III still have called for a crusade against south-west France? Would their northern countrymen still have besieged the city and forced the people of Carcassonne to abandon it? The citizens left with nothing more than the shirts on their backs and the sins in their hearts* (as one droll contemporary chronicler put it).

*It could have been worse. In Beziers, the previous heretic city they had besieged, every man, woman and child (20,000 people in total), whether heretic or loyal Christian, were put to the sword with the chilling words 'kill them all, God will know his own'.

And, more importantly, would Carcassonne's signature cassoulet have ended up flesh-free and looking a little like this?

The answer to all these questions is 'probably'.

FOOD NERD FACT: Although, obviously as the history nerds all chime in, the pumpkin would most likely have been eggplant as, like zucchini, tomatoes and capsicum, pumpkin was still unknown at that time. Eggplant originated in India but was known in China as early as 544 AD. Ironically it was cultivated by the Arabs in time for earlier Crusaders to discover it and bring it back to their European homes.

1.2 kg butternut pumpkin, peeled, deseeded and cut into 3 cm chunks
2 leeks, trimmed and cut into 2 cm thick rounds
2 celery stalks, thickly sliced
2 large rosemary sprigs
2 tablespoons olive oil
sea salt and freshly ground black pepper
½ bunch flat-leaf parsley, leaves and stalks separated and finely chopped
2 garlic cloves, crushed
1 tablespoon smoked paprika
125 ml (½ cup) white wine
625 ml (2½ cups) vegetable stock
400 g can cannellini beans, rinsed and drained
140 g (2 cups) chunky stale breadcrumbs
40 g butter, melted

Preheat the oven to 200°C/180°C fan-forced.

Place the pumpkin, leek, celery and rosemary in a large roasting tin and drizzle with half the olive oil. Season well and toss to coat, then roast for 50 minutes.

When the veggies have 10 minutes of roasting time to go, heat the remaining olive oil in a saucepan over medium heat. Add the parsley stalk, garlic and paprika and cook, stirring, for 1 minute or until aromatic. Pour in the wine and cook, stirring, for 5 minutes or until reduced by half. Add the stock and bring just to the boil.

Scatter the cannellini beans over the roasted veggies (do not stir), then pour over the stock mixture. Roast for a further 15 minutes.

Place the chopped parsley leaves, breadcrumbs and melted butter in a bowl. Season with salt and pepper and toss until really well combined.

Sprinkle the breadcrumb mixture over the veggie mixture and roast for 15 minutes or until a golden crust has formed on top.

MEATY ADDITION: Add 4 large or 6 small Pan-fried sausages (see page 270) to the pan just before sprinkling with the breadcrumbs.

Primavera bake with pea & pumpkin seed pesto

SERVES: 4 **PREP:** 20 mins **COOKING:** 45 mins

The Italian way of combining the green bounty of spring in a number of different dishes is a joy, whether as a sauce for pasta or as a fricassee to seasonal goodness. Here, it becomes the simplest of tray bakes that is best in spring but good all year round when there's fresh greenery at the market.

3 zucchini, cut into 1.5 cm thick slices
6 lemon thyme sprigs
60 ml (¼ cup) extra-virgin olive oil, plus extra to serve
sea salt and freshly ground black pepper
2 bunches asparagus, trimmed
120 g sugar snap peas, trimmed
500 ml (2 cups) vegetable stock
600 g coliban potatoes, peeled and cut into 2 cm chunks
150 g goat's cheese, broken into large pieces (or a non-dairy alternative that makes your vegan heart skip with joy, like cashew cheese and a sprinkling of nutritional yeast)

PEA & PUMPKIN SEED PESTO
150 g (1 cup) frozen peas
boiling water
45 g (¼ cup) pumpkin seeds
2 garlic cloves, crushed
½ cup flat-leaf parsley leaves, plus extra to serve
⅓ cup mint leaves, plus extra to serve
60 ml (¼ cup) extra-virgin olive oil
1 tablespoon freshly squeezed lemon juice
sea salt and freshly ground black pepper

Preheat the oven to 180°C/160°C fan-forced.

Place the zucchini and thyme in a shallow roasting tin and drizzle with 2 tablespoons of the olive oil. Toss to coat and season well with salt and pepper. Roast for 20 minutes. Add the asparagus and sugar snap peas and roast for a further 20–25 minutes or until tender.

Meanwhile, get the stock boiling in a saucepan over medium–high heat. Add the potato and cook for 5–8 minutes or until just tender. Drain and return to the pan. Add the remaining oil, season well with salt and pepper and toss to coat.

While your veggies are cooking, make the pesto. Place the peas in a heatproof bowl, cover with boiling water and set aside for 3 minutes to soften. Drain and leave to cool slightly.

Blitz the pumpkin seeds and garlic in a food processor until finely chopped. Add the peas, parsley and mint and blitz until well combined. Add the olive oil and lemon juice and blitz until almost smooth but still a little chunky. Season to taste.

Spread three-quarters of the pesto over a platter and top with the potato, then the roasted veggies. Scatter over the goat's cheese and remaining pesto and drizzle with a little extra olive oil. Sprinkle over some extra parsley and mint leaves, and serve.

MEATY ADDITION: Sprinkle the top of the bake with 6 chopped rashers Crispy bacon (see page 268) or Crispy prosciutto shards (see page 269). It is also delicious as a side dish with Roast chicken (see page 262).

Greek baked eggplant

SERVES: 6 PREP: 15 mins COOKING: 1 hour 5 mins

I came up with this recipe on a dark winter's night of fridge shaking as the solution of what to do with eggplants a wee bit past their prime. It works because the skins get deliciously chewy in the oven, the tomato sauce intensifies and the feta brings a salty accent that is more Greek than Provençal or Neapolitan.

3 eggplants (about 400 g each)
80 ml (⅓ cup) olive oil, plus extra
    for greasing
1 onion, finely chopped
2 garlic cloves, crushed
2 teaspoons Greek or regular
    dried oregano
700 g bottle passata
400 g can chickpeas, rinsed
    and drained
sea salt and freshly ground
    black pepper
150 g Greek feta, crumbled into
    large pieces
black olive tapenade and oregano
    leaves, to serve

Preheat the oven to 200°C/180°C fan-forced. Generously grease a large roasting tin.

Halve the eggplants lengthways and score a 1 cm wide border around the edge of each half. Score within the border in a crisscross pattern, then scoop out the flesh and roughly chop it.

Heat 1 tablespoon of the olive oil in a large frying pan over medium–high heat, add the onion and cook, stirring, for 5 minutes or until softened. Add the remaining oil and the chopped eggplant flesh and cook, stirring, for 8–10 minutes or until tender. Add the garlic and dried oregano and cook for 30 seconds or until aromatic.

Pour the passata into the pan, along with the chickpeas and cook, stirring, for 20 minutes or until the mixture has reduced and thickened and pulls away from the side of the pan. You want it to be nice and pulpy. Season well with salt and pepper.

While the sauce is cooking, place the eggplant shells cut-side down in the prepared tin, cover with foil and bake for 20 minutes or until slightly softened.

Turn the eggplant shells over and fill with the tomato mixture. Sprinkle over the feta and bake for a further 30 minutes or until the eggplant is tender and the tops are golden. Finish with dollops of olive tapenade and sprinkle with fresh oregano leaves.

MEATY ADDITION: Serve with Slow-roasted lamb shoulder (see page 264) as part of a shared meal.

PREPARE IN
15
MINUTES

Pumpkin, potato & peanut Thai red curry

SERVES: 4 PREP: 15 mins COOKING: 1 hour 5 mins

Lawd luv a tray bake. Less washing up and loads of crusty burnished bits around the edges to pick at as a cook's treat.

1 tablespoon melted coconut oil
1 onion, cut into wedges
2 tablespoons Thai red curry paste
70 g (¼ cup) crunchy peanut butter
½ bunch coriander, leaves picked, stalks and roots cleaned and finely chopped
400 ml can coconut cream
2 tablespoons soy sauce or tamari
juice of 1 lime
4 kaffir lime leaves
2 tablespoons coarsely grated palm sugar
1.2 kg butternut pumpkin, peeled, deseeded and cut into 5 cm pieces
3 large coliban potatoes, peeled and quartered lengthways
80 g (½ cup) salted roasted peanuts, coarsely chopped
2 tablespoons coconut flakes, toasted
steamed rice, to serve

Preheat the oven to 200°C/180°C fan-forced.

Heat the coconut oil in a flameproof roasting tin over medium heat. Add the onion and cook, stirring, for 2–3 minutes or until softened. Add the curry paste, peanut butter and coriander stalk and root and cook for 1 minute or until aromatic. Stir in the coconut cream, soy sauce or tamari, half the lime juice, the kaffir lime leaves and sugar until well combined and bubbling.

Remove the tin from the heat. Add the pumpkin and potato and carefully toss until well coated. Place in the oven and bake for 1 hour or until the vegetables are tender and starting to char around the edges.

Squeeze over the remaining lime juice, top with the peanuts, toasted coconut flakes and coriander leaves and serve with steamed rice.

Braised & fried

It used to be that if I wanted a sure-fire winner of a dish I'd crumb something, fry it and serve it with mayo. Nothing much has changed, even in these vego-friendly pages. The same basic primordial rules of crunchy/creamy and sweet/salty apply, and you'll find plenty in the pages that follow.

My must-try favourites here are the Andhra golden potato curry and the carrot korma – a real eye opener to serve to your most carnivorous friends – while the leeky potato gems and Sichuan pumpkin fritters with my tamarind and chipotle ketchup are great with drinks. Make mine a Tanqueray and tonic, obviously! Also do take time to check out all the falafels – you won't regret it.

Crunchy vegetable croquettes

MAKES: 18 PREP: 30 mins (plus 4 hours 30 mins chilling) COOKING: 25 mins

This is an excellent example of a D.F.V dish (see page 9). I've taken to wrapping things in leaves – wasabi leaves, betel leaves, shiso leaves (to be honest, 90 per cent of the time it's lettuce leaves!), and then throwing on a green garnish to fool the eye into thinking that yes, this dish is really fresh and good for you. That is until it's too late and you are snared; dragged down into the tumbling helix of those two sets of unholy paradigms.

150 g broccoli, cut into florets
80 g (½ cup) frozen baby peas
100 g butter
100 g (⅔ cup) plain flour, plus
    40 g (¼ cup) extra
375 ml (1½ cups) full-cream milk
170 g jarred marinated artichoke
    hearts, drained and finely chopped
    (or 100 g marinated artichokes
    from the deli)
2 spring onions, white and green
    parts thinly sliced
1 tablespoon finely chopped
    oregano leaves
¾ teaspoon sea salt
freshly ground black pepper
250 g fresh breadcrumbs
5 eggs
vegetable oil, for deep-frying
2 baby cos lettuces, leaves separated

CHEAT'S GARLIC MAYO
250 g (1 cup) whole-egg mayonnaise
3 small garlic cloves, crushed
1½ tablespoons freshly squeezed
    lemon juice

Cook the broccoli in a saucepan of boiling water for 3 minutes. Add the peas and cook for another 2 minutes or until just tender. Drain well. Transfer the broccoli to a chopping board and very finely chop.

Melt the butter in the now empty saucepan, over medium–high heat until foaming. Stir in the flour for 1 minute. Remove from the heat and stir in one-third of the milk, then gradually stir in the remaining milk, ensuring there are no lumps. Return to medium–high heat and cook, stirring, for a further 2–5 minutes or until very thick. You will know it's thick enough when your wooden spoon enthusiastically resists your stirring efforts. It needs to be really thick, man …

Stir the broccoli, peas, artichoke, spring onion, oregano and salt into the bechamel, and season to taste with pepper. Transfer to a shallow container and set aside to cool slightly. Cover and place in the fridge for 4 hours or overnight to set.

Later, or the next day, make the garlic mayo. Combine the ingredients in a bowl. Place in the fridge until you are ready to serve.

Line a baking tray with baking paper. Place the extra flour and breadcrumbs in separate bowls. Lightly beat the eggs in a third bowl. Using floured hands, roll 2 tablespoons of the cooled broccoli–bechamel mixture into an 8 cm long croquette. Roll this croquette in the flour, shaking off the excess, then dip in the egg and then in the breadcrumbs to coat. Place on the prepared tray. Repeat with the remaining mixture to make 18 croquettes, then repeat to give a second coating to all the croquettes and place in the fridge to chill for 30 minutes.

Pour enough vegetable oil into a large saucepan to come 5 cm up the side and heat over medium–high heat to 170°C or until a cube of bread dropped in the oil browns in 20 seconds. Working in batches so you don't overcrowd the pan, deep-fry the croquettes, turning occasionally, for 2–3 minutes or until golden and crisp. Remove with a slotted spoon and drain on a tray lined with paper towel.

Serve your croquettes with the lettuce leaves for wrapping and garlic mayo on the side.

MEATY ADDITION: Replace the broccoli with 120 g chopped rashers Crispy bacon (see page 268) or Spicy chorizo coins (see page 269).

Leeks with cheese snow

SERVES: 4 as a side PREP: 5 mins COOKING: 10 mins

There is a strong anarchic streak running through some of the ideas in this cookbook which, I suspect, is in direct response to the big wank perpetrated by some top chefs around the world. I am not innocent. It's a wank that we have been guilty of promulgating on the television show I was involved in.

For example, my reaction to a six-hour prep time for a dessert made with malt, milk and yeast is to mix a couple of spoons of Horlicks and roughly crushed Maltesers into softened vanilla ice-cream. This avoids using any ingredients more often seen in a laboratory and is almost as delicious.

This dish is another aberrant interpretation of a far more complex inspiration.

4 thin leeks
1 × 250 g block cream cheese, frozen hard (remove the foil but freeze in the cardboard packet)

BLACK PEPPER VINAIGRETTE
60 ml (¼ cup) olive oil
2 tablespoons white wine vinegar
1 teaspoon coarsely ground black pepper
1 teaspoon honey
large pinch of sea salt

Remove the dark green leaves from the leeks and wash the leeks well. Give them a trim, leaving the white end of the leek totally sealed. Get rid of any straggly roots.

To make the vinaigrette, whisk together all the ingredients in a bowl.

Place two leeks in a flat-bottomed microwave-safe dish (a pie plate works well) or just put them directly on the turntable. Microwave on high for 4–6 minutes or until tender, a little squidgy and a bit bendy. Repeat with the remaining leeks.

When the leeks are cooked, cut off the sealed ends and cut them in half lengthways. (Be careful as the leeks will be hot.)

Place the leeks on a serving platter and drizzle with the dressing. Coarsely grate a generous amount of cream cheese over the top to look like snow and serve.

 TIP: If you like finer, light snow, grate as soon as the cream cheese comes out of the freezer. For longer, creamier strands, leave the frozen block at room temperature for 2 minutes, then coarsely grate. You won't use the whole block, but keep it in the freezer for next time (and there will be a next time!).

MEATY ADDITION: Serve with Roast chicken (see page 262) or Crispy-skinned salmon fillets (see page 275).

Popcorn 'chicken' cauliflower

SERVES: 6 as a snack or starter **PREP:** 20 mins (plus overnight soaking) **COOKING:** 25 mins

Contrary to what the old cliche says, usually you CAN judge a book by its cover. Likewise you can usually judge a recipe by its title. But not this time. This is basically Indian-style pakoras with a cashew cream and chilli caramel. There is no popcorn in it at all! Nor is there any chicken! Unless you want it (see the meaty addition below). Needless to say this is another D.F.V dish.

500 g cauliflower, cut into bite-sized
    florets
200 g (1 cup) chickpea flour (besan)
½ teaspoon baking powder
¼ cup coarsely chopped coriander
2 teaspoons cumin seeds
2 teaspoons garam masala
1 teaspoon ground turmeric
½ teaspoon chilli powder
1 long green chilli, finely chopped
sea salt and freshly ground
    black pepper
vegetable oil, for deep-frying

COCONUT CASHEW CREAM
290 g (2 cups) raw cashews
boiling water
125 ml (½ cup) coconut cream
1 tablespoon freshly squeezed
    lemon juice
sea salt and freshly ground
    black pepper

CHILLI CARAMEL
200 g palm sugar, finely chopped
2 long red chillies, deseeded and
    thinly sliced (or more if you like
    things spicy)
1 tablespoon freshly squeezed
    lime juice

Start your cashew cream a day ahead (it will keep in the fridge for up to 3 days). Place the cashews in a heatproof bowl and cover with plenty of boiling water. Set aside to soak overnight.

Drain the soaked cashews and place in a high-powered blender or food processor. Add the coconut cream and lemon juice and season well, then process until smooth and creamy. Place in the fridge until you are ready to serve.

Place the cauliflower in a large microwave-safe bowl. Add 1 tablespoon of water and cover with plastic wrap. Microwave on high for 5 minutes or until slightly softened. Drain and place on a plate lined with paper towel to dry.

Now make your chilli caramel. Place the sugar and 80 ml (⅓ cup) of water in a small saucepan over low heat. Cook, stirring, for 2 minutes or until the sugar has dissolved. Increase the heat to high and bring to the boil, then reduce the heat to medium and simmer, without stirring, for 5–8 minutes or until syrupy. Remove from the heat and set aside until the bubbles subside. Stir in the chilli and lime juice.

Place the chickpea flour, baking powder, coriander, cumin, garam masala, turmeric, chilli powder and green chilli in a large bowl and season well. Make a well in the centre, pour in 160 ml of water and whisk until smooth. Add the cauliflower and stir until well coated.

Pour enough vegetable oil into a large saucepan or wok to come 8 cm up the side and heat over medium–high heat to 170°C or until a cube of bread dropped in the oil browns in 20 seconds. Working in batches so you don't overcrowd the pan, carefully drop dessertspoons of the cauliflower mixture into the oil and cook for 3 minutes or until crisp and golden. Remove with a slotted spoon and drain on a plate lined with paper towel. Keep warm.

Place the cauliflower in a serving bowl and season well with salt. Drizzle with the chilli caramel and serve with the cashew cream for dunking.

MEATY ADDITION: Reduce the cauliflower by half and add 250 g chopped peeled and deveined raw prawns or even-sized pieces of chicken thigh fillets to the batter. Make sure you cook them through.

Smash 'em green fritters

SERVES: 4 PREP: 15 mins COOKING: 25 mins

Ain't just the Hulk who'll smash these green fritters; they will sustain any aspiring superhero.

reserved celery leaves (see below)
1 tablespoon sea salt
olive oil, for shallow-frying
4 eggs
1 large avocado, thinly sliced
  crossways

GREEN FRITTERS

75 g (½ cup) self-raising flour
20 g (¼ cup) shredded parmesan
1 cup roughly chopped kale and/or
  silverbeet leaves (we like a mix of
  50/50 but use just one if you like)
1 large celery stalk, finely chopped,
  leaves reserved for the celery salt
2 spring onions, white and green
  parts thinly sliced
100 g Greek feta, crumbled
finely grated zest of 1 lemon
sea salt and freshly ground
  black pepper
2 eggs, lightly beaten
60 ml (¼ cup) full-cream milk

Preheat the oven to 180°C/160°C fan-forced.

Place the reserved celery leaves on a baking tray and bake for 5–8 minutes or until crisp but not browned. Transfer to a mortar and pound with the pestle until roughly crushed. Add the salt and pound until well combined.

To make the fritters, combine the flour and parmesan in a bowl. Add the kale and/or silverbeet, celery, spring onion, feta and lemon zest, season to taste and mix until well combined. Make a well in the centre and add the eggs and milk, then mix to combine.

Pour enough olive oil into a large frying pan to come 5 mm up the side and heat over medium heat. Working in batches of four, add heaped dessertspoons of the fritter batter to the pan and cook for 3–4 minutes each side or until golden brown and crisp. Remove and drain on a tray lined with paper towel. Cover loosely with foil to keep warm. Repeat with the remaining batter, adding extra oil to the pan as needed (but let the oil come to temperature before resuming frying).

While your fritters are cooking, heat 1 tablespoon of oil in a second frying pan over medium–high heat. Crack the eggs into the pan, then cover and cook for 2–3 minutes or until the whites on top are just set.

Divide the fritters among serving plates. Top with the fried eggs and avocado and sprinkle with the celery salt.

MEATY ADDITION: Top with 200 g smoked salmon slices or 8 rashers Crispy bacon (see page 268).

Tofu schnitzel fingers with idiot slaw

SERVES: 4 **PREP:** 20 mins (plus 20 mins chilling) **COOKING:** 25 mins

Some dishes are like a conjuring act – you can't believe they are possible. This is one of them. Cook it and be amazed that it tastes any good at all. This is perhaps the greatest proof of the famous 'everything is better crumbed' dictum that I have espoused elsewhere in this book.

BTW, as I sometimes dress like a camp music hall magician who has seen better days this recipe seems doubly right for this book. Tah-dah! This becomes very D.F.V if you add Japanese mayo.

50 g (⅓ cup) plain flour
100 g (2 cups) panko breadcrumbs
2 eggs
600 g firm tofu, cut into 1 cm
   thick slices
¼ white or red cabbage, hard core
   removed and leaves finely shredded
1 tablespoon rice wine vinegar
sea salt
grapeseed or vegetable oil, for
   shallow-frying
coriander leaves, to serve

FAKE HP SAUCE
80 g (¼ cup) finely chopped plump
   Medjool dates
2 whole cloves
60 ml (¼ cup) malt vinegar
115 g tamarind puree
60 ml (¼ cup) tomato sauce
2 tablespoons treacle
1 tablespoon soy sauce or tamari
1 tablespoon brown sugar, plus
   extra if needed
1 teaspoon garlic powder
¼ teaspoon ground allspice
sea salt

Sprinkle the flour and breadcrumbs over separate plates. Lightly beat the eggs in a shallow bowl.

Dip the tofu slices in the flour and shake off the excess. Dip in the egg and then in the breadcrumbs, pressing firmly to coat. Arrange on a plate in a single layer and place in the fridge to chill for 20 minutes.

Meanwhile, make your sauce. Combine the chopped dates, cloves, vinegar and 60 ml (¼ cup) of water in a small saucepan and cook gently over low heat for 3–5 minutes or until the date has softened and broken down. Press the date mixture through a fine sieve into a bowl and discard any solids left in the sieve. Wipe out the pan, then return the date liquid to the pan.

Add all the remaining sauce ingredients (except the salt) and cook gently over low heat, stirring occasionally, for 5 minutes or until thickened. Taste and adjust the flavour by adding salt and more brown sugar if required. The flavour should be fruity, then tangy, then sweet. Leave the sauce to cool.

Toss the cabbage with the vinegar and season with salt.

Pour enough grapeseed or vegetable oil into a heavy-based frying pan to come 1 cm up the side and heat over medium heat. Working in batches so you don't overcrowd the pan, carefully add the tofu and cook for 2–3 minutes each side or until golden. Transfer to a plate lined with paper towel to drain.

Divide the tofu and cabbage among plates, scatter a few coriander leaves over the cabbage and serve with the sauce.

 TIP: There are more music hall antics in the sauce, which is like the most convincing rubber-faced impressionist ever. While people will be impressed by the impression of HP Sauce, don't worry if you don't have time to make it. Just use a shop-bought version instead. Okonomiyaki sauce from your local Japanese supermarket will work just as well. Yes, Japanese mayo is a good idea, but even better if you spike it with some liquid smoke or Maggi liquid seasoning.

MEATY ADDITION: Omit half the tofu and replace with 4 chicken tenderloin fillets. Crumb as you would the tofu and proceed with the recipe.

Sichuan pumpkin doughnuts with tamarind & chipotle ketchup

SERVES: 4–6 PREP: 20 mins COOKING: 1 hour

Chewy like Japanese mochi, based on a recipe that could be either Korean or Sichuan and with a ketchup that was the result of emptying a few random jars in the fridge, this is a true mongrel of a dish.

My dog is a mongrel and I love her very much indeed. I love this recipe almost as much, as has everyone who tried these doughnuts over the summer.

1.2 kg whole butternut pumpkin, unpeeled, halved lengthways and deseeded
sea salt and freshly ground black pepper
500 g glutinous rice four (you will not use all of this unless the pumpkin is very wet)
vegetable oil, for deep-frying
55 g (⅓ cup) sesame seeds

TAMARIND & CHIPOTLE KETCHUP
110 g tamarind puree
60 g canned chipotle chillies in adobo sauce, rinsed and deseeded, roughly chopped (add more for a hot version or less if you prefer it mild)
60 g (¼ cup) brown sugar, plus extra to taste
sea salt, to taste
apple cider vinegar, to taste

TO SERVE
250 g creme fraiche
1 bunch coriander, leaves picked

Preheat the oven to 200°C/180°C fan-forced. Place the pumpkin halves, cut-side up, in a roasting tin. Season well and roast for 35–40 minutes or until soft and tender.

Now's a good time to make the tamarind and chipotle ketchup. Combine the tamarind puree, chipotle chilli and sugar in a bowl and use a stick blender to blitz until smooth. Taste and season with salt, apple cider vinegar and extra brown sugar to get a balance you like. Set aside.

Remove the flesh from the pumpkin, transfer to a bowl and mash until smooth. Stir in enough rice flour until you have a thick spoonable batter that's a little thicker than thick double cream. If it looks like a puree add more flour.

Pour enough vegetable oil into a large saucepan to come halfway up the side and heat over medium–high heat to 180°C or until a cube of bread dropped in the oil browns in 15 seconds. Start with a tester doughnut. Take a heaped teaspoon of batter and, holding the spoon over a large plate, sprinkle the batter with sesame seeds (the plate will capture any sesame seeds that fall off. There will be many!). Now use a second teaspoon to carefully scrape the batter into the hot oil. Fry for 3–4 minutes or until golden on all sides. If the doughnut has flattened out too much you'll need to add more flour to the batter.

Working in batches and without overcrowding the pan, continue to make and fry the doughnuts. Remember to push up the heat a little as you add them, to counter the impact of the cold batter on the oil's heat. Jiggle the pan and use the tip of a metal spatula to persuade any recalcitrant doughnuts not to stick to the base of the pan. When golden on the bottom, flip the doughnuts over in the oil and fry until golden all over. Use a slotted spoon to transfer them to a plate lined with paper towel to drain, then place in a large baking dish in the oven (that's still warm from cooking the pumpkin) while you cook the rest.

Dollop the creme fraiche onto a serving plate and top with the doughnuts. Add blobs of the tamarind and chipotle ketchup and scatter over any remaining sesame seeds and the coriander leaves.

Ratatouille spring rolls

MAKES: 15 PREP: 20 mins COOKING: 30 mins

They might sound weird but these spring rolls are actually rather wonderful, thanks to the wet resistance of the zucchini and capsicum, the rich, sweet tomato sauce and the contrasting crispness of the pastry.

I first had them during a few awe-inspiring days on safari near the Kruger National Park in South Africa, so I can definitively say that they can be equally well employed as a snack before a big game drive, or as a substantial canape to go with the perfect gimlet overlooking a waterhole where hippos, rhinos and lions conduct an uncomfortable and suspicious cohabitation.

P.S. Respect to the talented kitchen team at Sabi Sabi Earth Lodge who had the original idea.

2 tablespoons olive oil
2 large zucchini, cut into 1 cm thick, 7 cm long batons
1 large green capsicum, cut into 1 cm thick, 7 cm long batons
½ teaspoon dried oregano
2 garlic cloves, crushed
6 Lebanese eggplants, finely chopped
140 g (½ cup) tomato paste
100 g pitted green olives, quartered
¼ cup coarsely chopped flat-leaf parsley
1 tablespoon cornflour
15 spring roll wrappers
vegetable oil, for deep-frying

SPICED TOMATO SAUCE
125 ml (½ cup) tomato sauce
2 teaspoons soy sauce or tamari
1–2 teaspoons sriracha chilli sauce (depending on how spicy you like things)

Heat half the olive oil in a large frying pan over medium–high heat, add the zucchini, capsicum and oregano and cook for 8 minutes or until softened (but still with a little bite) and lightly golden. Add the garlic and cook, stirring, for 30 seconds or until aromatic. Transfer to a plate and set aside.

Heat the remaining oil in the pan, add the eggplant and cook for 4–5 minutes or until soft and golden. Add the tomato paste and cook, tossing, for 2–3 minutes or until the eggplant is well coated and the tomato turns a slightly darker colour. Stir in the olives and parsley, then set aside to cool.

Mix the cornflour and 1 tablespoon of water in a bowl until smooth.

Place one spring roll wrapper on a work surface. Lay three vegetable batons diagonally across the pastry square, then spoon over a generous tablespoon of the tomato eggplant mixture.

Brush opposite corners of the pastry with the cornflour paste, then fold in the sides and roll up to enclose the filling. Repeat with the remaining ingredients to make 15 spring rolls.

Pour enough vegetable oil into a large saucepan to come halfway up the side and heat over medium–high heat to 180°C or until a cube of bread dropped in the oil browns in 15 seconds. Working in batches so you don't overcrowd the pan, add the spring rolls and cook for 2–3 minutes or until golden. Remove with a slotted spoon and drain on a tray lined with paper towel.

Meanwhile, combine the spiced tomato sauce ingredients in a bowl.

Serve the spring rolls with the spicy sauce for dipping.

Ghost pop nuggets

MAKES: 22 **PREP:** 30 mins (plus 30 mins chilling) **COOKING:** 30 mins

The ragtag army of food lovers I travel with and I have a set of rules for when we are in new foreign climes doing dinners, demos or food festivals.

1) *Visit the market.*

2) *Visit the supermarket.*

3) *Make sure you eyeball everything that you've been promised (as sometimes other chefs and promoters lie about whether they've fulfilled their commitments).*

4) *Don't take on anything that you can't do yourself without any promised support (at a pinch).*

5) *Keep smiling.*

6) *Don't eat anything with smiling teeth or that's grey in colour.*

7) *Seek out the wild life.*

8) *Always support the choicest local drinking establishments – this is often interchangeable with rule 7.*

9) *Don't get caught.*

Rule 2 revolves around our desire to check out the local junk-food aisle to see what it says about their greatest loves, whether it's fruit chutney-flavoured crisps in South Africa, pollock roe-flavoured ones in Tokyo or Tom Yum Twisties in Thailand. These snacks have a powerful culinary value and unique emotional pull that can even eclipse that of the country's national dish. So it is with ghost pops – an airy, crisp puff the size of a large tooth that has an almost mesmeric hold over some sections of the populace of Cape Town, Johannesburg and Durban. This is my first attempt to capture the magic of these in recipe form. There will be more!

400 g purple-fleshed sweet potato, peeled and roughly chopped
200 g parsnip, peeled and roughly chopped
1 tablespoon olive oil
½ small onion, finely chopped
80 g (1 cup) coarsely grated cheddar
sea salt and freshly ground black pepper
3 eggs
70 g (¼ cup) tomato paste
3 teaspoons Vegemite
¼ teaspoon ground nutmeg
18 drops of liquid smoke
120 g (2½ cups) panko breadcrumbs
vegetable oil, for deep-frying
sweet chilli sauce and whole-egg mayo (or creme fraiche), to serve

Cook the sweet potato and parsnip in a saucepan of boiling water for 10 minutes or until tender. Drain and mash, then set aside to cool for 5 minutes.

Meanwhile, heat the olive oil in a frying pan over medium heat, add the onion and cook, stirring, for 2–3 minutes or until softened.

Add the onion and cheddar to the mashed vegetables and stir until well combined. Season well with salt and pepper.

Whisk together the eggs, tomato paste, Vegemite, nutmeg and liquid smoke in a bowl.

Tip the breadcrumbs onto a plate.

Roll level tablespoons of the vegetable mixture into nuggets (try to get them a little kidney shaped). Dip one nugget at a time into the egg mixture, shaking off the excess, then coat in the breadcrumbs. Transfer to a tray. Repeat to give a second coating, then place in the fridge to chill for 30 minutes.

Pour enough vegetable oil into a large saucepan to come halfway up the side and heat over medium–high heat to 170°C or until a cube of bread dropped in the oil browns in 20 seconds. Working in batches so you don't overcrowd the pan, deep-fry the nuggets for 3–4 minutes or until golden and crisp. Remove with a slotted spoon and drain on a tray lined with paper towel.

Swirl the sweet chilli sauce into the mayo (or creme fraiche) and serve with the hot nuggets.

FALAFELS

Every dish has its moment in the sun ... this is the falafel's time so let's shout about how they can be so much more than meatless fried chickpea balls!

Coy beetroot & hazelnut falafels

MAKES: 26
PREP: 25 mins (plus 30 mins chilling)
COOKING: 25 mins

2 beetroot bulbs (about 400 g), peeled and roughly chopped
400 g can brown lentils, rinsed and drained
2 spring onions, white and green parts sliced
2 garlic cloves, crushed
⅓ cup mint leaves, plus extra small leaves to serve
45 g (¼ cup) roasted hazelnuts, coarsely chopped
40 g (¼ cup) spelt flour (or plain wholemeal flour)
1 tablespoon nutritional yeast
finely grated zest of 1 lemon
2 teaspoons ground cumin
2 tablespoons sesame seeds (ideally black)
¼ white cabbage, finely shredded
1 green apple, cored and cut into matchsticks
1 tablespoon freshly squeezed lemon juice
1 tablespoon olive oil
300 g goat's cheese (or a vegan alternative)
1 tablespoon chopped dill fronds
your choice of milk, to loosen (optional)
sea salt and freshly ground black pepper
canola or vegetable oil, for deep-frying
warmed small flatbreads, to serve

Place the beetroot in a food processor and blitz until finely chopped. Add the lentils, spring onion, garlic, mint, hazelnuts, flour, nutritional yeast, lemon zest and cumin and blitz until well combined. Spoon into a bowl and stir in the sesame seeds.

Roll heaped tablespoons of the beetroot mixture into 26 balls and flatten slightly. Place on a tray lined with baking paper, then chill in the fridge for 30 minutes to firm up a little (this will also prevent them from falling apart during deep-frying).

Meanwhile, toss the cabbage, apple, lemon juice and olive oil in a bowl.

Combine the goat's cheese and dill in a bowl. If the cheese is a little dry, add a few teaspoons of milk to loosen it to a spreadable consistency. Season to taste.

Pour enough canola or vegetable oil into a large heavy-based saucepan to come two-thirds of the way up the side. Heat over medium–high heat to 180°C or until a cube of bread dropped in the oil browns in 15 seconds. Working in batches of four, deep-fry the falafels, turning occasionally, for 2–3 minutes or until golden brown. Remove with a slotted spoon and drain on a large plate lined with paper towel.

Spread the flatbreads with the goat's cheese mixture and top with the cabbage and apple slaw, then the warm falafels. Sprinkle with extra mint leaves, then roll up and enjoy.

Happily Australian roast pumpkin & pumpkin seed falafels with green tahini sauce

MAKES: 14
PREP: 20 mins (plus 30 mins chilling)
COOKING: 1 hour 10 mins

280 g Kent pumpkin, unpeeled, deseeded and
   cut into 3 cm thick wedges
olive oil spray
sea salt and freshly ground black pepper
100 g (½ cup) pumpkin seeds
150 g (1 cup) cooked white quinoa
½ small red onion, roughly chopped
3 garlic cloves, crushed
½ cup coriander leaves
1 tablespoon cornflour
2 teaspoons ground cumin
canola or vegetable oil, for deep-frying

GREEN TAHINI SAUCE

1 bunch coriander, leaves picked (reserve
   a few leaves to serve)
1 bunch flat-leaf parsley, leaves picked
½ bunch mint, leaves picked
2 garlic cloves, crushed
2 teaspoons cumin seeds, toasted
1 teaspoon sea salt
185 g (¾ cup) tahini
2 large ice cubes
60 ml (¼ cup) freshly squeezed lemon juice

Preheat the oven to 200°C/180°C fan-forced. Line a baking tray with baking paper.

Place the pumpkin wedges on the prepared tray, spray with olive oil and season well with salt and pepper. Roast for 40 minutes. Sprinkle the pumpkin seeds around the pumpkin and roast for a further 15 minutes or until the pumpkin is tender and the pumpkin seeds are toasted. Set aside to cool slightly.

While the pumpkin cools, place the quinoa, onion, garlic, coriander, cornflour and cumin in a food processor and blitz until combined.

Spoon the pumpkin flesh away from the skin and add to the food processor, along with the pumpkin seeds. Blitz until well combined.

Roll heaped tablespoons of the pumpkin mixture into 14 balls and flatten slightly. Place on a tray lined with baking paper, then chill in the fridge for 30 minutes to firm up a little (this will also prevent them from falling apart during deep-frying).

Give the food processor a quick wash, then make your tahini sauce. Put all the ingredients and 80 ml (⅓ cup) of water in the food processor and blitz until smooth.

Pour enough canola or vegetable oil into a large heavy-based saucepan to come two-thirds of the way up the side. Heat over medium–high heat to 180°C or until a cube of bread dropped in the oil browns in 15 seconds. Working in batches of four or five, deep-fry the falafels, turning occasionally, for 2–3 minutes or until golden brown. Remove with a slotted spoon and drain on a large plate lined with paper towel.

Serve the falafels warm with the reserved coriander leaves scattered over the top and the green tahini sauce on the side.

Parsnip & date falafels for the Damascus road trip

MAKES: 28
PREP: 20 mins (plus 30 mins chilling)
COOKING: 45 mins

2 parsnips (about 300 g), peeled and roughly chopped
400 g can chickpeas, rinsed and drained
150 g Medjool dates, pitted and coarsely chopped
2 spring onions, white and green parts sliced
1 cup flat-leaf parsley leaves
50 g (⅓ cup) chickpea flour (besan)
30 g (¼ cup) almond flour
2 teaspoons cumin seeds, toasted
2 teaspoons smoked paprika
finely grated zest of 1 lemon
70 g (⅔ cup) flaked almonds, coarsely chopped
    (or use pine nuts)
sea salt and freshly ground black pepper
canola or vegetable oil, for deep-frying
cashew cheese loosened with a little water or
    Greek-style yoghurt, to serve

ZUCCHINI HERB SALAD
3 zucchini, sliced into 5 mm thick ribbons and chargrilled
½ small red onion, thinly shaved (ideally with a mandoline)
1 bunch flat-leaf parsley, leaves picked
1 bunch mint, leaves picked
finely grated zest and juice of ½ lemon
1 tablespoon extra-virgin olive oil
sumac, to serve (optional)

Cook the parsnip in a saucepan of boiling water for 10 minutes or until tender. Drain and set aside to cool.

Place the parsnip in a food processor, add the chickpeas, date, spring onion, parsley, flours, cumin, paprika and lemon zest and blitz until well combined. Spoon into a bowl. Add the flaked almonds and season with salt and pepper, then mix together well.

Roll heaped tablespoons of the parsnip mixture into 28 balls and flatten slightly. Place on a tray lined with baking paper, then chill in the fridge for 30 minutes to firm up a little (this will also prevent them from falling apart during deep-frying).

Meanwhile, get your zucchini herb salad ready. Toss the zucchini, onion, parsley and mint in a bowl. In a jug, whisk together the lemon zest and juice and olive oil.

Pour enough canola or vegetable oil into a large heavy-based saucepan to come two-thirds of the way up the side. Heat over medium–high heat to 180°C or until a cube of bread dropped in the oil browns in 15 seconds. Working in batches of four or five, deep-fry the falafels, turning occasionally, for 3–4 minutes or until golden brown. Remove with a slotted spoon and drain on a large plate lined with paper towel.

Now toss the dressing through the salad and sprinkle with sumac, if you like. Serve with the warm falafels and cashew cheese or yoghurt.

Old-school falafels with something different

MAKES: 22
PREP: 20 mins (plus overnight soaking and
        30 mins chilling)
COOKING: 35 mins

200 g (1 cup) dried chickpeas
1 small white onion, roughly chopped
¼ cup flat-leaf parsley leaves
¼ cup coriander leaves
3 garlic cloves, peeled
1 teaspoon sea salt
1 teaspoon bicarbonate of soda
55 g chickpea flour (besan), plus extra
    if needed
2 teaspoons ground cumin
⅛ teaspoon cayenne pepper
1 teaspoon ground coriander
1½ tablespoons freshly squeezed
    lemon juice
2 tablespoons sesame seeds
260 g (1 cup) thick natural yoghurt
2 tablespoons tahini
canola or vegetable oil, for deep-frying
50 g butter

Place the chickpeas in a bowl, cover with plenty of cold water
and leave to soak overnight. Drain.

Place the chickpeas, onion, parsley, coriander leaves, garlic, salt,
bicarbonate of soda, chickpea flour, cumin, cayenne pepper, ground
coriander and 1 tablespoon of the lemon juice in a food processor. Pulse
until finely chopped but not pureed. Transfer to a large bowl and stir in the
sesame seeds. Add a little extra chickpea flour if the mixture looks too wet
to form into falafel.

Line a tray with baking paper. Shape with a falafel mould or use wet hands to
roll heaped tablespoons of the chickpea mixture into 22 balls and flatten slightly
(you need to press firmly). Place on the prepared tray, then chill in the fridge for
30 minutes to firm up a little (this will also prevent them from falling apart during
deep-frying).

Combine the yoghurt, tahini and the remaining lemon juice in a bowl.

Pour enough canola or vegetable oil into a large heavy-based saucepan to come
two-thirds of the way up the side. Heat over medium–high heat to 180°C or until
a cube of bread dropped in the oil browns in 15 seconds. Working in batches of
four, deep-fry the falafels, turning occasionally, for 6 minutes or until golden brown.
Remove with a slotted spoon and drain on a large plate lined with paper towel.

Melt the butter in a large frying pan over medium heat, then cook, stirring
occasionally, for 3 minutes or until light golden. Remove from the heat and let
it cool for a couple of minutes.

Spread the yoghurt mixture on a plate and create a pool in the centre. Fill with
the burnt butter and serve with the warm falafels.

KFC – crispy fried carrot – Southern style

SERVES: 4 as a starter **PREP:** 15 mins (plus 10 mins chilling) **COOKING:** 20 mins

If the (honorary) colonel had been born in 1990 rather than 1890, would he have swapped his signature white suit for a colourful embroidered Guatemalan calico smock and linen pants to deliver us those secret herbs and spices around slabs of bitey carrot instead? I like to think so.

And it should be noted that in the right light, and wearing a black satin western string bow, I could easily double for Colonel Harland David Sanders.

300 g (2 cups) plain flour
100 g (⅔ cup) cornflour
2 tablespoons sweet paprika
2 teaspoons onion powder
2 teaspoons garlic powder
2 teaspoons ground cumin
large pinch of cayenne pepper
sea salt and freshly ground
   black pepper
125 ml (½ cup) buttermilk
1 egg
5 carrots, halved crossways, then cut
   lengthways into 1 cm thick slices
250 g (1 cup) whole-egg mayonnaise
1 tablespoon sriracha chilli sauce
vegetable oil, for deep-frying

Combine the flour, cornflour, paprika, onion powder, garlic powder, cumin and cayenne pepper in a large shallow dish. Season with salt and pepper.

Whisk together the buttermilk and egg in a shallow bowl.

Toss the carrot in the flour mixture to lightly coat, shaking off the excess, then dip in the buttermilk mixture. Dip into the flour mixture again to coat. Don't panic – your carrot will have clumps of mixture attached but they end up becoming the tasty little crispy bits. Place on a tray and chill in the fridge for 10 minutes to help the coating stick.

Meanwhile, spoon the mayonnaise into a bowl and swirl through the sriracha.

Pour enough vegetable oil into a large saucepan to come halfway up the side and heat over medium–high heat to 170°C or until a cube of bread dropped in the oil browns in 20 seconds. Working in batches of four or five so you don't overcrowd the pan, deep-fry the carrot for 3–4 minutes or until golden and crisp. Remove with a slotted spoon and drain on a tray lined with paper towel.

Season the crispy fried carrot with salt and serve with the sriracha mayo.

Leeky tots – aka new-age potato gems

SERVES: 4 **PREP:** 45 mins (plus overnight soaking and 30 mins chilling) **COOKING:** 35 mins

I luv me a potato gem and these are frankly one of the dirtiest, filthiest, vegetarian-ist things in this whole darn book. Eat them hot dipped into the smokey almond mayo, which isn't really a mayo, so you can at least feel virtuous about that.

900 g even-sized sebago potatoes, peeled and left whole

40 g butter

2 leeks, trimmed white part cut into 1 cm thick rounds, light green part finely chopped

40 g plain flour

40 g (½ cup) coarsely grated smoked cheddar, plus an extra 20 g finely grated

sea salt and freshly ground black pepper

canola or vegetable oil, for deep-frying

3 jalapeno chillies, deseeded and thinly sliced into coins

SMOKEY ALMOND MAYO

80 g (½ cup) smoked almonds, soaked in warm water overnight

1½ smoked garlic cloves, crushed (or use ½ garlic clove and ¼ teaspoon smoked paprika if you can't get smoked garlic)

large pinch of mustard powder, plus extra to taste

60 ml (¼ cup) grapeseed oil

1 tablespoon freshly squeezed lemon juice, plus extra to taste

sea salt and freshly ground black pepper

Cook the potatoes in a large saucepan of boiling salted water for 12–15 minutes or until you can insert a skewer into a potato but it still feels firm with a little resistance. Drain and set aside for 10 minutes to cool slightly.

Meanwhile, melt half the butter in a small saucepan over medium heat. Add the white part of the leek and cook, stirring, for 5 minutes or until softened. Transfer to a bowl and set aside to cool. Repeat with the remaining butter and light green part of the leek. Leave in the pan and set aside (you'll be using it in the mayo).

To make the mayo, drain the almonds and place in a high-powered blender. Add the reserved green part of the leek, the garlic, mustard powder, grapeseed oil and lemon juice and process until finely chopped. Add 60 ml (¼ cup) of warm water and blitz until smooth, adding a little extra water if you prefer a thinner consistency. Season well with salt and pepper and check the balance of the mustard and lemon juice, adding a little extra if necessary. Place in the fridge until you are ready to serve.

Coarsely grate the potato and place in a bowl (be warned: it'll be sticky). Add the flour, white part of the leek and the coarsely grated cheddar and season with salt and pepper. Use your hands to mix it together really well, so the flour is well blended.

Line a tray with baking paper. Roll level tablespoonfuls of the potato mixture into 2 cm thick gems, pressing firmly so they stick together. Place on the tray, then chill in the fridge for 30 minutes.

Pour enough canola or vegetable oil into a large saucepan to come halfway up the side and heat over medium–high heat to 180°C or until a cube of bread dropped in the oil browns in 15 seconds. Working in batches so you don't overcrowd the pan, deep-fry the potato gems for 2–3 minutes or until golden and crisp. Remove with a slotted spoon and drain on a tray lined with paper towel.

Add the jalapeno chilli to the oil and fry for 30 seconds or until crisp. Remove with a slotted spoon and drain on paper towel.

Transfer the gems to a serving dish and top with the chilli, finely grated smoked cheddar and a little salt. Check the mayo – it will have thickened in the fridge, so stir in a little more water if necessary to make it dunkable. Serve with the potato gems.

Mission stew

SERVES: 4 PREP: 15 mins COOKING: 1 hour 25 mins

Inspiration comes from many funny places. This dish is named after some friends called Mich and Stu. I once drunkenly ran their names together, then immediately had the idea for a dish to match because I love both stew and the Mission District of San Francisco. It's been an area of bars, restaurants and entertainment since the Gold Rush days but takes its name from the Mission Dolores, founded there in 1776 and dedicated to Saint Francis of Assisi by Spanish colonisers. In fact, California was part of Mexico until it was 'liberated' by Col Stephen Kearny during the Mexican–American War of 1846–8. It is still home to some great cheap Mexican joints.

HISTORY NERD FACT: The Mexican–American War was driven by President James K Polk's desire to redraw the border with Mexico. This land grab was not sanctioned by Congress. In fact, the House of Reps passed a vote to censure Polk for 'unnecessarily and unconstitutionally' starting the war with Mexico. In the eventual Treaty of Guadalupe Hidalgo, Mexico ceded 500 000 square miles of land to the US that became the states of New Mexico, Utah, Nevada, Arizona, Texas and much of western Colorado. Many of the famous generals in the imminent American Civil War became battle hardened on this campaign, although famous Union general Ulysses S Grant described this Mexican War as 'one of the most unjust ever waged by a stronger against a weaker nation'.

Interestingly, just like another President with a profound interest in the border with Mexico, Polk was a rank outsider in the 1844 presidential election but Bradbury'd the nomination when the front runners all failed to secure the required two-thirds of the votes for automatic nomination. But unlike Donald J Trump, Polk made an election promise to only serve one term and actually resigned when his term came to an end in 1849.

1 tablespoon olive oil
1 red onion, roughly chopped
1 red capsicum, roughly chopped
½ bunch coriander, leaves picked, stalks and roots cleaned and finely chopped
2 garlic cloves, crushed
2 teaspoons ground cumin
2 teaspoons ground coriander
½–1 teaspoon chilli powder
400 g can diced tomatoes
1 litre (4 cups) vegetable stock
500 g sweet potato, peeled and cut into 3 cm chunks
2 × 425 g cans black beans, rinsed and drained
420 g can corn kernels, drained
200 g green beans, trimmed and cut into 3 cm lengths
sea salt and freshly ground black pepper
1 avocado
1 tablespoon sour cream
sliced pickled jalapeno chilli and chargrilled or warmed tortillas, to serve

Heat the olive oil in a large saucepan over medium–high heat. Add the onion and capsicum and cook, stirring, for 5 minutes or until slightly softened. Add the chopped coriander, garlic, cumin, ground coriander and chilli powder and cook, stirring, for 1 minute or until aromatic. Add the tomatoes and 750 ml (3 cups) of the stock and bring to the boil. Stir in the sweet potato. Cover and simmer for 45 minutes or until the sweet potato is just tender.

Add the black beans and corn and simmer, uncovered, for 15 minutes or until the mixture has thickened slightly.

Remove 250 ml (1 cup) of the stew and set aside to cool slightly.

Stir the green beans into the remaining stew and season with salt and pepper. If you like your stew a little wetter add the remaining 250 ml (1 cup) of stock at this point. Simmer, uncovered, for a further 10 minutes or until the green beans are just cooked.

While the stew finishes cooking, mash the avocado and stir in the sour cream.

Blitz the reserved cup of stew in a blender until smooth (or use a stick blender). Stir the pureed mixture into the stew.

Divide the stew among serving bowls and top with a dollop of the avocado cream to swirl through. Scatter over the coriander leaves and pickled jalapeno and serve with tortillas.

Tuscan bean stew with balsamic

SERVES: 4 PREP: 25 mins COOKING: 50 mins

Tuscans are so famous for their love of beans that their nickname is the 'mangiafagioli' (or bean eaters), but what can lift these creamy beany bowls of joy to another level is the addition of a few choice drops of balsamic. This condiment had drifted over the northern border from Emilia-Romagna to a basic little cafe in Greve in Chianti when I first tried it, and it made me ridiculously excited. Adding a little of this sweet but acidic black vinegar really punched up the flavours, making it even higher on the fuzzy warmth scale.

Here we've cheated by cooking down regular balsamic to a syrup, but if you can find an expensive bottle of thicker aged balsamic (something with over a decade of age), please spend the dollars and use that.

1 tablespoon olive oil
2 onions, roughly chopped
2 celery stalks, roughly chopped
1 carrot, roughly chopped
5 garlic cloves, crushed
400 g can cannellini or haricot beans, rinsed and drained
500 ml (2 cups) vegetable stock
400 g can diced tomatoes
2 fresh or dried bay leaves
2 rosemary sprigs
400 g can borlotti beans, rinsed and drained
400 g can butter beans, rinsed and drained
sea salt and freshly ground black pepper
2 tablespoons balsamic vinegar
2 tablespoons apple cider vinegar
1 tablespoon raw sugar

TUSCAN CHEESE TOASTS
1 tablespoon olive oil
½ bunch Tuscan cabbage or kale, leaves stripped and thickly shredded
2 tablespoons coarsely chopped flat-leaf parsley
sea salt and freshly ground black pepper
small crusty breadstick
olive oil spray
2 garlic cloves, peeled
100 g (1 cup) coarsely grated mozzarella

Heat the olive oil in a flameproof casserole dish over medium heat. Add the onion, celery and carrot and cook, stirring, for 5 minutes or until softened. Add the garlic and cook, stirring, for 30 seconds or until aromatic.

Add the cannellini or haricot beans, stock, tomatoes, bay leaves and rosemary to the dish. Bring to a simmer, then cover and cook gently for 10 minutes. Remove the lid and simmer for a further 20 minutes or until the vegetables are just tender.

Add the borlotti and butter beans to the dish and simmer for 5 minutes or until heated through. Season with salt and pepper, then set aside for 10 minutes to cool slightly. Place 250 ml (1 cup) in a jug and blend with a stick blender until smooth. Stir back into the stew and place over medium heat. Cook, stirring, for 5–8 minutes or until warmed through and thickened.

While your stew simmers away, make a balsamic syrup by simmering the balsamic vinegar, cider vinegar and raw sugar in a small frying pan over medium heat for 3 minutes or until thick and syrupy.

About 15 minutes before your stew is ready, make your cheese toasts. Preheat the grill on high. Heat the olive oil in a frying pan over medium heat, add the cabbage or kale and cook, stirring, for 3 minutes or just until the cabbage starts to wilt. Stir in the parsley and season with salt and pepper.

Slice the bread in half lengthways and then crossways into quarters. Place the bread slices on a baking tray and spray with olive oil. Grill for 2 minutes or until lightly toasted on both sides. Rub the cut side of each slice with the garlic cloves. Top with the cabbage or kale and sprinkle with the mozzarella. Grill for 5–8 minutes or until the cheese is melted and golden. Season with salt.

Dot the balsamic reduction over the stew like a beany Dalmatian and serve with the Tuscan toasts on the side.

MEATY ADDITION: Replace the butter beans with 4 sliced Pan-fried Italian pork sausages (see page 270).

Tandoori carrot korma

SERVES: 4 **PREP:** 20 mins **COOKING:** 2 hours

Roast carrots in a hot oven until they are soft and a little burnt in places and you have a vegetable that can sit happily in any of your favourite Indian curries, whether that's a butter chicken sauce or tikka masala sauce. Better still is to use a creamy nut-driven sauce made famous by India's Mughal rulers back when their empire was the richest in the world. I like the way the burnt edges on the carrots look a bit like tandoori chook. But then I'm still a little bit in love with meat.

1.5 kg carrots, cut into 3 cm long
   barrels
60 ml (¼ cup) peanut or vegetable oil
3 red onions, halved and thinly sliced
3 blades of mace (no mace? Use star
   anise instead)
3 garlic cloves, crushed
3 cm knob of ginger, peeled and
   finely grated
2 teaspoons brown sugar, plus extra
   to taste
1 teaspoon ground coriander
½ teaspoon ground cumin
2 teaspoons apple cider vinegar
1½ teaspoons soy sauce or tamari
1 teaspoon sea salt
400 g can diced tomatoes
freshly squeezed lemon juice, to taste
125 g raw cashews, ground in
   a food processor to a fine meal
2 green cardamom pods, crushed
1 teaspoon curry powder
150 ml vegetable stock (optional)

TO SERVE
steamed brown rice
coriander leaves
grated raw cashews

Preheat the oven to 180°C/160°C fan-forced.

Place the carrot on a baking tray and drizzle with 2 tablespoons of the peanut or vegetable oil. Toss until well coated, then roast for 1½ hours or until soft. Transfer half the carrot to a plate and set aside.

Increase the oven temperature to 200°C/180°C fan-forced. Return the remaining carrot to the oven and roast for a further 20 minutes or until golden and even a little burnt in places. Turn off the oven and leave the carrot inside until they have cooled slightly but are still warm. This will dry them out a little more and make them almost chewy. Yum!

Meanwhile, heat the remaining oil in a large frying pan over low heat. Add the onion and mace and cook very slowly, stirring occasionally but more frequently towards the end, for 30–40 minutes or until the onion is nicely browned and caramelised.

Add the garlic and ginger to the onion and cook, stirring, for 4 minutes or until starting to caramelise. Add the sugar, ground coriander and cumin and cook, stirring, for 2 minutes, then add the vinegar, soy sauce or tamari and salt and cook, stirring, for 1–2 minutes or until reduced and you have deglazed the pan. Add the tomatoes and season with salt, sugar and a little lemon juice to taste. Cook, stirring, for 15 minutes or until thick and pulpy. Remove the mace and stir in the cashew meal, then cook for 5 minutes or until heated through. Remove from the heat and set aside for 5 minutes to cool slightly.

Transfer the tomato mixture to a food processor and blitz, scraping down the side occasionally, until smooth. Return the tomato mixture to the pan and stir in the cardamom pods and curry powder. Then add all the carrot to the pan (for a thinner curry add 150 ml of stock at this point). Return to medium heat and stir for 2–3 minutes or until heated through.

Serve the carrot korma on brown rice with coriander leaves and grated cashews sprinkled over the top.

 TIP: Don't waste the coriander stalks. Finely chop the stalks of ½ bunch of coriander and stir through the steamed brown rice.

Sri Lankan beetroot & cashew curry with cauliflower rice

SERVES: 6 **PREP:** 20 mins **COOKING:** 1 hour 15 mins

Sri Lanka is a magical place, not least because they make a whole curry built around the cashew nut. This version adds the sweet nobility of roast beetroot to the party. What I especially love is the way, in Sri Lanka, they temper their curries with a little coconut milk and a few curry leaves at the end of cooking. It just seems to lift the whole dish. Because coconut underpins this curry, cauliflower rice is the perfect accompaniment. Coconut and cauliflower love each other so much.

1 kg beetroot bulbs, trimmed
1 tablespoon ground coriander
2 teaspoons ground cumin
1 teaspoon ground cardamom
1 tablespoon coconut oil
4 dried red chillies, tops removed and seeds tapped out
2 tablespoons almond butter (see TIPS)
330 ml coconut milk
250 ml (1 cup) vegetable stock
300 g (2 cups) raw cashews
60 ml (¼ cup) vegetable oil
about 30 curry leaves
coconut cream, to serve

CAULIFLOWER RICE
1 small head cauliflower (or half a large one), base trimmed, leaves removed
150 g (1 cup) sunflower seeds
55 g (1 cup) flaked coconut, toasted
1 tablespoon coconut oil
1 teaspoon sea salt

Preheat the oven to 200°C/180°C fan-forced.

Wrap each beetroot bulb in foil and place in a roasting tin. Roast for 1 hour or until tender when pierced with a skewer. Leave to cool slightly, then remove the foil. Put on some kitchen gloves to stop your hands turning pink and peel the beetroot. Cut the larger bulbs into quarters and leave any smaller ones whole.

Meanwhile, place the ground coriander, cumin and cardamom in a small frying pan over medium heat and toast for 1–2 minutes or until aromatic. Add the coconut oil and chillies and cook until the coconut oil has melted. Add the almond butter, coconut milk and stock and bring to a simmer. Simmer for 15 minutes or until reduced by half.

While this is happening, start your cauliflower rice. Cut the florets off the cauliflower and roughly chop the stem. Place the stem and florets in a food processor and use the pulse button to blitz into crumbs.

Heat your largest frying pan over medium heat until hot. Add the cauliflower and cook, tossing, for 5 minutes to slowly toast and dry out. When the steam has stopped rising off the cauliflower, add the sunflower seeds, flaked coconut and coconut oil. Cook, tossing, for 30 minutes or until everything has tanned up nicely. Season with salt.

Add the beetroot to the curry sauce and cook, stirring, for 3 minutes. Stir in the cashews and cook, stirring, for another 5 minutes or until the cashews have softened very slightly. Don't stir again.

Just before serving, heat the vegetable oil in a small saucepan over medium–low heat, add the curry leaves and cook until crisp but not brown. Remove with a slotted spoon and drain on paper towel.

Divide the curry among serving bowls, swirl in the coconut cream and top with the fried curry leaves. Serve with the cauliflower rice.

 TIPS: Make your own almond butter by blending 160 g (1 cup) of almonds, 125 ml (½ cup) of grapeseed oil, 1 teaspoon of ground cumin and a good pinch of salt.

If you don't want to make cauliflower rice, brown rice works really well, too.

MEATY ADDITION: There is no animal protein that can improve this curry.

Tofu kung pao

SERVES: 4 **PREP:** 15 mins **COOKING:** 30 mins

Biff, bang, pow! I always thought this dish was named after those onomatopoeic comic book frames in Marvel and DC Comics when some epic confrontation between good and evil was taking place with flying fists and whirling hammers, such is the in-yer-face impact of the flavours of this stir-fry. Not so. The truth is that it was named for a leading Sichuan bureaucrat of the late 19th century whose title was Gongbao or 'palace guardian'.

I suppose 'Palace Guardian Golden Tofu' does have a superhero ring all of its own. Ka-pow!

125 ml (½ cup) vegetable stock
80 ml (⅓ cup) light soy sauce
2 tablespoons Shaoxing rice wine
2 tablespoons black vinegar
2 teaspoons caster sugar
2 teaspoons cornflour
125 ml (½ cup) peanut oil
80 g (½ cup) raw peanuts
375 g firm tofu, cut into 2 cm cubes
8 spring onions
1 red capsicum, cut into strips
1 green capsicum, cut into strips
6 dried red chillies, tops removed
and seeds tapped out
4 cm knob of ginger, peeled and
finely grated
2 garlic cloves, crushed
1 teaspoon Sichuan peppercorns,
crushed using a mortar and pestle
steamed brown rice, to serve

Combine the stock, soy sauce, Shaoxing rice wine, vinegar, sugar and cornflour in a small bowl.

Heat the peanut oil in a wok or large frying pan over medium–high heat, add the peanuts and cook for 2 minutes or until lightly golden. Remove with a slotted spoon and drain on a tray lined with paper towel.

Reheat the oil in the wok or pan over high heat until just smoking. Add half the tofu and stir-fry for 5–8 minutes or until golden. Transfer to the tray. Repeat with the remaining tofu. Set the oil aside to cool slightly, then drain, leaving 1 tablespoon of the oil in the wok.

Meanwhile, trim the spring onions and cut the white parts of six of them into 3–4 cm lengths. Thinly slice the remaining two spring onions on the diagonal.

Heat the reserved oil in the wok over high heat. Add the red and green capsicum and dried chillies and stir-fry for 3–4 minutes or until slightly charred and starting to soften. Add the spring onion lengths, ginger, garlic and Sichuan pepper and stir-fry for 2 minutes or until aromatic.

Add the soy sauce mixture to the wok or pan and stir-fry for 2–3 minutes or until the sauce boils and thickens. Return the tofu and peanuts and stir-fry until well coated and heated through. Sprinkle with the thinly sliced spring onion and serve with steamed rice.

 TIP: Successful wok cookery revolves around harnessing 'the breath of the wok' (or wok hei), the intense heat that can be generated to quickly sear and catch ingredients. Don't be afraid of getting the wok really hot when cooking this dish – you want to bring some smokiness – but add just a little oil to transfer this heat to your ingredients without deep-frying them.

MEATY ADDITION: Reduce the tofu to 200 g and add 2 sliced Barbecued or chargrilled beef steaks (see page 266) when you return the tofu and peanuts to the pan.

The name-dropper's roasted couscous royale

SERVES: 4 PREP: 30 mins COOKING: 50 mins

I've eaten roast quail with Tony Bourdain while discussing the best place to lose a body along the New Jersey turnpike, and risotto with Antonio Carluccio and Michele Roux while arguing about whether Italian or French food was greater. I've shared the table with the great US chef Dan Barber at Noma, and Andoni Aduriz at Vue de Monde, and come away from both encounters lightbulb-lit with ideas. But the first of all these memorable meals with clunk, clunk, clunk name-dropping potential was dinner with rock and roll great Sleepy LaBeef.

Known as the human jukebox for the prodigious and comprehensive songbook of rockabilly and rock and roll tunes he carried in his head, this great bear of a man and I shared a couscous royale and discussed the similarity of this Moroccan dish with some of the classics from the Louisiana bayous where he recorded appearances on the same famous Louisiana Hayride TV, and radio show that gave Elvis his first break.

Like my own broken record, I can't help repeating this story every time I cook this recipe. Sorry if you've heard it before, but I can remember every moment of that night with a crystal clarity that I wish I could also turn to much more momentously important things than couscous and stewed vegetables – delicious though they are.

½ butternut pumpkin (about 650 g), peeled and deseeded, cut into 3 cm pieces
2 carrots, thickly sliced
2 zucchini, thickly sliced
60 ml (¼ cup) extra-virgin olive oil
sea salt and freshly ground black pepper
1 onion, cut into wedges
3 garlic cloves, crushed
1 tablespoon tomato paste
2 teaspoons ras al hanout (see TIP)
400 g can crushed tomatoes
large pinch of saffron threads
250 ml (1 cup) vegetable stock
400 g can chickpeas, rinsed and drained
110 g pitted green olives
380 g (2 cups) couscous
500 ml (2 cups) boiling water
40 g butter
25 g (¼ cup) flaked almonds, toasted
coriander leaves, to serve
harissa swirled through thick natural yoghurt, to serve

Preheat the oven to 200°C/180°C fan-forced. Line a large baking tray with baking paper.

Spread out the pumpkin, carrot and zucchini on the prepared tray and drizzle with 2 tablespoons of the olive oil. Season well. Roast, turning halfway through, for 50 minutes or until tender and golden.

Meanwhile, heat the remaining oil in a large heavy-based saucepan or tagine over medium heat, add the onion and cook, stirring occasionally, for 5 minutes or until slightly softened. Add the garlic and cook, stirring, for 30 seconds or until aromatic. Add the tomato paste and ras al hanout and cook, tossing, for 2 minutes or until aromatic and the onion is well coated. Add the tomatoes, saffron and stock and bring to a gentle simmer. Simmer, stirring occasionally, for 15–20 minutes or until the mixture has thickened slightly.

Add the chickpeas and olives to the tomato mixture and cook, stirring, for 2–3 minutes or until heated through. Season well.

While your tagine simmers away, place the couscous in a heatproof bowl. Cover with the boiling water and set aside for 5 minutes or until the liquid has been absorbed. Place the butter on top and stir it in as you fluff up the grains with a fork.

Place the couscous on a large serving platter and top with half the roast vegetables and half the tomato mixture. Repeat with the remaining vegetables and tomato mixture, then sprinkle with the almonds and coriander. Serve with the harissa yoghurt.

 TIP: If you'd like to make your own ras al hanout, here's how it's done. Use a spice grinder or mortar and pestle to grind 1 teaspoon each of ground ginger, ground cinnamon, cumin seeds and coriander seeds with ¼ teaspoon each of ground nutmeg, cardamom seeds, hot paprika, turmeric and ground allspice, 4 whole cloves, ½ teaspoon black peppercorns and a good pinch of sea salt.

MEATY ADDITION: Add 4 chopped Barbecued or chargrilled chicken thigh fillets (see page 261) with the chickpeas to serve 6.

Dal makhani

SERVES: 4–6 **PREP:** 15 mins (plus overnight soaking) **COOKING:** 1 hour 10 mins

From the same guys who gave you the very first butter chicken comes this prince of dals: rich, deep and creamy dal makhani or 'butter dal'.

It's amazing that one chef and one restaurant in Delhi lay claim to creating so many of the dishes that are now seen as Indian signatures around the world, such as butter chicken, Seekh kebab, barrah kebab and this vegetarian lentil and kidney bean dish.

So, all hail to chef Kundan Lal Jaggi, his partners Kundan Lal Gujral and Thakur Das Mago, and the pioneering kitchens of the Moti Mahal in Delhi. We revere you as we revere Escoffier, Careme, Bocuse, Adria and Redzepi.

200 g (1 cup) dried black lentils
100 g (½ cup) dried red kidney beans
sea salt and freshly ground
   black pepper
2 tablespoons vegetable oil
1 white onion, finely chopped
3 cm knob of ginger, peeled and sliced
3 garlic cloves, peeled
2 long green chillies, deseeded and
   finely chopped
2 teaspoons cumin seeds
1 tablespoon ground coriander
½–1 teaspoon chilli powder
   (depending on how hot you like it)
400 g tomato puree
5 whole cloves
4 green cardamom pods, crushed
4 fresh or dried bay leaves
1 cinnamon stick
80 g butter, cubed, plus extra
   melted butter for drizzling
60 ml (¼ cup) pouring cream
coriander leaves, to serve

Place the lentils and kidney beans in a large bowl. Cover with cold water and soak overnight.

Drain the lentils and beans and place in a large saucepan or stockpot. Cover with plenty of cold water and season with salt. Bring to the boil over high heat, then reduce the heat to medium–low and simmer for 25–30 minutes or until just tender. Drain, reserving 250 ml (1 cup) of the cooking liquid.

Heat the oil in a large saucepan over medium heat, add the onion and cook, stirring, for 5–8 minutes or until very soft. Add the ginger, garlic, green chilli and cumin seeds and cook for 2 minutes or until aromatic. Add the ground coriander and chilli powder and stir until combined.

Add the tomato puree, cloves, cardamom pods, bay leaves, cinnamon stick and reserved cooking liquid to the pan. Bring to a gentle simmer over low heat. Add the lentils and beans and simmer for 25 minutes or until thick and creamy. Stir in the butter and simmer for a further 5 minutes or until well combined.

Spoon into serving bowls and finish with a swirl of cream and melted butter. Top with coriander leaves and serve.

Thai green curry with eggplant & green beans

SERVES: 4 **PREP:** 15 mins **COOKING:** 30 mins

Chicken? Who needs chicken?

1 tablespoon coconut oil
1 large onion, cut into wedges
¼ cup homemade green curry paste (see below) or 2 tablespoons store-bought paste
400 ml can coconut milk
2 kaffir lime leaves
250 ml (1 cup) vegetable stock
3 Lebanese eggplants, thickly sliced diagonally
230 g can sliced bamboo shoots, drained and cut into small matchsticks
150 g green beans, trimmed and halved diagonally
1 tablespoon Vegan 'fish' sauce (see page 44) or regular fish sauce if you are okay with it
2 teaspoons coarsely grated palm sugar or caster sugar
juice of ½ lime
steamed jasmine rice, to serve

GREEN CURRY PASTE

2 coriander sprigs, leaves picked, stalks and roots cleaned and coarsely chopped
6 long green chillies, deseeded and roughly chopped
2 Thai green chillies, finely chopped
4 Asian shallots, cut into chunks
4 garlic cloves, chopped
2 kaffir lime leaves, shredded
2 Thai basil sprigs (save the leaves to serve)
2 lemongrass stalks, white part only, finely chopped
2 cm knob of galangal, peeled and finely chopped
1 tablespoon coriander seeds, toasted
2 teaspoons white peppercorns

To make the curry paste, place all the ingredients in a blender and blitz to a paste. Add a few tablespoons of water to help loosen it a little but it's fine if it's a bit fibrous and chunky. (You could be very old school and do this in a mortar and pestle but that can be quite a laborious process.)

Heat the coconut oil in a wok or large frying pan over high heat, add the onion and stir-fry for 2–3 minutes or until softened slightly. Add the curry paste and stir-fry for 1 minute or until aromatic.

Add the coconut milk and kaffir lime leaves to the wok or pan and bring to the boil. Reduce the heat and simmer for 10 minutes or until the oil comes to the surface. Add the stock and bring to the boil. Add the eggplant, then reduce the heat and simmer for 10 minutes or until tender.

Add the bamboo shoot, beans, fish sauce, sugar and lime juice to the curry and cook for 3–4 minutes or until the beans are tender crisp.

Serve the curry with jasmine rice and topped with the reserved Thai basil leaves.

MEATY ADDITION: Add peeled and deveined raw prawns or sliced chicken breast to the curry with the green beans.

Butter 'chicken' curry with mushrooms

SERVES: 4 **PREP:** 20 mins **COOKING:** 40 mins

As a cook, the most flattering thing that can ever happen is when someone tells you their family loves one of your recipes. Even better if they make that recipe every week. However, the pinnacle is when that person is one of your personal food heroes. So it is with the creamy sauce of this Indian butter chicken recipe which has popped up meatily in previous cookbooks of mine. It turns out to be just as delicious as a vego version slathered over roast pumpkin, roast celeriac or even mushrooms, as they are so gainfully employed here in this recipe.

Add a drop of liquid smoke to the curry to echo the market heritage of this dish.

1 kg very ripe tomatoes, roughly chopped

1 large red onion, roughly chopped

60 g butter

550 g portobello mushrooms, cut into 1 cm thick slices

1 tablespoon olive oil

5 green cardamom pods, crushed

3 large garlic cloves, crushed

3 cm knob of ginger, peeled and finely grated (you need about 2 tablespoons)

1 teaspoon ground coriander

½ teaspoon ground mace

2 tablespoons tomato paste

¼ teaspoon chilli powder

90 g (⅓ cup) thick natural yoghurt

1 tablespoon caster sugar

1 teaspoon garam masala

sea salt

100 ml pouring cream

stems from ¼ bunch coriander, finely chopped, to serve

1 green chilli, deseeded and finely chopped, to serve

steamed rice, to serve

Place the tomato and onion in a large frying pan over medium heat and bring to a simmer. Cook, stirring occasionally, for 20 minutes or until the tomato is thick and the liquid has reduced. Transfer the mixture to a jug and use a stick blender to blitz until smooth. In batches, strain through a fine sieve into a jug, pressing with the back of a spoon or ladle to push the mixture through. Discard what's left in the sieve.

While your tomato is cooking, melt 20 g of the butter in a separate large frying pan over medium–high heat. Add one-third of the mushroom and cook for 3–5 minutes each side or until golden. Transfer to a bowl. Repeat in two more batches with the remaining butter and mushroom.

Wipe out the frying pan, then add the olive oil and heat over medium–high heat. Add the cardamom pods, garlic, ginger, ground coriander and mace and cook for 1–2 minutes or until aromatic.

Add the tomato mixture, tomato paste and chilli powder to the spices and stir to combine. Remove from the heat and stir in the yoghurt and sugar. Return to low heat and cook very gently (so you don't curdle the yoghurt), stirring frequently, for about 10 minutes or until the sauce has thickened slightly.

Reserve about eight slices of mushroom, then add the remaining mushroom to the sauce, along with the garam masala and salt to taste. Cook, stirring, for 5 minutes or until heated through. Taste and adjust the seasoning if necessary. Divide among shallow bowls, top with the reserved mushroom slices and swirl in the cream. Scatter the chopped coriander and chilli over the top and serve with steamed rice.

MEATY ADDITION: Reduce the mushrooms to 250 g and add 4 chopped Barbecued or chargrilled chicken thigh fillets (see page 261) to the sauce.

Miso–almond butter corn cake stack

SERVES: 4 **PREP:** 30 mins **COOKING:** 35 mins

Whether for breakfast, brunch or a light supper, these crispy fritters are further proof that corn has a deep and abiding love affair with miso and butter.

They are also the result of one of my regular collaborations with **delicious.** *magazine food guru Phoebe Rose Wood for my column in that wonderful magazine. These collabs are one of the great pleasures of my month and, with her inestimable help, they always result in something waaaaaaaay more delicious than if I had just been working on the ideas on my own.*

I cite exhibit A, these fritters!

They also appeared (as a non-vego version) on the cover of last February's **delicious.**, *meaning that they are now much more famous than me and will be demanding their own make-up trailer and entourage next time they come round to my house for brunch. I blame Phoebe for that, too …*

4 eggs, 2 separated
4 corn cobs, husks and silks discarded,
  kernels removed (or 500 g frozen
  corn, thawed)
125 g plain flour
1 teaspoon baking powder
1 teaspoon ground cumin
4 spring onions, white parts thinly
  sliced, green parts shredded
1 bunch coriander, leaves picked,
  stalks thinly sliced
sea salt and freshly ground
  black pepper
sunflower oil, for shallow-frying
2 avocados, sliced or mashed
lime wedges and creme fraiche,
  to serve (optional)

MISO–ALMOND BUTTER

1 tablespoon caster sugar
1 tablespoon rice wine vinegar
100 g blanched almonds, toasted
80 g (¼ cup) white miso paste
100 g unsalted butter, at room
  temperature

CHILLI CARAMEL

150 g palm sugar, finely grated
1 teaspoon smoked paprika
6 long red chillies, deseeded and thinly
  sliced (use more if you love heat!)
2 teaspoons rice wine vinegar

To make the miso–almond butter, place the sugar and vinegar in a saucepan over medium heat and cook, stirring, for 1–2 minutes or until the sugar has dissolved. Set aside to cool slightly, then transfer to a blender. Add the almonds, miso and butter and blitz until well combined. Transfer to a bowl and set aside.

To make the chilli caramel, place the palm sugar and 100 ml of water in a small saucepan and bring to the boil over high heat. Reduce the heat to low and simmer, without stirring, for 5 minutes or until reduced slightly. Stir in the paprika, chilli and vinegar and cook, stirring occasionally, for 6–8 minutes or until thickened slightly. Remove from the heat.

Take two bowls. Place two egg whites in one and set aside. Put the two egg yolks and the whole eggs in the other bowl and lightly beat with a fork.

Combine the corn kernels, flour, baking powder, cumin, white spring onion, coriander stalk, 2 teaspoons of salt and a pinch of pepper in a bowl. Add the beaten egg and mix well.

Use a balloon whisk to whisk the two egg whites just to soft peaks, then gently fold through the corn mixture.

Pour enough sunflower oil into a non-stick frying pan to come 1 cm up the side and heat over medium heat. Working in batches, add ⅓ cup of batter for each corn cake to the pan and let it spread slightly, then cook for 3 minutes each side or until golden and cooked through.

Serve the fritters as a stack sandwiched with the avocado and miso–almond butter. Drizzle over the chilli caramel and top with the coriander leaves and spring onion greens.

Yes, lime wedges and creme fraiche can also be added!

Chilli san carne with parsnip chips

SERVES: 4 PREP: 20 mins COOKING: 30 mins

Chilli con carne originated in San Antonio, sold by street vendor 'Chilli Queens' and in disreputable slum chilli parlours inspired by the cooking of Canary Island settlers who arrived in 1731 and were notoriously heavy-handed with cumin. So, isn't it logical to make San Antonio's famous dish 'san carne' or without meat?

1 tablespoon olive oil
1 large red capsicum, roughly chopped
1 red onion, roughly chopped
300 g cauliflower, cut into small florets
2 garlic cloves, crushed
2 tablespoons chopped chipotle chilli in adobe sauce
2 teaspoons ground cumin
1 teaspoon dried oregano
2–3 jalapeno chillies, deseeded and finely chopped
1 bunch coriander, leaves picked, stalks and roots cleaned and finely chopped
2 × 400 g cans diced tomatoes
250 ml (1 cup) vegetable stock
sea salt and freshly ground black pepper
400 g can kidney beans, rinsed and drained
80 g (2 cups) shredded silverbeet leaves
sour cream (or use Vegan sour cream; see page 26) or avocado mashed with lime juice, to serve

CRISPY PARSNIP CHIPS
1 tablespoon sea salt
1 teaspoon chilli flakes, plus extra to serve (optional)
½ teaspoon ground cumin
vegetable oil, for deep-frying
4 parsnips, peeled, then peeled into ribbons

Heat the olive oil in a large saucepan over medium–high heat, add the capsicum, onion and cauliflower and cook, stirring, for 5 minutes or until softened. Add the garlic, chipotle chilli, cumin, oregano, jalapeno and coriander stalk and root and cook, stirring, for 1 minute or until aromatic. Add the tomatoes and stock and bring to the boil. Reduce the heat to medium and simmer, covered, for 15 minutes or until the cauliflower is tender and the sauce has thickened slightly. Season with salt and pepper.

Remove 1 cup of the chilli mixture and set aside to cool.

Meanwhile, make the parsnip chips. Combine the salt, chilli and cumin in a bowl. Pour enough vegetable oil into a large saucepan to come 5 cm up the side and heat over medium–high heat to 170°C or until a cube of bread dropped in the oil browns in 20 seconds. Working in batches so you don't overcrowd the pan, deep-fry the parsnip for 1 minute or until golden and crisp. Remove with a slotted spoon and drain on a tray lined with paper towel. While still hot, sprinkle with the chilli salt mixture.

Place the cooled cup of chilli mixture in a blender and blitz until smooth. Return to the main chilli mixture, along with the kidney beans and silverbeet, and stir until heated through and the silverbeet has wilted.

Top with the coriander leaves and your choice of sour cream or avocado (or both!). Sprinkle a few chilli flakes over the top (if using) and serve with the parsnip chips and remaining chilli salt for sprinkling, if desired.

MEATY ADDITION: Replace the cauliflower with 300 g Pan-fried beef mince (see page 266).

Easy African peanut & sweet potato stew

SERVES: 4 PREP: 15 mins COOKING: 40 mins

In 2018, MasterChef contestant Chloe Carroll was way ahead of the curve when she made us the most delicious version of this Ghanaian classic with chicken. Soon after, US trend-spotters were predicting that this African stew would be the big dish of 2019. I reckon they went a little too early and that 2020 will be the beginning of the decade we start embracing African dishes like West African suya skewers, Mozambique prego rolls, and Botswanan seswaa (pounded beef) with pap and slow-cooked Sengalese poulet yassa (where the chicken is flavoured with the unlikely combination of lemon, chilli, ginger and Dijon mustard).

If you want to be further on trend, serve this stew with jollof rice. This is long-grain rice fried with tomato paste, onion, chilli, red capsicum and spices, such as nutmeg and ginger. It is claimed by many countries in West Africa but most vocally Nigeria and Ghana.

2 tablespoons peanut oil
1 large onion, finely chopped
3 garlic cloves, crushed
3 cm knob of ginger, peeled and finely grated
2 fresh or dried bay leaves
1 teaspoon ground cumin
1 teaspoon ground coriander
½–1 teaspoon chilli flakes
2 tablespoons tomato paste
400 g can diced tomatoes
375 ml (1½ cups) vegetable stock
130 g (½ cup) crunchy peanut butter
500 g sweet potato, peeled and cut into 3 cm chunks
400 g can chickpeas, rinsed and drained
80 g baby spinach leaves
steamed white rice, to serve
chopped unsalted peanuts, to serve

Heat the peanut oil in a large saucepan over medium heat, add the onion and cook, stirring, for 5 minutes or until softened. Stir in the garlic, ginger, bay leaves, cumin, ground coriander and chilli flakes and cook, stirring, for 30 seconds or until aromatic. Add the tomato paste and cook, stirring, for 2 minutes.

Add the tomatoes, stock and peanut butter to the pan and stir until the mixture comes to the boil. Reduce the heat to medium–low and add the sweet potato, then cover and cook, stirring occasionally, for 10 minutes.

Stir the chickpeas into the stew and cook for 15 minutes or until the sweet potato is tender. Add the spinach and cook for 1–2 minutes or until wilted.

Serve with steamed rice and a sprinkling of peanuts.

MEATY ADDITION: Reduce the sweet potato to 300 g and replace with 4 quartered chicken thigh fillets.

Andhra golden potato curry

SERVES: 4–6 **PREP:** 30 mins **COOKING:** 25 mins

I discovered this super-intense curry sauce on a trip to Hyderabad – one of my favourite cities in the world. It's quick and easy to make and goes equally well with hard-boiled eggs fried with turmeric or with yesterday's leftover roast potatoes. Serve with your favourite flatbread, roti or paratha, or it's great with rice, too. One of the key secrets here is caramelising the ginger and garlic properly, plus the use of curry leaves and long green chillies as so much more than a garnish. They add a wonderful herbaceous freshness to the rich, sour curry base.

160 ml sunflower oil

2 tablespoons yellow mustard seeds

¼ cup loosely packed curry leaves, plus 4 extra sprigs to serve

4 red onions, coarsely grated and drained

10 garlic cloves, finely grated

10 cm knob of ginger, peeled and finely grated

2 teaspoons ground coriander

1 teaspoon cumin seeds

1¼ tablespoons ground turmeric

2 tablespoons tomato paste

2 tablespoons tamarind puree

2 teaspoons caster sugar

½ teaspoon sea salt

2 teaspoons chilli powder, ideally Kashmiri

1 teaspoon sweet paprika

500 g cooked potatoes (yesterday's roast spuds or waxy and pre-boiled)

3 long green chillies, halved lengthways, deseeded if you want to cut the heat

coriander leaves, to serve

warm flatbreads or steamed brown rice, to serve (optional)

Heat 1½ tablespoons of the sunflower oil in a large deep frying pan over medium–high heat, add the mustard seeds and cook, stirring occasionally, for 1–2 minutes or until the seeds pop. Add the curry leaves and cook, stirring, for 1–2 minutes or until the leaves turn bright green.

Add the onion to the pan and cook, stirring occasionally, for 6 minutes or until softened. Scrape the onion mixture to the side of the pan. Add 1 tablespoon of the remaining oil and the garlic and ginger to the other side of the pan and cook for 3 minutes or until lightly caramelised.

Stir the onion and the ginger and garlic mixture together. Add the ground coriander, cumin seeds and 3 teaspoons of the turmeric and cook, stirring frequently, for 3 minutes to develop the flavour. Stir through the tomato paste, tamarind, sugar, salt and 250 ml (1 cup) of water. Keep warm over low heat, stirring occasionally. Add a splash more water if it's drying out too much.

Now mix the chilli powder, paprika, remaining turmeric and 1½ tablespoons of the remaining oil in a large frying pan over medium–high heat. Add the potatoes and cook, stirring occasionally, until golden, warmed through and a little crusty. Nestle the potatoes into the curry and cover to keep warm.

Wipe out the frying pan that had the potatoes in it and heat the remaining oil over high heat. Add the chillies and cook, stirring occasionally, for 4 minutes or until blistered on one side. Add the extra sprigs of curry leaves and cook, stirring, for 30 seconds or until bright green. Scatter this chilli mixture over the curry.

Top with coriander leaves and serve with flatbreads or brown rice if you need an extra carb.

 TIPS: Try sprinkling a few pinches of kesoori methi (dried fenugreek leaves, available from Indian stores) over the curry before serving. This herb brings an earthy flavour, a bit similar to celery, to anything that comes off the grill or out of the tandoor.

Head to delicious.com.au to find out how I make perfect roast spuds that will go brilliantly with this dish.

MEATY ADDITION: Replace the potato with 6 halved Barbecued or chargrilled chicken thigh fillets (see page 261) or 12 Meaty meatballs (see page 267).

Meat appendix

While this book is full of delicious recipes that just happen to be proudly vegetarian and vegan, we understand that sometimes you might require a little additional protein, and that's what this section is for. Pretty much everything suggested here will go with most of the recipes – even if the recipes are marvellous and complete on their own. Sometimes it's just nice to have options.

This book is free of rules and judgement, unlike my previous cookbooks. Some people still think of meat or seafood as the focus of a meal – and I don't feel there is anything wrong with that. If that sounds like you, then this section is designed so you can pick a protein you want to cook and then quickly find the ideal recipe in the front of the book to pair it with.

JUST ADD *more* PROTEIN!

Yes, you can take the meat-free recipes in this book and add a little extra protein for the carnivores in your life. Here's how to cook everything meat, seafood or fowl to add as you wish to the previous 127 proudly vegetarian and vegan recipes.

Just look at what you can do!

from

to

Avocado & friends
(see page 12)

Add sliced Barbecued or chargrilled
chicken thigh fillets (see page 261)

from

to

The impossible vegan caesar
salad (see page 38)

Replace the carrot bacon with Crispy
bacon (see page 268) or Crispy
prosciutto shards (see page 269)

from

to

Singapore noodles
(see page 110)

Toss in Pan-fried prawns
(see page 275)

from

to

Sunday roast tray bake with
crunchy roast potatoes
(see page 194)

Serve with Barbecued
butterflied lamb leg
(see page 264)

from

_to_

Grilled snow pea sandwiches
with ricotta butter & lemon
(see page 80)

Replace the cashews with
Crispy pork crackling
(see page 272)

from

_to_

Barbecued broccolini with
sunflower seed hummus &
lemon salt (see page 82)

Serve with sliced Barbecued
or chargrilled beef steaks
(see page 266)

from

_to_

The heretic's golden cassoulet
(see page 197)

Add Pan-fried sausages
(see page 270)

from

_to_

Leeks with cheese snow
(see page 208)

Serve with Roast chicken
(see page 262)

HOW TO COOK CHICKEN

Barbecued or chargrilled chicken skewers

MAKES: 8
PREP: 15 mins (plus 30 mins soaking and 5 mins resting)
COOKING: 10 mins

800 g chicken thigh fillets, cut into 3 cm pieces
olive oil, for drizzling
sea salt and freshly ground black pepper

Soak eight bamboo skewers in water for at least 30 minutes so they don't scorch on the barbie, or use metal skewers.

Thread the chicken evenly onto the skewers, drizzle with oil and season well with salt and pepper.

Preheat a barbecue grill or large chargrill pan over medium–high heat. Cook the skewers for 3–4 minutes each side or until cooked through. Transfer to a baking tray, cover loosely with foil and rest for 5 minutes before serving.

GOES WITH:

Mexican sweet potato street salad (see page 64)
Roasted red cabbage with dates & Vietnamese mint (see page 158)

Barbecued or chargrilled chicken breast fillets

SERVES: 4
PREP: 5 mins (plus 5 mins resting)
COOKING: 10 mins

4 chicken breast fillets, skin on
1 tablespoon olive oil
sea salt and freshly ground black pepper

Pat the chicken dry with paper towel.

Preheat a barbecue grill or large chargrill pan over high heat.

Drizzle the oil over the chicken and season well with salt and pepper.

Add the chicken to the barbecue or pan, skin-side down, and sear for 1 minute, then reduce the heat to medium and cook for 8 minutes or until golden and crisp. Increase the heat to high. Turn the chicken over and cook for a further 2–3 minutes or until just cooked through. Transfer to a baking tray, cover loosely with foil and rest for 5 minutes. Thinly slice and serve.

GOES WITH:

Devilled egg salad (see page 29)
Cauliflower steaks with red hummus (see page 75)

Barbecued or chargrilled chicken thigh fillets

SERVES: 4
PREP: 5 mins (plus 5 mins resting)
COOKING: 30 mins

olive oil, for drizzling
800 g chicken thigh fillets
sea salt and freshly ground black pepper

Drizzle the olive oil over the chicken and season well with salt and pepper.

To barbecue the chicken thigh fillets, preheat a barbecue with a lid to hot. Quickly sear the chicken on both sides, then place in the centre of the barbecue. Switch off the burners directly under the chicken and reduce the burners on either side to low. Close the barbecue lid and gently finish cooking the thighs for 12–15 minutes. Turn the heat back up to high. Turn the chicken over and sear for 1–2 minutes or until nicely charred. Transfer to a baking tray, cover loosely with foil and rest for 5 minutes.

To chargrill the chicken thigh fillets, heat a chargrill pan over medium–high heat. Add the chicken and cook for 8 minutes each side or until nicely charred and cooked through. Transfer to a baking tray, cover loosely with foil and rest for 5 minutes.

Serve the chicken thighs whole, sliced or chopped.

GOES WITH:

Avocado & friends (see page 12)
Barbecued potato salad with tamarind caramel,
  mint & yoghurt (see page 14)
The twofer salad (see page 37)
Corn in a cup (see page 79)
The name-dropper's roasted couscous royale (see page 241)
Butter 'chicken' curry with mushrooms (see page 247)
Easy African peanut & sweet potato stew (see page 252)
Andhra golden potato curry (see page 254)

Poached chicken breast fillets

SERVES: 4
PREP: 10 mins (plus 45 mins standing)
COOKING: 5 mins

1 litre (4 cups) chicken stock
4 chicken breast fillets
2 spring onions, white part only
2 fresh or dried bay leaves
1 teaspoon black peppercorns

Pour the chicken stock into a deep frying pan or large saucepan. Add the chicken and enough water to cover, then add the spring onion, bay leaves and peppercorns.

Bring to the boil over medium heat, then remove from the heat and cover with a tight-fitting lid. Set aside for 45 minutes to poach in the liquid. Use tongs to transfer the chicken to a chopping board, then slice or shred to serve.

GOES WITH:

The golfer's salad (see page 21)
Sunflower seed risotto (see page 100)
Cheat's ramen with udon (see page 117)

Roast chicken

SERVES: 4
PREP: 10 mins (plus 20 mins standing)
COOKING: 1 hour 10 mins

1 × 2 kg whole chicken
1 small lemon, halved
80 ml (⅓ cup) olive oil
sea salt and freshly ground black pepper

Preheat the oven to 200°C/180°C fan-forced. Remove the chicken from the fridge 30 minutes before roasting.

Pat the chicken and cavity dry with paper towel. Fold the wing tips underneath the bird and place the lemon halves inside the cavity. Rub half the oil all over the chicken and season well with salt and pepper.

Place the bird on a wire rack in a shallow baking dish or tin and cover the breast with a strip of foil so it won't dry out. Roast the chicken for 40 minutes, then remove the foil. Drizzle the remaining oil over the chicken breast, then roast for a further 30 minutes.

Test the thickest part of the leg with a thermometer – it is ready when it reaches 68°C. (If you don't have a thermometer, insert a knife into the thickest part of the leg. If the juices run clear it's ready; if they are still a bit pink, cook it for another few minutes.) Remove the chicken from the oven and turn over so it is breast-side down. Cover loosely with foil and leave to rest for at least 20 minutes so the residual heat finishes cooking the bird. Transfer to a board to carve.

GOES WITH:

#2 The handmaid's tale undressed (& unrolled) (see page 44)
Oozy, melty, cheesy pupusas – emigrated (see page 63)
*Middle Eastern butter-roasted white cabbage wedges
  (see page 176)*
Leeks with cheese snow (see page 208)

Middle Eastern inspired
Cover chicken fillets or a whole chicken with a spice rub of two parts crushed coriander seeds to one part cumin seeds. Add a little harissa or finely grated orange zest.

French inspired
Cover chicken fillets in a paste made from lemon juice, olive oil, crushed garlic, Dijon mustard and thyme or tarragon. For a whole roast chicken, use butter instead of oil and make sure you rub it under the skin (carefully, so you don't tear the skin).

Italian inspired
Cover chicken fillets or a whole chicken in a paste made from lemon juice, olive oil and garlic blitzed with oregano or marjoram.

Thai inspired
Cover chicken fillets or a whole chicken in a paste of coriander root and stalk, lime juice, grated galangal (if you have it), palm sugar, fish sauce, chopped and pounded lemongrass and red chilli.

Mexican inspired
Cover chicken fillets or a whole chicken in a paste of coriander root and stalk, lime juice, ground coriander and a few cumin seeds. Add chilli flakes, chipotle chillies in adobo sauce or fresh green chillies, to taste.

Indian inspired
Combine yoghurt with curry powder or tandoori paste, grated ginger and garlic and toss with chicken fillets or brush over a whole chicken.

Takeaway Chinese inspired
Combine soy sauce or tamari, honey, lemon juice and grated ginger and toss with chicken breast fillets or brush over a whole chicken.

Decadent
Marinate chicken fillets or a whole chicken in a mix of maple syrup, smoked paprika or powdered chipotle, miso and a little cider vinegar.

HOW TO COOK LAMB

Barbecued butterflied lamb leg

SERVES: 6
PREP: 5 mins (plus 30 mins marinating and 15 mins resting)
COOKING: 30 mins

1.5 kg butterflied boneless lamb leg
juice of 1 lemon
2 tablespoons olive oil
3 garlic cloves, crushed
sea salt and freshly ground black pepper

Place the lamb flat in a large glass or ceramic dish. Combine the lemon juice, olive oil and garlic in a bowl, then rub all over the top of the lamb. Season with salt and pepper, then set aside at room temperature for 30 minutes.

Preheat a barbecue grill on medium. Add the lamb and cook for 5 minutes each side. Transfer the lamb to a roasting tin (or foil tray if you like less washing up).

Place the tin in the centre of the barbecue. Switch off the burners directly under the lamb and reduce the burners on either side to low. Close the barbecue lid and the temperature should gradually come up to about 200°C. Roast the lamb for 20 minutes for medium, or until cooked to your liking. Transfer the lamb to a plate, cover loosely with foil and rest for 15 minutes before serving.

GOES WITH:

Middle Eastern butter-roasted white cabbage wedges (see page 176)

Sunday roast tray bake with crunchy roast potatoes (see page 194)

Slow-roasted lamb shoulder

SERVES: 4–6
PREP: 15 mins (plus 15 mins resting)
COOKING: 3 hours 20 mins

1.2 kg lamb shoulder, boned and opened out flat
250 ml (1 cup) chicken stock
2 tablespoons apple cider vinegar
1 rosemary sprig (or use 3 thyme sprigs)
1 garlic clove, thinly sliced
2 teaspoons instant coffee powder
sea salt and freshly ground black pepper

Preheat the oven to 160°C/140°C fan-forced.

Using a sharp knife, make slits in the fatty top of the lamb. Place the lamb in a roasting tin and drizzle with the stock and vinegar. Pull off the little leafy sprigs on the rosemary and insert into the slits with the garlic, then rub the instant coffee into the slits as well. Season with salt and pepper, then cover with foil and roast for 3 hours or until the lamb is tender and pulls apart easily with two forks.

Increase the oven temperature to 180°C/160°C fan-forced. Remove the foil and roast the lamb for a further 20 minutes or until it has a golden crust.

Remove the lamb from the oven, cover loosely with foil and rest for 15 minutes. Shred the meat and serve.

GOES WITH:

#3 The Aleppo herb rice salad bowl (see page 46)
Greek baked eggplant (see page 200)

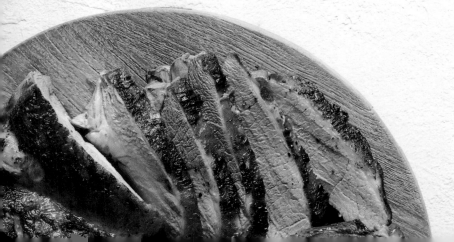

Barbecued or chargrilled lamb skewers

MAKES: 8
PREP: 10 mins (plus 30 mins soaking and 5 mins resting)
COOKING: 10 mins

800 g lamb fillet, cut into 4 cm pieces
1 tablespoon olive oil
sea salt and freshly ground black pepper

Soak eight bamboo skewers in water for at least 30 minutes so they don't scorch on the barbie, or use metal skewers.

Thread the lamb evenly onto the skewers, drizzle with oil and season well with salt and pepper

Preheat a barbecue grill or large chargrill pan over medium–high heat. Cook the skewers, turning occasionally, for 6 minutes for medium, or until cooked to your liking. Transfer to a baking tray, cover loosely with foil and rest for 5 minutes before serving.

GOES WITH:

#6 The crunchy granola Sunday bowl (see page 52)
Roasted red cabbage with dates & Vietnamese mint (see page 158)
Imam bayildi – the best eggplant dish ever … from Turkey (see page 188)

> ### Indian inspired
> Rub a finely blitzed paste of onion, yoghurt, mint, salt and lemon juice onto the lamb before threading onto skewers.
>
> ### Xinjian inspired
> Rub a spice mix of two parts ground cumin seeds to one part ground Sichuan pepper onto the lamb before threading onto skewers.
>
> ### Italian inspired
> **Shoulder and leg:** Marinate in a mixture of olive oil, rosemary, sliced and squeezed lemons, salt and loads of garlic.
> **Cutlets:** Slather with a paste of blitzed onion, olives, anchovies, flat-leaf parsley, garlic, lemon, olive oil, salt and pepper.
>
> ### Middle Eastern inspired
> **Skewers and cutlets:** Marinate in pomegranate molasses with a squeeze of lemon juice for no more than 30 minutes.
> **Slow-roasted shoulder:** Using a mortar and pestle, crush two parts coriander seeds to one part cumin seeds, then rub all over the lamb before cooking.

Barbecued or chargrilled lamb cutlets

SERVES: 4
PREP: 5 mins (plus 30 mins marinating)
COOKING: 10 mins

2 tablespoons olive oil
2 garlic cloves, thinly sliced
finely grated zest and juice of ½ lemon
12 lamb cutlets, French-trimmed
sea salt and freshly ground black pepper

Combine the oil, garlic, lemon zest and juice in a shallow glass or ceramic dish. Add the lamb and season well with salt and pepper. Turn to coat the lamb on both sides in the marinade, then cover and place in the fridge for 30 minutes.

Preheat a barbecue grill or large chargrill pan over high heat. Cook the lamb cutlets for 4 minutes each side for medium, or until cooked to your liking. Transfer to a baking dish, cover loosely with foil and rest for 2–3 minutes before serving.

GOES WITH:

Ancient grain salad version 22.0 (see page 18)
Sifnos summer salad revisited (see page 34)

HOW TO COOK BEEF

Barbecued or chargrilled beef steaks

SERVES: 4
PREP: 5 mins (plus 5 mins resting)
COOKING: 10 mins

4 × 3 cm thick beef scotch fillet, rump or sirloin steaks
olive oil, for drizzling
sea salt and freshly ground black pepper

Allow the steaks to come to room temperature.

Preheat a barbecue grill or a large chargrill pan over medium–high heat until it is nice and hot.

Sparingly drizzle the steaks with oil and massage it over the meat. Season well on one side with salt just before hitting the grill or pan.

If your steaks have a seam of fat running around one edge, first hold the steak with your trusty tongs and sear this fatty edge until browned, then cook on the seasoned side. Otherwise place the steaks, seasoned-side down, on the grill or pan. After 6 minutes, or when the meat changes colour at least halfway up the side, flip it over. Using your superior powers of anticipation, season the tops of the steaks with salt and pepper a minute before you reach the turnover point.

Cook for a further 3 minutes (ie, half the time the steaks have been cooking on the first side) for medium–rare. If you prefer your steak medium, wait until the first juices bubble up on the surface before flipping, then cook for another 2–3 minutes. Transfer to a plate and rest uncovered in a warm place for 5 minutes.

GOES WITH:

Barbecued broccolini with sunflower seed hummus & lemon salt (see page 82)

Sunday roast tray bake with crunchy roast potatoes (see page 194)

Tofu kung pao (see page 238)

Pan-fried mince

SERVES: 4
PREP: 5 mins
COOKING: 20 mins

1 tablespoon olive oil
500 g beef mince (you can also use lamb, pork, veal or chicken mince)

Heat half the olive oil in a frying pan over medium–high heat. Add half the mince and cook, breaking up any lumps with a wooden spoon, for 5–8 minutes or until golden. Transfer to a bowl and repeat with the remaining oil and mince. Cooking the mince in batches allows it to caramelise rather than stewing in the pan.

GOES WITH:

Easy potstickers (see page 91)

Mushroom Ned Ned noodles (see page 102)

Vegan bolognese (see page 123)

Lentil shepherd's pie with celeriac mash (see page 179)

Chilli san carne with parsnip chips (see page 251)

Meaty meatballs

MAKES: 25
PREP: 20 mins
COOKING: 20 mins

2 tablespoons olive oil
1 onion, finely chopped
2 garlic cloves, crushed
600 g beef mince (you can also use pork and veal, lamb
  or chicken mince)
200 g fresh ricotta
½ bunch flat-leaf parsley, leaves picked and finely chopped
50 g (1 cup) panko breadcrumbs
1 egg, lightly beaten
sea salt and freshly ground black pepper

Preheat the oven to 180°C/160°C fan-forced.

Heat half the olive oil in a frying pan over medium
heat. Add the onion and cook, stirring, for 3–4 minutes or
until soft. Add the garlic and cook, stirring, for 30 seconds
or until softened and aromatic. Transfer to a large bowl.

Add the mince, ricotta, parsley, breadcrumbs and egg to the
bowl. Don't overwork the mixture – just basically pull the
ingredients together. Season with salt and pepper.

Clean your hands and then dunk them in water. With wet
hands, roll heaped tablespoons of the mixture into balls,
making them as even as possible.

Heat the remaining oil in a large frying pan over medium–high
heat. Add the meatballs in two batches and cook, turning, for
4 minutes or until golden. Transfer to a roasting tin.

Once all the meatballs are browned, bake for 10 minutes or
until cooked through.

GOES WITH:

Caprese 'neatball' bake (see page 184)
Andhra golden potato curry (see page 254)

TWIST THEM

Depending on the dish you are adding them to, you can
mix up the flavours of these meatballs to match.

Italian: Use beef or pork and veal mince and add
1 tablespoon dried oregano.
Indian: Use chicken mince and add 2 teaspoons
ground cumin, 2 teaspoons curry powder and
1 teaspoon garam masala.
Middle Eastern: Use lamb mince and add
¾ teaspoon ground allspice and ¾ teaspoon
ground cinnamon.
Asian: Use chicken mince and add 1 finely chopped
lemongrass stalk, 1 finely chopped red chilli and
1 teaspoon finely grated ginger.

Barbecued or chargrilled whole beef fillet

SERVES: 4
PREP: 5 mins (plus 5 mins resting)
COOKING: 15 mins

650 g beef eye fillet
1 tablespoon olive oil
sea salt and freshly ground black pepper

Preheat a barbecue grill or chargrill pan over high heat. Toss
the beef in the olive oil to coat and season well with salt and
pepper. Cook the beef for 7 minutes each side for rare or until
cooked to your liking. Transfer to a plate, cover loosely with foil
and rest for 5 minutes, then thinly slice.

GOES WITH:

Grilled plums with milky haloumi & rocket (see page 22)
#4 The #blessed bento bowl (see page 49)

French inspired
Rub the beef fillet with Dijon mustard to coat. To fancy
things up, mix crushed garlic and finely chopped soft
herbs of your choice (tarragon, flat-leaf parsley, chervil,
thyme, etc.) into the Dijon before coating the beef.

Malaysian inspired
Marinate the beef fillet in kecap manis. Leave the
marinade on the beef to get a quick bark on the meat
when it's quickly cooked to rare.

Vietnamese inspired
Whisk together oyster sauce, fish sauce, lots of crushed
garlic, a splash of red wine and a few drops of Maggi
seasoning, then use to marinate your beef fillet.

Spanish inspired
Make a spice rub of sweet paprika, cumin seeds, finely
grated orange zest and crushed garlic and rub over the
the beef fillet to coat.

Korean inspired
Slather the outside of the beef fillet with gochujang,
ssamjang or a mixture of the two.

Italian inspired
Make a paste with blitzed onion, olives, anchovies, flat-
leaf parsley, garlic, finely grated lemon zest and olive oil,
and season to taste. Slather over the beef fillet to coat.

HOW TO COOK PORK

Crispy bacon

SERVES: 4
PREP: 5 mins
COOKING: 5–20 mins (depending on method)

4 (about 100 g) hickory-smoked streaky bacon rashers (or any good-quality streaky bacon)

STOVETOP: Heat a frying pan over medium heat. Add the bacon and cook, allowing the fat to render out, for 4–5 minutes each side or until crisp. Transfer to a plate lined with paper towel to drain.

OVEN: Preheat the oven to 220°C/200°C fan-forced. Place the rashers in a single layer on a baking tray and bake, turning halfway through, for 15–18 minutes or until crisp. Transfer to a plate lined with paper towel to drain.

MICROWAVE: Place two rashers between sheets of paper towel. Microwave on high for 1½–2 minutes, depending on the power of your microwave. Repeat with the remaining rashers.

CHOPPED: Heat a frying pan over medium heat. Add the chopped bacon and cook, stirring, for 3–4 minutes or until golden and crisp. Transfer to a plate lined with paper towel to drain.

GOES WITH:

Barbecued potato salad with tamarind caramel, mint & yoghurt (see page 14)

Green goddess salad (see page 25)

The impossible vegan caesar salad (see page 38)

Leek carbonara with strozzapreti (see page 88)

Our mac 'n' cheese with chunky garlic bread topping (see page 126)

The other BLT – 'bacon', lettuce & tomato sandwich (see page 133)

Decadent vego souffles with creamed leek, cheddar & jalapeno (see page 138)

Cheesy whole roasted cauliflower (see page 153)

Sumiso prairie tray bake (see page 182)

Primavera bake with pea & pumpkin seed pesto (see page 198)

Crunchy vegetable croquettes (see page 207)

Smash 'em green fritters (see page 212)

Fried lap cheong

SERVES: 4
PREP: 5 mins
COOKING: 5 mins

175 g lap cheong (about 6 sausages)

Slice the sausages thinly if you are after a crispy finish, or more thickly (about 8 mm) for slightly more sweetness and chew.

Heat a non-stick frying pan over medium–high heat. Add the lap cheong and cook, stirring occasionally, for 3–5 minutes or until golden (a lot of fat will render out of the sausage). Use a slotted spoon or tongs to transfer to a plate lined with paper towel to drain.

GOES WITH:

San choi bao for Buddha (see page 17)
Very special fried rice – hold the spam (see page 124)

Spicy chorizo coins

SERVES: 4
PREP: 5 mins
COOKING: 10 mins

1 tablespoon olive oil
2 chorizo sausages, thinly sliced into coins

Heat the olive oil in a large frying pan over medium heat. Working in batches, cook the chorizo for 2 minutes each side or until golden and crisp. Transfer to a plate lined with paper towel to drain.

GOES WITH:

The creamiest coddled egg (see page 143)
Crunchy vegetable croquettes (see page 207)

Crispy prosciutto shards

SERVES: 4
PREP: 5 mins
COOKING: 10 mins

8 slices prosciutto

Preheat the oven to 180°C/160°C fan-forced. Line a baking tray with baking paper.

Place the prosciutto on the prepared tray in a single layer and bake for 8–10 minutes or until crisp. Set aside to cool completely, then break into large shards.

GOES WITH:

Green goddess salad (see page 25)
The impossible vegan caesar salad (see page 38)
Leek carbonara with strozzapreti (see page 88)
Decadent vego souffles with creamed leek, cheddar & jalapeno (see page 138)
Primavera bake with pea & pumpkin seed pesto (see page 198)

Pan-fried sausages

SERVES: 4
PREP: 5 mins
COOKING: 15 mins

1 tablespoon olive oil
8 good-quality pork sausages (or beef, lamb
    or chicken, of course)

Heat the olive oil in a large non-stick frying pan over
medium–low heat. Cook the sausages, turning every
2–3 minutes, for 10–15 minutes or until golden and
cooked through. (This might take a little longer if the
sausages are very thick.)

GOES WITH:

Caprese 'neatball' bake (see page 184)
The heretic's golden cassoulet (see page 197)
Tuscan bean stew with balsamic (see page 232)

Slow-roasted pork shoulder

SERVES: 6–8
PREP: 5 mins (plus 2 hours drying and 15 mins resting)
COOKING: 4 hours 15 mins

1.25 kg boned rolled pork shoulder, scored
60 ml (¼ cup) olive oil
2 teaspoons sea salt

Place the pork, skin-side up, on a plate and pat the skin dry with
paper towel. Place in the fridge, uncovered, for at least 2 hours
but for the best results leave it overnight.

Preheat the oven to 220°C/210°C fan-forced.

Place the pork, skin-side up, on a wire rack in a roasting tin.
Rub the olive oil over the skin and sprinkle with the salt. Roast
for 30 minutes. Baste with any juices, then cover with a large
piece of baking paper and then foil.

Reduce the oven temperature to 160°C/140°C fan-forced.
Roast, basting every hour, for 3 hours or until the meat is tender.
Remove the foil and paper and roast for a further 45 minutes,
allowing the skin to crackle up. Set the pork aside and rest
uncovered for 15 minutes. Remove the rind and shred or slice
the meat to serve.

GOES WITH:

Oozy, melty, cheesy pupusas – emigrated (see page 63)
Corn in a cup (see page 79)

Chinese or Vietnamese inspired
Rub the pork shoulder with five spice powder or
marinate in char siu sauce – either shop-bought or
make your own with honey, hoisin, brown sugar, soy
sauce or tamari and five spice powder.

French inspired
Mop the pork shoulder with a mix of white wine
vinegar and Dijon mustard before and during cooking.
Keep any crackling dry.

Caribbean inspired
Blitz up pineapple chunks with ground allspice, sea
salt and green chillies (if you like heat). Use as a quick
marinade for the pork shoulder.

Spanish inspired
Marinate the pork shoulder in an adobo of smoked
paprika, dried oregano, crushed garlic, olive oil and
lots of sherry vinegar or red wine vinegar.

Barbecued or chargrilled pork cutlets

SERVES: 4
PREP: 5 mins (plus 5 mins resting)
COOKING: 10 mins

4 pork cutlets
1 tablespoon olive oil
sea salt and freshly ground black pepper

Pat the pork dry with paper towel and allow to come to room temperature.

Preheat a barbecue grill or chargrill pan over medium heat. Drizzle the pork with the olive oil and season both sides well with salt and pepper.

Cook the cutlets for 3–4 minutes each side or until just cooked pink. Transfer the pork to a plate, cover loosely with foil and rest for 5 minutes before serving.

GOES WITH:

Grilled plums with milky haloumi & rocket (see page 22)
Mexican sweet potato street salad (see page 64)

Roast pork fillet

SERVES: 4
PREP: 5 mins (plus 5 mins resting)
COOKING: 20 mins

400 g pork fillet
sea salt and freshly ground black pepper
1 tablespoon olive oil

Preheat the oven to 200°C/180°C fan-forced.

Season the pork all over with salt and pepper.

Heat the olive oil in an ovenproof frying pan over medium–high heat. Add the pork and cook for 1–2 minutes each side or until golden all over. Transfer the pan to the oven and roast for 15 minutes for medium, or until cooked to your liking. Transfer the pork to a plate, cover loosely with foil and rest for 5 minutes. Thinly slice to serve.

GOES WITH:

#1 The #blessed Brazil rice bowl (see page 43)
#6 The crunchy granola Sunday bowl (see page 52)

Crispy pork crackling

SERVES: 4
PREP: 5 mins (plus 2 hours drying)
COOKING: 50 mins

500 g piece pork rind
olive oil, for brushing
1 tablespoon sea salt

Preheat the oven to 220°C/200°C fan-forced.

Place the rind on a baking tray lined with baking paper and pat the skin dry with paper towel. Place in the fridge, uncovered, for about 2 hours.

Score the pork skin at 1 cm intervals. Place the rind on a wire rack over a baking tray, then brush with olive oil and sprinkle with the salt.

Roast for 45–50 minutes or until bubbled and crackled. Set aside for 5 minutes to cool slightly, then use a sharp knife to cut into shards.

GOES WITH:

Grilled snow pea sandwiches with ricotta butter & lemon (see page 80)

The devil's miaow (with addictive caramel brussels) (see page 161)

Roast pork belly

SERVES: 4–6
PREP: 5 mins (plus 2 hours drying and 15 mins resting)
COOKING: 2 hours 30 mins

1 kg piece pork belly
2 teaspoons olive oil
2 teaspoons sea salt

Place the pork on a baking tray lined with baking paper and pat the skin dry with paper towel. Place in the fridge, uncovered, for at least 2 hours but for the best results leave it overnight.

Preheat the oven to 250°C/230°C fan-forced.

Score the pork skin at 1 cm intervals. Place the pork on a wire rack in a roasting tin, skin-side up, then rub the olive oil over the skin and sprinkle with the salt. Roast for 30 minutes or until the skin is crispy.

Reduce the oven temperature to 160°C/140°C fan-forced. Pour 250 ml (1 cup) of water into the base of the tin (without touching the skin), then continue to roast, topping up the water as necessary, for a further 1½–2 hours or until the meat is tender. Set the pork aside and rest uncovered for 15 minutes before slicing.

GOES WITH:

Ancient grain salad version 22.0 (see page 18)
Barbecued broccolini with sunflower seed hummus
  & lemon salt (see page 82)

HOW TO COOK SEAFOOD

Baked white fish fillets

SERVES: 4
PREP: 10 mins
COOKING: 15 mins

4 × 200 g skinless chunky white fish fillets
   (such as blue eye), pin-boned
1 tablespoon olive oil
1 lemon, halved
sea salt and freshly ground black pepper
4 dill fronds or flat-leaf parsley sprigs

Preheat the oven to 200°C/180°C fan-forced. Tear off four pieces of baking paper about 40 cm long or large enough to wrap each fish fillet.

Place a fish fillet in the centre of each piece of paper. Drizzle each portion with a teaspoon of olive oil and squeeze over a little lemon juice. Season well with salt and pepper and top with a dill frond or parsley sprig.

Fold the long sides of paper over to enclose the fish and flavourings and tuck the short ends under the parcels to secure. Place on a baking tray and bake for 10–15 minutes (depending on the thickness of the fillet) or until the fish flakes when tested with a fork. Unwrap and serve.

GOES WITH:

Barbecued carrots & toasted crunchy brown rice with green mole (see page 66)
One-pan Bangkok pumpkin (see page 187)

Generally, I reckon it's best to keep the flavour of the fish clean of any marinade or rub unless you are adding a crust when cooking, but I make an exception for baked fish. Lay cuisine-appropriate herbs or other aromatics in the parcel or, if using a whole fish, in cavity before baking.

Pan-fried prawns

SERVES: 4

PREP: 5 mins

COOKING: 5 mins

20 g butter
1 tablespoon olive oil
16 raw prawns, peeled and deveined
1 garlic clove, crushed
1 tablespoon lemon juice
sea salt and freshly ground black pepper

Heat the butter and olive oil in a large frying pan over medium–high heat until the butter is melted and foaming.

Add the prawns and garlic and cook for 3–4 minutes or until the prawns curl and change colour. Drizzle with the lemon juice and season well with salt and pepper. Remove from the heat and serve.

GOES WITH:

Green goddess salad (see page 25)
Burnt butter spaghettini (see page 105)
Singapore noodles (see page 110)

Crispy-skinned salmon fillets

SERVES: 4

PREP: 5 mins (plus 30 mins standing)

COOKING: 10 mins

4 × 200 g salmon fillets, skin on, pin-boned
sea salt
1 tablespoon olive oil

Place the salmon fillets, skin-side up, on a plate and pat dry with paper towel. Sprinkle the skin with plenty of salt, then set aside for 30 minutes.

Use the blunt edge of a knife to scrape the salt off the salmon skin and pat the skin dry with paper towel.

Place the salmon, skin-side down, in a cold large frying pan. Drizzle the olive oil into the pan, then place over medium heat. Cook for 4–5 minutes or until the skin is golden and crisp. Carefully turn the salmon over and cook for a further 2 minutes or until cooked to your liking. Serve.

GOES WITH:

The twofer salad (see page 37)
Leeks with cheese snow (see page 208)

Barbecued white fish fillets

SERVES: 4

PREP: 5 mins (plus 30 mins standing)

COOKING: 10 mins

4 × 200 g chunky white fish fillets (such as blue eye), skin on, pin-boned
1 tablespoon olive oil
sea salt and freshly ground black pepper

Place the fish fillets, skin-side up, on a plate and pat dry with paper towel. Set aside for 30 minutes.

Preheat a barbecue flat plate on medium. Drizzle the fish fillets with a little olive oil and season with salt and pepper, then barbecue, skin-side down, for 3 minutes.

Carefully turn the fillets over and cook for a further 2–3 minutes (depending on the thickness) or until the flesh flakes easily when tested with a fork. Serve.

GOES WITH:

Devilled egg salad (see page 29)
Cauliflower steaks with red hummus (see page 75)

THANK YOU

It's taken three years, many phones calls, endless emails and more than a few meetings and fully colour-coded spreadsheets to pull this book together; to shape it into something of which we are all very proud.

At the receiving end of so many of these frantic communications has been my long-term collaborator and recipe wizard Michelle Southan, who takes my ideas and recipes and then, simply, makes them better. She also contributes many of her own brilliant ideas that have accumulated here over the long gestation period of this book. While Lucy Heaver not only pulled everything together with the skill of a master puppeteer but, as a long time vegetarian, she helped me dodge some of the pitfalls of previous cookbooks on the subject. She kept us honest even when I really, really wanted to add just the teeniest bit of bacon or splash of fish sauce. She is, I suppose, my muse for this book as well as the truest weather vane any author could want.

This is my first book with stylist Lee Blaylock and you'll notice her sure and elegant hand in every image here, all evocatively captured with consummate skill by photographer Mark Roper. Mark is the most measured, funny and charming man with whom to spend days on end in a studio. If you want to lick the pages of this book then Lee and Mark are mainly to blame.

As is Caroline Griffiths who once again led the kitchen team with Emma Guapa and support from Meryl Batlle. They cooked everything you see here and helped fix anything that might have been confusing, too complex or just plain wrong. Thank you!

Pan Mac's Ingrid Ohlsson very much helped shape this book from the very earliest days and made me work hard to ensure that this is a book for everyone, and one that celebrates plant-based and meat-free food in all its tasty glory – whether you want to add more protein or not. I can't think of anybody I'd rather be pushed by … While publicity guru, Tracey Cheetham, baking wizard Charlotte Ree and the team of Cate Paterson, Kate Butler, Katie Crawford and Ross Gibb made sure you knew about the book and could buy it.

In the engine room, praise be for talented designer Kirby Armstrong, editor Rachel Carter, typesetter Megan Ellis, proofreader Megan Johnston and Helena Holmgren who compiled the invaluable indexes.

So many of the ideas for this book and its recipes have come from time spent with the inspirational team at *delicious.* magazine, taste.com.au and delicious. on Sunday in *Stellar*. Thank you so much to Kerrie McCallum, Samantha Jones, Phoebe Rose Wood, Fiona Nilsson, Toni Mason, Brodee Myers-Cooke and Michelle Southan, again! You are still, still, still the best in the business. I love you all dearly and it's so much fun 'working' with you.

I also want to take this chance to say thank you for the last time to my old *MasterChef* family: Tim, Marty, Jodie, Maureen, Charmaine, DJ Deadly, Bennie, Matt, Koops, Steph, Pauly, Dobbs, Butch, Roey and Davey the wonder 1st; Heidi, Cyril and Tian; and Daz, Lockie, Foxy, Dre, Brett, Sasha, Carly, Leigh, BC, Zoe, Scotty, Pete, Tiff, Caleb, Carla, Archie, Tropical Tommy, Little Josh and Joshie, along with all the story team: Rob, Mounya, Minnie, Simon, Kelly, Nat and Ben. And, of course, above all, the other two wheels on the tricycle that was my life for 11 years, Gary and George.

Outside my TV and writing jobs I get to work with some amazing people. Thank you to the team at Alfred and all at Diageo, Andrew, Paul, Sara and Simone at Canstar, and my new besties at IKEA, Ivana and Nicole.

Then there's my 'other' family who also shouldered so much of the load this year, the wise counsel (and council) represented by my manager, Henrie Stride, Lena Barridge, social media guru Charlotte James, David Vodicka and Yasmin Naghavi from Media Arts Lawyers, and Aaron Hurle.

I have also relied heavily on the help and support of my real family this year – thank you Sadie, Will, Jono and Emma, you are the reason everything is worthwhile. I love you MORE.

One final note, keep in touch with me on Facebook, Twitter and Instagram at @mattscravat. Send me pics of what you cook from this book. I'd love that!

Onwards and upwards, always x

INDEX

EXTENDED INDEX

THE WOMBAT SECTION — EATS ROOTS

TUBERS TO TOOT YOUR HORN

CHEESY

GRAINS, PULSES & LEGUMES

HERBALICIOUS

chilli & tomato salad 79
chipotle mayo 64
Crispy bacon 268
crispy parsnip chips 251
Crispy pork crackling 272
Crispy prosciutto shards 269
Crunchy vegetable croquettes 207
Devilled egg salad 29
fake HP sauce 214
Fried lap cheong 268
garlic yoghurt sauce 63
Ghost pop nuggets 221
gochujang sauce 137
Green goddess salad 25
Green hummus 58
green mole sauce 66
green tahini sauce 223
instant mustard mayo 133
labne 52
Leeks with cheese snow 208
napoli sauce 118
One-pan Bangkok pumpkin 187
Oozy, melty, cheesy pupusas — emigrated 63
Pan-fried prawns 275
Pan-fried sausages 270
pea & pumpkin seed pesto 198
peppery basil pesto 144
Popcorn 'chicken' cauliflower 211
red hummus (aka muhammara) 75
Roast onion (aka French onion) hummus 57
sichuan chilli sauce 102
Sifnos summer salad revisited 34
Smokey sweet potato hummus 57
smokey almond mayo 228
spiced tomato sauce 218
Spicy chorizo coins 269
spinach bechamel 99
sunflower seed hummus 82
tamarind & chipotle ketchup 217
tangy herb salad 149
The impossible vegan caesar salad 38
The twofer salad 37
Tuscan cheese toasts 232
vegan sour cream 26
zucchini herb salad 224

GOES WELL WITH CHICKEN

#2 The handmaid's tale undressed (& unrolled) 44
#7 The Japanese #blessed bowl of virtue 55
Andhra golden potato curry 254
Avocado & friends 12
Barbecued potato salad with tamarind caramel, mint
    & yoghurt 14
Butter 'chicken' curry with mushrooms 247
Cauliflower steaks with red hummus 75
Cheat's ramen with udon 117
Corn in a cup 79
Crunchy eggplant schnitzels 150
Devilled egg salad 29
Easy African peanut & sweet potato stew 252
Easy potstickers 91
Grilled snow pea sandwiches with ricotta butter & lemon 80
Leeks with cheese snow 208
Mapo dofu comes to town 92
Mexican sweet potato street salad 64
Middle Eastern butter-roasted white cabbage wedges 176
Oozy, melty, cheesy pupusas — emigrated 63
Popcorn 'chicken' cauliflower 211

Roasted red cabbage with dates & Vietnamese mint 158
Sunflower seed risotto 100
Thai green curry with eggplant & green beans 244
The golfer's salad 21
The name-dropper's roasted couscous royale 241
The other, other KFC — Korean Fried Cauliflower 137
The twofer salad 37
Tofu schnitzel fingers with idiot slaw 214

GOES WELL WITH BEEF

#4 The #blessed bento bowl 49
Andhra golden potato curry 254
Barbecued broccolini with sunflower seed hummus & lemon
    salt 82
Caprese 'neatball' bake 184
Chilli san carne with parsnip chips 251
Grilled plums with milky haloumi & rocket 22
Lentil shepherd's pie with celeriac mash 179
Mushroom Ned Ned noodles 102
Mushroom stroganoff with parsley-flecked noodles 95
Sunday roast tray bake with crunchy roast potatoes 194
Tofu kung pao 238
Vegan bolognese 123

GOES WELL WITH LAMB

#3 The Aleppo herb rice salad bowl 46
#6 The crunchy granola Sunday bowl 52
Ancient grain salad version 22.0 18
Greek baked eggplant 200
Imam bayildi — the best eggplant dish ever …
    from Turkey 188
Lentil shepherd's pie with celeriac mash 179
Middle Eastern butter-roasted white cabbage wedges 176
Roasted red cabbage with dates & Vietnamese mint 158
Sifnos summer salad revisited 34
Sunday roast tray bake with crunchy roast potatoes 194
Vegetarian mushroom moussaka 157

GOES WELL WITH PORK

#1 The #blessed Brazil rice bowl 43
#2 The handmaid's tale undressed (& unrolled) 44
#6 The crunchy granola Sunday bowl 52
Ancient grain salad version 22.0 18
Barbecued broccolini with sunflower seed hummus
    & lemon salt 82
Barbecued haloumi with grilled peaches & green couscous 71
Barbecued potato salad with tamarind caramel, mint
    & yoghurt 14
Caprese 'neatball' bake 184
Cheesy whole roasted cauliflower 153
Corn in a cup 79
Creamy pumpkin & leek risotto 120
Crunchy vegetable croquettes 207
Dadaist sausage rolls for Barry Humphries 140
Decadent vego souffles with creamed leek, cheddar
    & jalapeno 138
Green goddess salad 25
Grilled plums with milky haloumi & rocket 22
Grilled snow pea sandwiches with ricotta butter & lemon 80
Leek carbonara with strozzapreti (aka priest strangler
    pasta) 88
Mapo dofu comes to town 92
Mexican sweet potato street salad 64
Oozy, melty, cheesy pupusas — emigrated 63
Our mac 'n' cheese with chunky garlic bread topping 126
Pea, ricotta & feta filo pie 174
Primavera bake with pea & pumpkin seed pesto 198

San choi bao for Buddha 17
Singapore noodles 110
Smash 'em green fritters 212
Sumiso prairie tray bake 182
The creamiest coddled egg 143
The devil's miaow (with addictive caramel brussels) 161
The heretic's golden cassoulet 197
The impossible vegan caesar salad 38
The most mortally totally decadent tartiflette potato tray
    bake 191
The other BLT — 'bacon', lettuce & tomato sandwich 133
Tofu kung pao 238
Tuscan bean stew with balsamic 232
Vegan bolognese 123
Very special fried rice — hold the spam 124
Zucchini nests with eggs, kale, capers & olives 134

GOES WELL WITH SEAFOOD

#4 The #blessed bento bowl 49
Barbecued carrots & toasted crunchy brown rice with
    green mole 66
Burnt butter spaghettini 105
Cauliflower steaks with red hummus 75
Cheat's puttanesca with orecchiette 113
Devilled egg salad 29
Green goddess salad 25
Leeks with cheese snow 208
One-pan Bangkok pumpkin 187
Popcorn 'chicken' cauliflower 211
Red capsicum, black olive & caramelised onion
    pissaladiere 162
Singapore noodles 110
Smash 'em green fritters 212
Thai green curry with eggplant & green beans 244
The creamiest coddled egg 143
The twofer salad 37
Zucchini slice version 5.0 149

A PLUM BOOK

First published in 2019 by Pan Macmillan Australia Pty Limited
Level 25, 1 Market Street, Sydney, New South Wales Australia 2000

Level 3, 112 Wellington Parade,
East Melbourne, VIC 3002, Australia

A CIP catalogue record for this book is available from the National Library of Australia:
http://catalogue.nla.gov.au

Design by Kirby Armstrong
Edited by Rachel Carter
Typesetting by Megan Ellis
Index by Helena Holmgren
Prop and food styling by Lee Blaylock
Food preparation by Caroline Griffiths, Meryl Batlle and Emma Warren
Hair and make-up by Dyan Gregoriou

Colour + reproduction by Splitting Image Colour Studio
Printed in China by 1010 Printing International Limited

We advise that the information contained in this book does not negate personal responsibility
on the part of the reader for their own health and safety. It is recommended that individually
tailored advice is sought from your healthcare or medical professional. The publishers and their
respective employees, agents and authors are not liable for injuries or damage occasioned to any
person as a result of reading or following the information contained in this book.

10 9 8 7 6 5 4 3 2 1